The Caregiver's Manual

A Guide to Helping the Elderly and Infirm

The Caregiver's Manual

A Guide to Helping the Elderly and Infirm

BY GENE B. WILLIAMS
AND PATIE KAY

ILLUSTRATIONS BY PATIE KAY

A CITADEL PRESS BOOK
Published by Carol Publishing Group

Dedication

To Bear

A Citadel Press Book
Published by Carol Publishing Group
Citadel Press is a registered trademark of Carol Communications, Inc.

Editorial Offices: 600 Madison Avenue, New York, N.Y. 10022
Sales and Distribution Offices: 120 Enterprise Avenue, Secaucus, N.J. 07094
In Canada: Canadian Manda Group, One Atlantic Avenue, Suite 105, Toronto, Ontario M6K 3E7
Queries regarding rights and permissions should be addressed to Carol Publishing Group, 600 Madison Avenue, New York, N.Y. 10022

Carol Publishing Group books are available at special discounts for bulk purchases, sales promotions, fund-raising, or educational purposes. Special editions can be created to specifications. For details contact: Special Sales Department, Carol Publishing Group, 120 Enterprise Avenue, Secaucus, N.J. 07094

Manufactured in the United States of America

10 9 8 7 6 5 4 3 2 1

Library of Congress Cataloging-in-Publication Data

Williams, Gene B.
   The caregiver's manual : a guide to helping the elderly and infirm / by Gene B. Williams and Patie Kay.
       p.   cm.
   "A Citadel Press book."
   ISBN 0-8065-1597-X
   1. Aged—Home care—United States—Handbooks, manuals, etc.
   2. Caregivers—United States—Handbooks, manuals, etc.   I. Kay, Patie.   II. Title.
   HV1461.W52   1995
   649.8—dc20   94-46621
                                                           CIP

Contents

Foreword

Consider how often we select a book whose author makes *claims* of having solved some human dilemma whose solution has eluded us all—increasing one's popularity, developing better communication skills or finding the way to a more meaningful life. What generally eludes the reader is a solid grasp of the implied one-two-three method of reaching such a goal. We seem to be deluged with generalities rather than specifics as to how to go about making recommended changes.

Yet there are books in which all the claims ring true.

Many years ago, I met the author of *Games People Play* and *What Do You Say After You Say Hello?* What intrigued me about Eric Berne, M.D., was that he wrote and said specific things about emotionally disabling problems—and, moreover, what to do about them! And it was because of his close attention to specifics that I became a teacher of his methodology.

The authors of this book have done much the same thing as Berne did, in that they have managed to present a huge body of factual information within *specific* as well as practical guidelines, and featuring the real-life stories and examples of individuals who have faced many of the same problems that have (or may yet) beset the rest of us.

If you have a loved one in crisis of one kind or another, you cannot help but find both tender solace and solid support in this book. This is especially true if you are confronted with the terminal illness of a relative. The authors literally brought me to tears more than once in the remembrance of that kind of experience, and I found myself wishing I'd had the wisdom of their advice at that earlier time.

It was a distinct pleasure to review this book, and it is equally so to recommend it without reservation.

William J. Collins, Ph.D.
Virginia Beach, Virginia
October 1994

Preface

I have stood where you're standing now. Surrounded by family, friends and an army of medical professionals, all offering advice and trying to help, I had never felt so alone in my life. I wasn't the patient—I was the caregiver.

I found myself balanced on the point of a sword, juggling patient care, marriage and a career. Everyone's emotions were on a roller coaster as we hurtled from crises to "good days" to catastrophes, interspersed with periods of relative calm. For every fact I received and instruction I was given, there were a hundred more I needed to know and wasn't told. Not because anyone was hiding anything, but because they assumed either that I already knew, or didn't need or want the information.

I needed an "instant" education. What I got was a discharge coordinator who said: "Get this prescription filled for your mother. Make an appointment with the doctor in three days. She should have someone staying with her. We have arranged for at-home care to check on her twice a week. Please sign here. Thank you. I hope you've enjoyed your stay with us. Please fill out our services questionnaire and mail it back."

In less than three minutes, I went from married career woman to caregiver. A caregiver who had no training. (I didn't even know there were thermometers that beeped to tell you they were ready to be read.)

For all of you who find yourself in a similar situation, we offer this book—and one piece of solace: You are not alone in your efforts.

Patie Kay

While she was still fairly young, my grandmother was the victim of a hit-and-run driver. All the years I knew her, she was in a wheelchair. Instead of letting this affect her, she merely went on with life, and in fact was the most cheerful person I've ever known. Coincidentally, Grandpa was also hit (separate accident). In his later years, the effects were more apparent; he could barely move. But, like Grandma, he never complained. In fact, one Christmas there he was outside, shoveling snow from the walk so the visitors would have it easier. To do this he had to brace the shovel handle against an arm that was nearly paralyzed, and use that arm as the fulcrum in swinging the snow away.

In my teen years there were many times when I had to spend a weekend at their farm taking care of one while the other was in the hospital. Due to their natures and personalities, though, it was easy. I didn't even mind having to cancel a date, or other plans.

Some years later, Grandma suffered a massive heart attack and was hospitalized. Within a week we got a call from the hospital: Grandma had passed away. In that call the nurse told us: "She did the strangest thing. Just before the coronary, she pressed the button to call me to the room and said, 'I'm sorry to bother you, but I think I'm going to die now. I wouldn't have called, but I didn't want you to come in later and find me. I didn't want you to be distressed.'"

That was my first real exposure to caregiving.

Physically, both were failing. Grandpa was in so much pain that at times he could barely carry on a conversation. Yet both were mentally sharp. In this there was no degradation at all: If either ever complained, I don't remember it. Until their deaths they remained independent, needing only occasional help with chores.

There were others, such as Dr. Billy Barr, a retired minister from our church, and his wife. We would help them with heavier chores, but they usually took care of the lesser tasks of their own home together. Up the street from us was Charles Kelly, a retired lawyer and judge. Physically he had terrible difficulties compounded by having become almost totally blind from cataracts. In his last years I was his chauffeur, a tour which gave me a wonderful chance to get to know him.

These people were all part of what continues to be the largest group of elders—those who merely need a little extra help in order to live at home. That some inevitably will suffer from a condition or situation which will make it necessary for them to move into some kind of facility is a hard reality. But caregiving simply is full of hard realities. And it is very much the purpose of this book to give you at least a starting point toward handling them as best you can.

Apparently you are at least considering providing care for a loved one—or perhaps you're already in it and are feeling overwhelmed. This guide begins with a perhaps surprisingly stern reality check, but then offers fast relief by letting you know that there are things you can take advantage of that will make the situation work for the best. Often the main one is common sense itself. Other times it's merely a bit of information or a new skill. It might also be the whereabouts of a service or agency that can help you quickly and efficiently.

This book will serve as a guide to knowing the options you have available, honestly assessing the situation and your abilities, gathering information and then making an informed—not an emotional or panicked—decision. The real guide, however, should be yourself—because you will know the situation, and the elder, probably better than anyone else. Ultimately, whether you decide to follow someone's advice or not (including ours) will be up to you, the situation notwithstanding.

We wish you the very best in all your caregivings.

Gene B. Williams

Introduction

If you run errands for an elder, occasionally fix a meal or do a minor repair around an elder's home, you are in the primary stages of caregiving. In fact, "caregiving" is a catch-all term that covers everything from minor assistance to full-time, round-the-clock care. It may be temporary or permanent. Especially with elder care, it may progress from the simple (running a few errands) to the complicated (caring for someone bedridden).

Just as there is no one clearly defined caregiving situation, there is no one clearly defined caregiver. Your relationship with the elder might be friend, neighbor, health care professional or employee. Typically, the caregiver will be a spouse or adult child (in both cases, usually female). There may or may not be other partners, relatives or friends who provide help and support—and if there is, sometimes, unfortunately, that support will evaporate as the situation continues.

In short, each situation is different and can be expected to change. Your own situation, and the reason you are reading this book, might fall into one of the tidy categories (adult daughter with children of her own) or might be quite different.

In 1900, only 4 percent of the American population was sixty-five or older. Ninety years later, the percentage reached 12.5. It is estimated that by 2050, more than one person out of five (20 percent) will be in the "senior" category. Even more amazing than this projected growth is the "centenarian boom" predicted to occur within the next sixty years. Since 1900, the chances of a person's living to his or her hundredth birthday has increased forty times: In 1989, America had 61,000 centenarians! Dr. Gregory Spencer, a demographer with the U.S. Census Bureau, has predicted that there will be 108,000 centenarians by the year 2000, 441,000 by 2025 and 1.3 million by 2050.

There are three primary reasons for increased lifespans: better medical care, life-sustaining technologies and healthier lifestyles. Since these advances are likely to continue, we can also expect to see people with chronic or terminal diseases in longer states of control or remission.

These longer life expectancies are having a profound effect on the lives of adult children. Many baby boomers (people born between 1945 and 1965) are still handling childrearing responsibilities while facing senior family members who also need care. These baby boomers are members of the "sandwich generation." Many baby boomers, as they start becoming seniors themselves beginning in 2010, will be faced with caring for parents in their eighties just at the time they are looking forward to their own "golden years" of retirement. This will be doubly hard on those who find themselves with an ailing spouse as well as an aging parent.

It has become increasingly difficult to provide the care these situations require because lifestyles have changed radically. In an earlier era, society was basically agricultural, and retirement was practically unknown. People worked as long as they were physically able. Many shared their homes with two or three generations or had immediate family close by; thus when senior members became incapacitated someone was available to provide care.

This situation changed with the Industrial Revolution. Manufacturing jobs lured many away from farms and into a structured, task-specific, "town" way of life. The family nucleus went from three generations (grandparents–parents–children) to two. Seniors who were previously venerated for their wisdom and work experience were being "retired" because they could no longer keep up with advancing technologies and younger workers.

The family circle used to be more compact geographically. The closer proximity encouraged closer emotional ties because family members interacted frequently. Growing to maturity with the family farm or business as a hub of activity encouraged lines of family communication to remain open. In most cases there were plenty of siblings, aunts, uncles and cousins in the same area, which made a support network readily available.

Today's family is much more complex. As family members have become increasingly diverse geographically, maintaining close contact is more difficult. Higher rates of divorce and remarriage have also created a merged or "blended" family situation, and therefore additional strains when elder care becomes necessary. When increased life expectancy is factored into the equation, it becomes obvious that almost every baby boomer will have to deal with this situation in some form—and probably without the traditional family support network.

Traditionally, female family members have been responsible for care of the elderly. This is understandable because, also traditionally, men were expected to leave the home each morning, go to work and earn the money needed to support the household. Like so many other traditions, this one is fading. And as more women enter the workplace, more men are becoming primary, or at least secondary, caregivers.

In 1986, the majority (55.5 percent) of those caring for an elder within the household were still female. Of those, 18 percent were daughters and 44 percent were spouses. Care given to an elder family member outside the caregiver's home fell to an even higher proportion of females (67 percent females, 33 percent males). Almost twice as many daughters were caregivers as were sons, and over 25 percent of the caregivers themselves qualified as elderly. As the family dispersed, care became the responsibility of either the closest adult child or that child's spouse.

The sexual revolution of the sixties increased the number of women in the work force. In 1986, approximately two-thirds of women who were caregivers also worked outside the home at least part-time. The economic climate of the nineties makes outside employment less of a choice and more of a necessity for today's woman. The income she brings to the household is important; her time is at a premium. Suddenly faced with an elder-care issue, she may find herself rearranging work schedules, reducing her full-time job to part-time status, taking an unpaid leave of absence or quitting work entirely.

Employed adult male children report the same conflicts as do adult female children, though they are less likely—and often less able—to rearrange working schedules to accommodate elder care. The unequal participation in elder care between male and female adult children probably reflects the traditional roles that baby boomers were raised with and the higher earning capacity of men in general, rather than a noncaring attitude on the part of men. With rare exception, men are still expected to be the primary breadwinners and don't have the options of working part-time or not at all.

More people in general, of both genders, are becoming caregivers. Although the role still falls more often to women, the proportion of men taking on the role is increasing. When faced with an elder-care situation, an adult child of either sex can be quickly and easily overwhelmed. But being unable to cope with the additional strain of care is not a weakness: The simple fact is that there are only twenty-four hours in each day, and the complexity of our lives puts ever more demands on those hours.

When it comes to balancing career, marriage and family with the additional responsibilities of elder care, many eventually will find it impossible to cope without assistance. Today's adult children, male and female alike, need to develop a working, practical knowledge of aging and caregiving, and a support system with both other family members and the community, in order to be able to cope satisfactorily with the problems of elder care. Particularly important is mutual support and cooperation within the family. New stresses can easily cause tempers and finances to run short. Relationships can become strained throughout the family.

In many ways, the situation posed is similar to having a new baby in the house—but there is a very real difference. Although that neonate is helpless and needs constant care, as time goes by the amount needed decreases. With the elder-care "patient," the demands and need for attention are bound to increase. Caregiving is needed because the body, and sometimes also the mind, is slowing down. With a child, the amount of care will become less in time. With elder care, the strain on the caregiver tends to increase.

Adding to all this are memories: Someone you once looked to for strength and competence no longer fits that mold or image. It's possible that the father who once bounced you on his knee now has an artificial knee that causes him pain when he moves—or the mother who used to spend hours in the kitchen making delicious meals suddenly can't remember to turn off the stove.

Obviously caregiving isn't easy at any level. It can even prove impossible at any level for some. Despite all its problems and pitfalls, however, it can still be one of life's more enriching experiences.

This guide can become, for you and others, a road map of sorts that anyone in a caregiving situation can use to help minimize its problems and enhance the love, peace and fulfillment that are possible in this act of dedication and thanks.

The Caregiver's Manual

A Guide to Helping the Elderly and Infirm

ONE

Overview of Aging

It's easy to find a seminar, class or book on parenting, child development or self-fulfillment. Traditionally, classes on various aspects of human physiology and psychology have been taught in colleges and universities. In both subjects, education may now begin as early as grade school. Thus you and your kids learn about birth, child care, growth, physical and mental development, nutrition (especially for the growing body), diseases, etc. What you won't find in either case is much information on aging and the elderly—and there is virtually nothing at all on how to care for a loved one who is becoming infirm.

Many people have little or infrequent interaction with the elderly, and what they do have is often distant. Concepts of "old" come from a society that worships youth and attempts to stave off the most dreaded thing in life—aging. No matter what we try, or how well we take care of ourselves, the years will pass and we will age.

Other cultures respect age. Ours does not. Decrepit, senile, feeble, infirm, declining years, dotage, doddering, timeworn, second childhood—all are words and concepts associated with being old. Our media characterize the negative aspects of aging and often poke fun at the elderly. But beneath the laughter is fear: Few want to think about facing this type of future themselves or want to watch someone they love experience it.

Fortunately, real aging is different from the popular concept. For example, many people think that an old person automatically ends up in a nursing home eventually. Actually, only about 5 percent of people over sixty-five are in long-term care facilities. This simple statistic points up the fact that 95 percent of our elders either manage on their own, manage with some assistance or are being cared for in some other manner.

In *Aging in America—Trends and Predictions*, 1991 edition, the U.S. Department of Health and Human Services reported that 71 percent of the noninstitutionalized elderly described their health as excellent or good when compared to that of others their age. This indicates that it's not unusual for the elder to overlook physical and mental degeneration. This is easily explained: Since the aging process takes place over a long period of time, and humans are naturally adaptable, the individual can adapt to slow changes, often without even noticing them.

The borderline between normal and abnormal changes often is vague, its delineation depending as it usually does on terminology and social interpretation. Be aware of what is "normal" for *your* elder, so that you will know when something is going on that may require medical intervention. An elder who seems "out of it" may simply be suffering from a hearing loss. And one who doesn't think as quickly as before isn't necessarily becoming senile. He or she is more likely to be simply slowing down—and that change is perfectly normal.

To understand what could be required of you as a caregiver, it is first necessary that you understand the "normal" aging process and how it affects your elder's life (and your own). We shall proceed toward both goals at the pace that each requires.

Acute and Chronic Health Problems

It is true that elders have more medical problems than do young adults, simply because their bodies have aged. In the past, common conditions such as infections or diseases that the young could throw off fairly easily could become life-threatening to the elder. With the advent of antibiotics, this is no longer the problem it used to be. Other new medical treatments and practices have solved still more difficulties. Even surgery has become less intrusive, making recovery easier.

Chronic (long-term or frequently recurring) conditions have become the bane of aging. The main culprits are heart disease, hypertension and arthritis. It is interesting to note that men are more prone to acute, life-threatening conditions, while women are more likely to develop chronic conditions that lead to physical impairment. There are indications that acute conditions are brought about largely by the stress of being the breadwinner. Current findings indicate that as more women fill traditionally male roles, the number of women suffering from "male conditions" (such as hypertension) is increasing. Whether or not the correlation is valid is not yet known. For the moment, it is important to recognize that there may be a shifting. In any case, it's a mistake to assume that an older man has hypertension, but it's a worse mistake to take for granted that an older woman does not.

Mental health problems can be every bit as devastating as physical ones. An elder may suffer mental illness from either functional or organic sources, or a combination of the two. *Functional* causes can include emotional stress (such as unexpressed fear, worry, or anger), psychoses or neuroses. *Organic* sources cover a wide range of chemical imbalances, reactions to medications, physical conditions (such as tumors or cerebral arteriosclerosis) and certain diseases, including Alzheimer's and COPD (Chronic Obstructive Pulmonary Disease). Most functional causes and about 15 percent of organic causes are curable. Many more of the problems can be managed with a combination of medication and therapy. The key is prompt diagnosis and treatment.

Many of the elder's medical problems can be helped with medication, diet, and/or exercise. For you as the caregiver, it's important that you keep a close eye on things. Sometimes, for example, a prescribed medication or other treatment will have an undesirable effect. By being aware and alert, you can help increase the benefits of the treatment while reducing the dangers.

Slowing and Gradual Degeneration

Although the capabilities of the human body decline with age, the rate and amount of the decline is an individual matter. One person may suffer from heart trouble at sixty-five while an eighty-five-year-old neighbor (or parent) is vigorous and strong. The chance of later-life illness is determined by a variety of factors, including heredity and past or present lifestyle.

As aging occurs, most people experience a general slowing of movement due to weakened muscles and stiffening joints. Things you did easily at twenty, like playing sports, become more physically challenging at thirty-five, even if you have a fairly active lifestyle. An elder may not walk as fast as when he or she was forty, but may be able to walk just as far, given enough time. Balance can also be affected to some degree. An aging person who can walk three miles through a mall may have problems on an uneven surface such as a nature trail, or may navigate stairs with little problem but become uncomfortable on a ladder.

Few elderly are afflicted with total deafness, though many suffer enough hearing loss to make life difficult. Hearing problems usually occur gradually and progress for some time before they are noticeable—even to the person who suffers from them. One reason for this phenomenon is our aforementioned unconscious and lifelong ability to adapt to our environment. Some people with hearing loss concentrate harder on what is being said and even lip-read to a degree. And then there is the marvelous capacity of the human mind to fill gaps: Several words of a sentence can be missing, but the handicapped listener may still be able to understand the entire meaning.

A tip-off is "selective hearing," which occurs when a person seems, in general, to hear only when he or she wants to. In most elders, there is no damage to the small bones of the ear. The problem is caused by the uncorrectable nerves becoming less effective, a deterioration which makes distinguishing between and among consonants a problem. Shouting at the person does little good (and often irritates the listener), because the increased volume tends to blur the vowel sounds as well. The trick is to speak more slowly, and certainly more clearly—though even that won't help all the time.

In some elders, a hearing problem can cause them to become withdrawn or paranoid, thinking everyone is talking quietly about them. A properly fitted (molded) hearing aid can go a long way toward alleviating the problem, though some elders consider even the suggestion of a hearing aid almost an insult. This reaction is due at least in part to the natural tendency of people to deny that they are losing some of their abilities and therefore need prosthetic assistance.

Loss of sight can cause similar psychological problems. As with hearing, the gradual dimming of vision is a normal part of aging and often takes a while to be noticed. Beginning in middle age, the shape of the eyeball becomes distorted and the lens loses elasticity. The problem becomes more pronounced without treatment and with advancing age—and lack of sight can cause people to lose confidence in their ability to cope and to get around in unfamiliar or less frequented places. Glasses can solve the problem for the most part, though in more serious cases corrective surgery is required. Improvements in this kind of surgery allow the majority of patients to enjoy dramatically improved eyesight. In a few cases, however, not much can be done other than to give the elder special training in coping with the worsening problem.

Thinking processes can slow down as elders become less able to absorb information at the same rate as younger people. Do not mistake this slowing for senility (which we will discuss later): A somewhat slowed thinking process is normal. In general, an elder is still as capable of learning new skills and gaining new information as ever—it all simply takes a little longer.

Memory loss can be the most frustrating of all the slowed mental capabilities. Distant events may be more easily recalled than last week's luncheon date or the time of today's appointment. When memory loss is coupled with slowed thinking processes, elders may have trouble making decisions based on current situations. For the caregiver, this means that lots of understanding and patience are required. However, don't make the mistake of treating the person like a child. Not only is this unfair, it could begin a pattern of dependency.

Personality Changes

Certain similarities between the young child and the elder are responsible for the misnomer "second childhood." Some accept this unfortunate label without thinking it through. The elder may indeed sometimes act like a child, but the reality is quite different. In most cases, the elder is slowing down physically and mentally, but is not becoming a child again and should never be treated as one.

Because the processing time for what is seen and heard by an elder is longer than it used to be, the reaction time is also hampered. This makes the performance of routine tasks more time-consuming. When coupled with the normal slowing of physical movement, the combination can make even ordinary tasks more difficult—and frustrating.

Some personality changes also occur, with the more dominant personality traits often becoming even more pronounced. While some people mellow with age, others become more irascible. A quiet, reserved person may become more shy, or even frightened, while a dominant person may turn more argumentative or demanding. A person who has been concerned with others' opinions may worry excessively over becoming a burden or even a nuisance. Someone who has shown little consideration for others may have even less now.

Added to this syndrome, and sometimes making it even more pronounced, are other factors. For example: An elder person may become more and more concerned about death, and could even start thinking that there's not much time left to make amends. Another might take on the attitude that age automatically means wisdom and take offense when someone younger doesn't instantly fall into line with his or her thinking.

In many cases, especially when the elder suffers from physical pain, either chronic or acute, there is a natural tendency for the affected person to become grumpy just as would anyone else, at any age, who is hurting. These instances must be dealt with by using a good deal of empathy if the caregiving is to be received as genuinely heartfelt.

Changes in Lifestyle

There is no magic door labeled GOLDEN YEARS that a person can walk through in order to make personal problems disappear. Instead, most personal problems follow us into old age, and some become much more acute as lifestyle, situations and health change. For instance, marital problems that may have been simmering for years suddenly erupt when a couple spend much more time than usual together in retirement.

Retirement can produce an identity crisis because of the loss of employment. A person who has spent a lifetime working can suddenly feel lost and useless. If the spouse (or whoever) begins to berate this person for being underfoot, the sense of uselessness is only increased.

Reduced income alone, even when it has been planned for, can cause fear. Someone young who loses a job may undergo depression and worry but can be comforted by knowing that there's a replacement job out there. For a person of retirement age, however, finding a new job can be difficult or even impossible.

In a youth-oriented, work-oriented society, retirement can also mean a loss of social status. This can be particularly hard on someone who has always been the breadwinner. Many times the center of that person's life has been work, and with that gone he or she may become covertly angry. (The condition is called displaced anger.) Without even recognizing that he or she is doing it, that party looks for self-justified reasons for venting built-up anger.

As the lifestyle of the elder changes, perceived and real losses of respect, love, position, and income contribute to feelings of uselessness and lowered self-esteem. The situation becomes more acute when combined with poverty, dangerous environments, or chronic worry. Any of these situations can raise tension in a marriage and various other relationships and can endanger physical or mental health. In severe cases, abuse and self-destructive impulses can occur.

As a caregiver, you need to be as much aware of personality and mental health changes as you are physical conditions. Part of your caregiving role may entail serving as a peacemaker and arbitrator. If the services of a psychologist or therapist is required, be certain you work with the professional to reinforce the needed behavioral changes.

Senility

Senility is not synonymous with aging. Many behaviors that are expressions of individual personalities are labeled "senile." Some elderly people suffering with treatable disorders have had their problems dismissed as senility, and with tragic results. A thorough physical examination is always recommended if judgment is impaired or there have been alarming shifts in personality or behavior.

Senile dementia is the disease that most closely resembles the stereotype of old-age senility. Elders with senile dementia may have trouble remembering where they are, confusing their own home with that of a friend—or vice versa. There may be problems with short-term memory, disorientation and impaired judgment. The elder may wander off and not be able to find the way back. Concentration, even on simple tasks, becomes very difficult. The person may withdraw and refuse to speak, or may express frustration in anger and aggressive or argumentative behavior.

Sudden-onset dementia, which is caused by damaged blood vessels in the brain (usually due to multiple strokes), accounts for about 20 percent of dementia cases. An individual's response to a stroke will vary, depending on which portion of the brain was affected and the number and intensity of the stroke(s). The symptoms of a stroke can appear singly or in combination. Some of these include speech pattern changes (misuse of words), slurred speech, lack of recognition of common objects or people formerly well known, and a change in body posture or motor skills (such as being able to write or hold a fork).

There are a number of pseudodementias, which are functional disorders that mimic organic causes. Remember that medical tests can often spot the true cause of a person's problem. Testing would probably include chest X rays and also skull X rays (for intracranial calcification). An angiogram will track blood flow to and through the brain. The EEG (electroencephalogram) detects abnormal brainwaves. A computerized axial tomography (CAT) scan checks for location of tumors or clots inside the brain. There are also blood, urine and thyroid tests. The interpretation of these tests would take into consideration the elder's medical history. (Having a primary-care physician, as discussed later, will increase the chances of accurate interpretation.)

Depression and Its Effects

Depression is a condition that everyone experiences at some time and to some degree. For some it can become so severe and so chronic (clinical depression) that professional help may be required.

Often it is a response to stress brought on by a loss. Another common cause is the feeling of deprivation, such as the sense that what has been wanted out of life wasn't achieved and now never will be. Complicating this is that as people age, their ability to cope with stress seems to diminish.

Anxiety contributes to depression. Excessive worrying leading to repetitive thoughts is a mental pattern associated with anxiety. Some outward symptoms of anxiety are agitation, nervousness and such irritating, repetitive motor mannerisms as pacing or finger tapping.

In conversations with a depressed person, a repetitive negative speech pattern can be discerned. That is, most positive statements will be countered by negative ones from a depressed individual. Conversational statements on his or her part will demonstrate both a lack of self-esteem and an attitude of hopelessness. You might hear statements like, "What did I do to deserve this?" "It's hopeless." "What's the use?" "I'm no good." "I can't even find the energy to try anymore." These and similar complaints may well be indicators of depression.

Depression, even clinical depression, does not always indicate suicidal tendencies (just as suicide does not always indicate depression). However, in elderly people depression is often, but not always, accompanied by a death wish.

In 1988, the suicide rate was almost nine times higher for elders than for the general population. The rates are probably even higher than reported because (1) passive suicides (those committed by nonviolent means, such as not eating or not taking the proper medication) are hard to detect; (2) many families, possibly due to feelings of guilt, shame, or both, are unwilling to report suspected suicide as the cause of death; and (3) the figures reflect only deaths listed as suicide on official death certificates.

The latest marked increase in elder suicide began in 1981 and is a trend peculiar to the United States. It puzzles health-care experts, who cite statistics supporting the premise that today's elderly are better off financially and physically healthier than ever before. Mental health professionals point out that technological advances that can prolong life (postpone death) have resulted in longer lives but not necessarily in more satisfying ones. As society's attitude about suicide changes, more elders are weighing the cost of extended life against the quality of life gained. Most elders who kill themselves do so by intentionally not taking life-sustaining medication, by overmedicating themselves, by drinking to excess and/or by not eating.

It must be noted that there are differences among depression, grieving and demoralization. Depression is general, and its blame is usually self-directed. Grieving does not habitually either show self-reproach or demonstrate a fall in self-esteem. Demoralization usually occurs in response to a specific event such as a loss, a crime in the neighborhood, a fender-bender or a fractured wrist.

Demoralization is usually not as serious as depression, but its reported incidence is higher.

Somatic Disorders

Somatic disorders are physical problems that are caused by a mental problem, often depression. They are seen in people of all ages, but the stresses and fears that often come with aging make the elderly particularly susceptible to them. The condition is sometimes referred to as hypochondria.

Even though they have mental origins, somatic disorders cause genuine pain and suffering. A number of things elders frequently complain of—including headaches, stomach trouble, constipation and trembly or shaky feelings—are among their common symptoms. However, hypochondria can also cause a person to writhe in pain, vomit, have difficulty breathing, be unable to digest food or run a high fever.

A thorough medical examination is the only way to establish, or to rule out, physical causes for such problems. If a somatic disorder is diagnosed, a therapist may be needed to help work through its mental causes. As a caregiver, remember that a hypochondriac is likely to be a person in need of attention and reassurance—which you may be able to provide.

Arthritis

More than 100 separate diseases of the cartilage and connective tissue are commonly referred to as arthritis. The two most common types are osteoarthritis and rheumatoid arthritis. Neither is curable. However, with proper diagnosis and treatment (such as physical therapies and exercise to maintain mobility, pain medication, anti-inflammatories, proper diet and weight management), the quality of life for the victims of arthritis most certainly can be improved.

Malnutrition

Malnutrition is a problem affecting approximately half of all elderly people. The aging body loses its ability to absorb and use nutrients from food—a condition that becomes worse as the elder becomes less active. Complicating matters, certain medications can increase the need for specific nutrients. The elder may need to begin vitamin and food-supplement therapies. Also discuss with the physician(s) a gentle exercise program, such as a daily thirty-minute walk or riding an exercise bike, as a means of stimulating the appetite.

An individual's eating habits are affected by many things beyond the normal effects of aging. Among these are loneliness, depression, medication, lack of money, lack of transportation to grocery stores, and no longer having the energy or ability to prepare foods. Check into senior services that provide a Meals on Wheels program or that offer a senior center for dining. Try a Dial-A-Ride program that offers transportation for seniors. Some church groups have volunteers who drive seniors or shop for them. Another solution is to prepare meals in advance for the elder to simply reheat, bake or microwave.

Drug Abuse

Drug abuse is a potentially disastrous problem among the elderly. When an elder takes a variety of different medications for a number of different complaints, or takes medication on a complicated schedule, it is quite easy to mismanage drugs. If the person has a problem with short-term memory, the potential for problems is even greater. The result can include unsuccessful treatment of the ailment, drug overdose, drug reaction or interreaction and, in some cases, death. This is a situation that needs careful monitoring by both caregivers and health professionals in order to prevent needless tragedy.

As a person ages, his or her physiology changes and the body responds to medications in a different manner than when the person was younger. For example, the dosage of a medication that worked perfectly in a person of fifty-five may cause that person to feel dizzy at seventy-five. This can happen even with medications that have been in use for many years and are well understood.

New medications are being released regularly. Unfortunately, not much is known about how the older body responds to the majority of these chemical compounds, since most testing is still being done with younger people, or even with the lower animals. Add to all this the normal (and natural) memory impairments that can cause the elder to skip a medication or take it twice, and you get an ugly picture of the potential for trouble.

Although drug abuse may be intentional or unintentional, the result of it will be the same. There are five common ways in which such abuse happens.

One stems from complaints of restlessness by the elder, such as not being able to sleep. A sedative is prescribed instead of a nondrug therapy, such as exercise and the elimination of naps. In many cases, the doctor will recommend the nondrug therapy yet provide the sedatives anyway for those "bad" nights—nights that may come far more often in the elder's mind than they do in fact.

The second is usually due to the elder's seeing a number of different doctors for a variety of ailments. This may result in prescriptions that interreact. A medication that is perfectly safe by itself may have terrible—even fatal—side effects when used with another that also is safe on its own.

The third is a misunderstanding of either the purpose of a medication or the instructions on how to use it. Coupled with this is not knowing its main effects and side effects.

The fourth is hypochondria. This may develop from loneliness, anxiety or depression—or simply from relying too much on pills to cure all ills. In addition, when the elder has a physical complaint, he or she receives more attention from the family and doctor. This comfort can make the complaint(s) feel genuine, when in reality their cause is psychological—the physical symptoms are real but do not have a physical cause.

The fifth is the unfortunate possibility that the elder may

intentionally take too much or too little of prescribed medication. Whether consciously or unconsciously, this could be a suicide attempt.

There are ways in which you can reduce the chance of drug abuse—intentional or unintentional. One of the most important is to work closely with the physicians who write the prescriptions and the pharmacists who fill them. Despite the common misconception, there is a substantial difference between a doctor and a pharmacist. Each is a specialist in his or her own way.

If possible, use the same pharmacy for all prescriptions. Most pharmacists keep track of all prescriptions filled for each individual, so they can quickly spot overuse of a particular drug or when two drugs are likely to cause an adverse reaction when used at the same time.

If a generic drug (one without a brand name) is offered or used to fill a prescription, make certain the doctor approves of the substitution. (Usually, the doctor will check a box on the prescription form that indicates whether a generic is allowed.) Whether a brand name or a generic is prescribed, be certain the pharmacist or doctor explains exactly what the drug is for and what reactions are possible.

KEEPING TRACK OF MEDICATIONS

Keeping track of medications is an important part of using them correctly. If the elder cannot be relied on to do this, it will be up to you as the caregiver. Your job isn't to act as the pharmacist but rather to keep accurate records of all medications and be sure that the primary-care physician is informed about their use. Do not rely on memory alone. It is a good idea to create both a drug book (Fig. 1-1) and a drug board (Fig. 1-2) to help you.

Keeping a Drug Book. Buy a steno book. Use one page per drug. For each drug, list the following information:

1. the drug's brand name and generic name
2. dosage

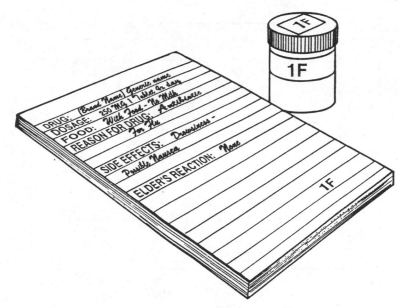

Fig. 1-1: Drug book

3. instructions for use
4. what the drug is for
5. possible side effects
6. elder's reaction to the drug

Assign each page a number. Write the same number on a label and affix it to the bottle containing that drug. The drug book should accompany the elder on every doctor visit, so the medications can be monitored easily.

Keeping a Drug Board. Buy an erasable memo board with a hard white wipe-off surface to hang on a wall. (Magnetic boards, for mounting on refrigerators or other metal surfaces, are also available.) Use an erasable marking pen (included with most boards sold) to section the board in the following way:

Time	Sun	Mon	Tue	Wed	Thur	Fri	Sat
7 AM	1F 3	1F 3	1F 3	1F 3	3	3	3
10 AM	4	2 4	4	2 4	4	2 4	4
Noon	1F	1F	1F	1F			
2 PM	4		4		4		
6 PM	1F	1F	1F	1F			
Bedtime	1F	1F	1F	1F			

Figure 1-2: Drug board

1. Across the top, list the days of the week.
2. Draw a vertical line between the days, from the top to the bottom of the board.
3. Down the right side of the board, list the times when medications are to be taken.
4. Draw horizontal lines between the times, from the left side to the right side of the board.

You now have the board divided into squares, with the day of the week at the top and the medication times at the side. Use the drug book to complete the drug board, as follows:

1. In the drug book, find the number you assigned each medication. Write that number in the appropriate square on the board. (You could write the name of the drug instead, but drug names are often long and can be similar to each other, so it is easier and less confusing to use this number system.)

2. Place the letter F after the number if the medication must be taken with food.

If the elder will be away from home when it is time to take medication, use the chart as a guide to placing pills in a small plastic sandwich bag that will be available to him or her when needed. Use one bag for each time of day. Affix a label to the outside of the bag that clearly specifies the time the medication is due and whether it is to be taken with food, as well as any other appropriate instructions.

As we have said, you don't need to become a pharmacist—but it *is* important that you take it upon yourself to understand the basics of the medications: What do they do? What are the predicted side effects? What precautions need to be taken, and which adverse side effects should you be watching for?

Not only can medications interact with each other, they can interact with the diet. Trudy was put on coumidin, a blood thinner. Neither she nor her daughter thought it was important to tell the doctor that she was a vegetarian. The result was that her diet was high in vitamin K, which caused the blood thinner to have unpredictable effects. The doctor tried to adjust the dosage, which only seemed to make matters worse. It wasn't until weeks later, after several scares, that the cause (her diet) was discovered. A change in medication solved the problem.

The lesson is to pay attention to everything. Don't make assumptions. Sometimes the answer is obvious—or would be to the doctor or pharmacist. Other times it's more subtle, such as Trudy's being a vegetarian.

The Primary-Care Physician

One of the best ways to help minimize elder health problems is to find and keep a good general practitioner. This doctor is referred to as the *primary-care physician* or *primary doctor.* If a specialist is required, the primary doctor will recommend one and hopefully will coordinate all the care the patient receives. (Don't rely on this. Take it upon yourself to be sure that the primary physician is always kept informed.)

Ideally, the primary doctor will know the elder's history and be aware of changes. For example, knowing that there is a history of stroke in the elder's family may indicate a more careful monitoring of a slight rise in blood pressure that in someone else would not be cause for alarm. The better the doctor and elder know and understand each other, the more likely they are to develop a strong, reliable relationship. This can be especially important if the elder is facing a serious medical condition or when a number of specialists are required. A good primary care doctor will get the needed answers and form a plan for cohesive medical care.

Although not all elders require physical care from their care-givers, many do. If you and the doctor have developed a working relationship, it will be much easier for you to gain the answers you need, should you ever have to assume more extensive physical care responsibilities.

It can't be stressed enough that you need to keep the primary doctor informed of *all* medications, including those purchased over the counter, that the elder is taking. Even aspirin or the alcohol in cough syrup can cause problems with some medications. When more than one doctor is involved, *do not* rely on all of them to be in communication. Take it upon yourself to keep an accurate list of the medications, their dosages and any side effects you notice.

Accepting Aging

Think about your own retirement for a moment. If you're now working full-time, you probably think of free time, hope for few monetary constraints, and in general think of enjoying life more. If you ever considered the physical problems of aging, it was likely in a vague way and doubtless associated with a more extreme age—perhaps eighty or ninety. It is difficult to imagine yourself responding more slowly to situations you are currently handling with ease, and to feel left out while the world and even your own family seems to move at supersonic speed. But these things happen.

Feelings of betrayal are common as a person ages. The body, and perhaps also the mind, no longer responds as it used to—yet, inside, the person still *feels* like the person of many years ago. Plenty of elders are heard to remark, "That character looking back at me in the mirror isn't how I see myself. I don't feel *that* old!" The need to feel independent, useful, loved and fulfilled does not diminish with age. As a caregiver, you must always keep these needs in the forefront of your mind.

You will walk a very thin line between caring and *over*caring for your loved one. It is ever so easy to rush in too soon, to do too much, and thereby to rob your elder of dignity, self-respect and independence. Without these elements, the quality of life suffers a tremendous blow, and your loved one may simply give up. When this happens, the strains of caregiving and receiving care alike will intensify long before the final stage of care arrives.

These are some of the problems and pitfalls of old age—but they are not by any means the whole story. Most elders *do* lead fulfilling lives. Their age-related limitations usually *are* manageable. And with love, compassion and tender care to support and comfort them, the last stages of their lives can truly be "golden years."

TWO

Taking on Elder Care: A Personal Decision

Many elders are able to continue living independently. Others can remain in their own homes with some assistance. Of the rest, about half live with adult children, many of whom are themselves raising families (while also moving toward their own retirement years).

If you're fortunate, you are looking at the challenge of elder care before it has reached a crisis level. Preplanning, with time to explore all options, is always the best aid in making serious decisions. If you are confronted with a need to make an immediate decision, relieve the pressure by considering the solution temporary. Make certain that everyone involved is aware that the decisions are on trial until a more permanent care plan can be adopted.

In any circumstances, the decision to undertake caregiving should be one that is well thought-out, in realistic terms rather than merely emotional, and discussed thoroughly with everyone who will be affected. At the very least, you and the elder will be directly affected. Always remember that if you have a spouse and children, your home is not just yours, it's theirs as well. So is your time and attention.

Emotional Impact

While the physical, legal and financial aspects of caregiving must be considered, nothing will influence the quality of your caregiving experience as much as the emotions involved. Here everything becomes intertwined. What others feel will affect you. What you feel will affect them. The feelings that you and all the others concerned experience, both positive and negative, will affect both your ability to give care and the length of time that you will be able to participate in a caregiving situation.

One extreme is the situation in which the elder is deeply loved by everyone involved, and there are no problems, no friction and no personality conflicts. The opposite extreme would be caring for an elder who has a background of being abusive toward family members. The elder may have changed. All parties involved may have even gone through extensive therapy and may feel certain that the problem no longer exists and all has been forgiven. However, the danger of role reversal, with you, the caregiver, becoming the abuser, is in fact very real and far too common. If there is abuse in your background, you are strongly advised to find an alternate means of elder care, for the sake of both the elder and yourself.

In between are the more realistic levels. There will be conflicts; denying that would be unrealistic and a sign that perhaps elder care isn't a viable solution in your case. Some of these conflicts seem to be unimportant when you see the elder for fairly short periods of time. But they can become much more serious when you and the elder are together more regularly. For example, if you have a tendency to get into arguments—even small ones— with the elder, the situation is very likely to be amplified if he or she has moved into your home (or vice versa).

Beyond this is the impact that caregiving will have on others around you. A spouse, or life partner, children, even friends and neighbors are going to be affected. Once again, denying or ignoring this reality is a warning that other options might be better. Take the time to thoroughly assess the relationships you are involved in before you begin to predict the impact that caregiving will have on each. Every relationship, like every caregiving situation, is unique.

On the other hand, caregiving can have a beneficial effect for you, your elder and your family as a whole. It offers intergenera-

tional contact and a chance for strengthening family ties, especially between grandparents and grandchildren. There is also
peace of mind, and sometimes the advantage of shared incomes
and workloads. Most of all there is an opportunity for love,
understanding and growth—a chance to resolve old feelings and
create new ones, and to explore aging as a natural part of life (and
perhaps resolve your own fears of it).

There is another intangible advantage. In today's society, the
number of hours spent at a job has increased, but, with the advent
of automation and computers, many of us work with machines
instead of people. Many jobs, while necessary to the economy,
offer little in the way of allowing us to feel that we have
contributed to making the world a better place. Add telecommut-
ing, shopping by phone, even the option of doing banking by
phone or through a computerized kiosk, and human contact is
again diminished. Caregiving reorders your priorities. You know
that what you do makes a difference in the quality of someone
else's life. It focuses your attention on the joys in the here-and-now
instead of somewhere in the future.

Will caregiving enhance your life? There are no pat answers—
but there are some strong indicators. Think about your relationship with your elder. Is it positive? Do you get along well together,
agreeing on most things? If you have a spouse and/or children,
consider of their relationship with the elder—and with you.
Harmony, an ability to cooperate and compassion for all concerned are the essential three ingredients for a positive caregiving
situation.

On the negative side, the benefits of combined incomes and
shared workloads can change as the elder's health and abilities
decline. Think about the elder's medical situation and especially
about how it might change in the future. Try to decide how far you
are willing to go with it—what you would and wouldn't be able to
handle in a caregiving situation.

The love and sharing aspects can quickly become negative if all
your time and energy are taken up by the elder, with the other
loved ones in your life being made to suffer by comparison. This is

every bit as real a concern as the finances. It's easy for others who need and deserve your attention to feel left out—and every bit as easy for both sides to become bitter.

How do you decide whether caregiving is a practical idea for you and your family? Begin with yourself. Before you broach the subject to anyone else, understand your own feelings and capacities, and become aware of what you personally can and can't do and are willing and not willing to do.

When the need for elder care arises, especially if it is because of an emergency situation, many times we push reality aside in the emotional need to solve the problem. Closest to the surface are feelings of helplessness and fear of losing a beloved elder. Of course, emotions of anger, resentment, frustration and jealousy usually are present to some degree as well, but they are not as readily acknowledged. Unfortunately, repressing so-called negative feelings doesn't make them go away; usually they resurface in other areas. Being less than affectionate with your spouse, irritable with the children, or snappish with friends or coworkers are just a few of the ways this can show up. Feelings of isolation, loneliness and depression may also be present. Try to understand and remember that these feelings are neither right nor wrong. They are simply *there*, often in defiance of all logic. What is important is how you act on those feelings.

A Typical Day

Suppose you are a woman who has a spouse, two children (ages eleven and thirteen) and a demanding job. Your parents live across town, and your mother has recently been diagnosed with a serious chronic condition requiring frequent medical attention. Your father at seventy-eight no longer drives, due to impaired vision.

A typical day for you begins at 6:00 A.M. when you get up, dress, bag lunches, toss in a load of laundry and dash for work by 7:30. At noon you call your mother to check on things and are told she's out of milk and bread. An afternoon meeting runs long and you can't leave work until 5:30 P.M. Stopping by the store for

Mom's groceries, you pick up a few of your own, then drop by the pharmacy to get her prescription.

It's almost 7:00 when you get to your parents' home, only to discover Mom has had a rough day and hasn't had the energy to make dinner. Your father has therefore tried to make grilled cheese sandwiches and—judging from the mess—has burned them. You call home to explain the situation and ask that someone toss the laundry into the dryer. Putting the groceries away, you discover that your folks are out of eggs, cheese and other staples—and that some of the vegetables in the refrigerator have spoiled. Another trip to the grocery store is needed before you can fix dinner.

After dinner, you talk with Mom as you straighten up the kitchen. She feels bad that you are cleaning up yet another mess and that you don't seem to have the time to just talk anymore. By the way, she suddenly reveals, the doctor called, saying that the test results are back and need to be discussed tomorrow at 3:15. Could you be there?

It's after 9:00 by the time you get home to find pizza boxes in the kitchen for the third time this week. Someone forgot about the laundry, and no one ran the dishwasher. Your daughter reminds you to meet with her school counselor about class changes at 4:00 tomorrow, and your son needs to be picked up from soccer practice at 5:30.

With these new pressures dropped on your shoulders, you swallow the anger and turn to cleaning up yet another kitchen. Finally, you sit down and put your feet up. It's 10:30, and you're thinking about tomorrow's balancing act. Your husband is bent over a desk, working on a batch of papers. With some hesitation you explain to him about the doctor's appointment, the meeting with the counselor and having to pick up your son after soccer practice. With a hurt look in his eyes, he gently reminds you that you've forgotten the proposal he's been working on at night for the last month. It was scheduled weeks ago to be presented tomorrow—with much of his career, and your financial future, relying on it. With so many other things on your mind, you simply couldn't remember that, too. Quietly he leaves the room, headed for the late-night news and bed.

This type of situation can be common in a caregiver's life. The circumstances seem to conspire to bring out every negative emotion we are capable of feeling. We usually top it off by feeling guilty for all the feelings we shouldn't feel. After all, a "nice" person, a "good" person, the person you always thought yourself to be, would be able to handle all this without so much as a whimper. Right? And your husband and the kids wouldn't complain if they were "nice" and "good." Right?

The answer is an emphatic *no!* You are not a robot, devoid of feelings and needs, made to function for everyone else's benefit. Neither are the others around you. We all are emotional beings who have varying needs that must be filled if we are to have any type of peace, contentment and joy.

Taking apart the situation described in the previous paragraphs, it's fairly easy to see how anyone could become angry and frustrated—on all sides. However, some of the other emotions are not quite as easy to discern.

Look for instance at the feeling of abandonment. The caretaker in the scenario just described may feel that she is about to lose either one or both of her parents. Not feeling supported by her husband or children, she takes on still another load of responsibility, thus contributing to her feelings of abandonment, loneliness and isolation. She loves her parents—they have always been there for her, and she feels it's time to give a little back, especially now that they need her so much. Secretly, however, she resents the vast amount of time that giving help takes and the damage it is doing to the rest of her life. She also resents the fact that her spouse and children are also mere human beings who need some sign of care and love—then gets even madder at herself and perhaps at her parents as well.

Jealousy and resentment become part of the equation, too. Everyone else appears to be going on with their lives. Her husband has his job, and the kids seem okay. Only *her* life appears to have been disrupted. Don't they love her enough to pitch in and help? Can't they at least be emotionally supportive and understand the pain she is going through? In many ways she feels torn and manipulated. If only she had someone to talk to about all this. Unfortunately, her husband seems unwilling to discuss the issue.

The caregiver is not the only one to feel jealous, resentful or abandoned. During their eighteen previous years of marriage, the caregiver and her husband had a close, caring relationship. They were friends in every sense of the word. They laughed, planned for the future and cheered each other on. Now the sharing has become sporadic and much more difficult—she's rarely home, and when she is, she has no time or energy left that's worth a darn.

The husband *thought* he was being supportive. He didn't yell about the fact that dinner wasn't made; he simply ordered pizza. He didn't reproach her for putting her parents first once again; he just went back to work on a proposal that was crucial to his job. After all, they had talked about the extra hours the proposal would require and the promotion he would get if it was successful. Now it seemed as though his friend didn't even care about it anymore. He tried not to show his hurt when she didn't remember the meeting date. He knew she had a lot on her mind, but he didn't know how to help her with it, and his attempts at giving comfort were rebuffed. He was ashamed of feeling jealous that her parents saw more of her than he did and embarrassed by his feelings of helplessness. He did what many people do when faced with a situation that makes them feel inadequate. He withdrew.

The children were another matter. They grew up knowing that their parents were active people but that, no matter what, Mom and Dad were always there when it counted. They were even there for things like soccer games, and slumber parties and family outings were always a treat. Now, though, home wasn't such a nice place to be. Mom was always over at Grandpa and Grandma's or was home yelling about things she never cared about before. And Dad didn't laugh anymore. Something was wrong, and nobody was telling them anything. When the children talked to their friends about it, the others said it sounded like the parents were going to get a divorce. Being worried and afraid made it hard for the kids to think about things like school and homework.

Things weren't any easier for the elders. They thought they had planned well for their retirement. Who could have foreseen this kind of necessary dependency? They hadn't wanted to be a burden to their daughter—but, regardless of how she denied it, they felt they had become one. They felt useless, depressed and guilty for the way things had turned out.

The elders were also afraid that their situation would only get worse. This made them angry and frightened. What would happen if their daughter stopped loving them and refused to help further? Unconsciously they began to ask for even more help, as a measure of reassurance that they were still loved, still valuable.

On top of all this, they all entertained some conviction of guilt for feeling the way they did. And the guilt didn't stop the upsetting feelings—it simply made everything seem that much worse.

Many times, simply discussing your feelings honestly will help you to put them in perspective and reduce imagined guilt relating to them. The only way a caregiving situation can truly work is if all people involved are willing to communicate openly and know that it is safe to say what they really feel. When feelings are discussed calmly, there is more chance that the other person will be able to see your point of view. (More tips on communication are given in chapter 12.) This all begins at the beginning—not after the fact.

It is very easy, especially in the beginning when an elder's need for care is new, to agree to provide a service for that person without considering the total impact. We are sure that we can do that for a week or even a month. But how about for a year? Five years? Take time to really think about the logistics of what you are agreeing to. Can you really prepare two dinners every night of the week and manage either the delivery of one dinner or the cleanup of a second kitchen when you prepare the meal there? How long can you manage this? What will it cost you in terms of time? Family commitments? Personal responsibilities? Decisions you make as the caregiver will of course affect others, too. The time to open communication is before the decision is made, not after it has caused emotions to flare.

It may seem easier if the elder were to live with you. It is true you would not have the drive time from one home to another and would face only half as much cleaning. However, the workload—even for simple things like cooking and laundry—increases markedly for the caregiver. Private time for that person, and for him or her to spend with the family without the company of the elder, may decrease greatly. It is obvious that this decision directly involves everyone living in the affected home.

Coping: Can You Do It?

When all the problems of caregiving are examined, especially if the situation is serious, many people immediately doubt their ability to cope with it. Most caregivers have no medical background, so they worry about the physical aspect of care. Giving injections, monitoring an erratic physical condition, helping someone bathe or do physical therapy at home—all can take on terrifying proportions in the mind of a new caregiver. Some people are so overwhelmed at the prospect that they convince themselves that only a nurse or some other trained person can handle the job. This simply isn't true for the majority of situations a caregiver ordinarily encounters. The skills needed are easily learned, and the professionals will teach them to you right the first time.

It used to be that cardiopulmonary resuscitation (CPR) was performed only by doctors in emergency room settings. Eventually, though, it was thought that other emergency personnel (such as police, fire and ambulance people) needed the skills. Now the general consensus is that everyone should know CPR. Many people fear giving injections. Take heart: Insulin-dependent diabetic children as young as eight or ten are taught the procedure of self-injection.

You will find, as you work in a caregiving situation, that—at least until the later stages—physical care is the least demanding part of your role. Caregiving involves much more than the physical care of someone else's body. An elder's mental and emotional well-being can play an even more important role in determining the quality of his or her life. You will of necessity learn to walk a tightrope between and among what the elder wants and needs, the physician's orders, and your own priorities. To keep your balance, you will need (rather more regularly than you'd like) to refer to certain capacities that have long served you well under other circumstances. Discussions on several of these now follow.

Do You Have the Right Attitude?

If your personality is essentially optimistic, viewing others and most situations as basically good, then your attitude about caregiving and your dependent elder will be more positive than otherwise. There is a good chance that you also will bring out the best in your elder.

Some other positive points of view and attitudes that a successful caregiver will have in mind at all times are:

- The elder has the right to be treated with dignity and respect, regardless of any physical or mental condition.
- The elder has the right to be kept informed of his or her medical condition, as well as other important aspects of daily life. The elder has the final decision in directing personal care and affairs. If this is not possible (due to impairment), that person is still to be kept informed as much as possible and is to participate in decisions made regarding care.
- The elder has the right to privacy and confidentiality.
- You must help the elder to maintain self-worth—the feeling of being a valued human being—regardless of his or her impairment.
- You need to express love and compassion. Liberal use of eye contact, smiles, attention and hugs are all important.

People with a pessimistic attitude communicate a distrust of most people and situations. They tend to dwell on both real and anticipated problems and complications without focusing on possible solutions. In a caregiving situation they may very well seek to control elders as a way to ease their own problems. This behavior could be very destructive to a healing situation.

Personality traits that can cause problems are:

- Being quick to anger
- Being highly critical and pointing out "failures." Example: "You never get the dishes clean when you wash them," or, "You're not going to wear that ugly thing, are you?"
- Withholding affection, and so treating elders as duty assign- ments rather than as needful people
- Treating elders as children, thus robbing them of their dignity and self-respect
- Denying competent elders control of their own lives

SENSE OF HUMOR   The ability to laugh at the absurdity of some of the incidents that will happen helps you, your family, and the elder to get the most joy out of the caregiving situation. Humor will generally keep frustration in perspective. Regardless of the seriousness of the situation (even if you are dealing with a terminal situation), laughter can truly be the best medicine. A joke, an old family anecdote retold or a silly response can bring a smile and chase some pain or depression, even if only for a moment.

Here's an example: A teen was assigned to care for his elderly grandfather on a farm located far away from anything and everyone. Grandma was in the hospital after a suspected second heart attack. Grandpa was a semi-invalid.

After several days of boredom (a lifetime to the teen), the phone rang. He answered, took the message and hung up. Grandpa asked, "Who was that?"

"It was Bertrice Wilson. She wanted Grandma."

"Did you tell Bertrice she couldn't have her?"

It took a moment for the ridiculous remark to sink in, but when it did the boy realized that his grandfather had a wonderful and natural sense of humor. It was a short step from there for him to realize that Grandpa was also in emotional pain from worry. By the end of the week, the two were closer than ever—and the next time someone was needed to help at the farm, the boy eagerly volunteered.

Can You Resist the Urge to Control?

It takes a wise person to understand that the only real control possible is that of oneself. You cannot control others' attitudes, desires or feelings. The best you can do is influence them by your reaction to their behavior.

The elder is an adult and, assuming competency, has the right to determine the course that his or her life will take; including accepting or rejecting a doctor's (or anyone else's) advice. This is probably the hardest fact for a caregiver to accept.

Suppose your mother is diagnosed with a terminal illness, and the doctor has said that if immediate treatments were taken and were successful, her life could be extended by a year or more. The side effects of the treatments will make her weak and sick. The cost will throw her and possibly you into poverty. Without treatments, she will be able to continue as she is for a short while but will grow steadily weaker and perhaps have only a few months to live.

Your mother fully understands the situation and decides to take a long-dreamed-of cruise instead of having treatments. You love your mother and want her in your life as long as possible, so the idea of taking a cruise seems foolish to you. You might even think her decision is a symptom of incompetency.

At this point, you don't think you can bear the thought of losing her, especially when there is a chance, however slim, that the treatments could work and she would live longer. But before you open your mouth and utter words you may live to regret, stop and think.

Suppose you succeed in changing your elder's mind. Will you be able to handle the guilt when you see her suffering from the side effects, knowing she is going through treatment only because you wanted her to? Suppose the treatment doesn't work—or even that it does and your mother lives for another few years but has missed that dream cruise, how will you feel?

Don't you feel it is your right to choose the path your life will follow? How can you demand the right of choice for yourself but deny that right to another competent adult? Elders know what gives their lives meaning and joy; what constitutes quality of life for them. They also know you love them and want them to live. Set your desires and beliefs aside, accept and love them enough to respect and support their decisions.

You cannot change other people, either. They must change on their own. Many times in a caregiving situation an elder who is fully aware of some condition and its consequences will refuse to follow a doctor's order or do something you know he or she shouldn't. Why would someone do that? The reasons are as varied as the elders themselves. Many elders fear losing the control over their own life and destiny as they have had throughout their adulthood. They want to maintain the right to continue controlling their actions, decisions and choosing their destiny. All the screaming, nagging, cajoling and logic in the world will not change their feelings. They may by physically forced to submit to someone else's will, but what will this do to their spirit?

Imagine for a moment that your father has dangerously high blood pressure. The doctor has absolutely forbidden salt, so you make sure all food is fresh and cooked without added salt. You have provided a salt substitute for table use, but still your father grabs the regular salt shaker and uses it liberally and on everything, fully aware that he is endangering his life by his actions. What can you do?

Your only chance to influence his behavior is to say: "Dad, I love you. I care about your life. The doctor has told you not to use salt because it makes your blood pressure even higher. It's up to you to decide if salt is more important to you than staying as healthy as possible, for as long as possible."

This statement must come calmly and lovingly from your heart, and you must not repeat it to the point where it becomes part of an ongoing struggle for control. There is a real difference between control and communication. Your job isn't to control the situation, or the person, but to keep communication open.

In the above scenario, your father obviously had a reason for his actions, but it was not communicated to you. Reassuring your father of his right to make his own decisions may also open communication so that you become aware of his motivations. Understanding motivations and actions, especially where control issues or a battle of wills is involved, can lead to compromise and peace. Suppose the reason for the additional salt was a lack of taste. A compromise could be asking the doctor about a small amount of salt in the diet or a salt substitute.

Perhaps your father stated, "Everybody's going to die someday. I see no reason to put up with tasteless food." The underlying motivation could be depression or anger over his condition; deciding he is guilty of bringing the condition on himself and seeks punishment; needing to feel in control regardless of the situation; he may feel the good part of his life is behind him and wants to hasten the end. In such cases, psychological intervention may be needed.

The important point at this juncture is that either trying to force the issue (exert your control) or ignoring it won't solve anything. At the very least, communication will help clarify the problem.

THE "ELEPHANT TRAINER" THEORY A psychology professor stood in front of a class and said, "Today, I will teach you how to get through life while maintaining as much peace as possible. This is not part of your course, and you don't need to remember this to pass a test."

In my old country there are elephant trainers. There are two kinds of elephant trainers: good elephant trainers and dead elephant trainers. An elephant trainer understands the elephant and tries to bring out its capabilities and teach it what to do. A trainer knows that some days the elephant will not cooperate, no matter what the trainer tries. In fact, some days the elephant will be nasty and try to attack the trainer. This is when everything will be decided. A bad elephant trainer will try to force his will on the elephant. The elephant will swat him with his trunk or step on him, and the trainer will most likely be dead. A good elephant trainer will get out of the elephant's way and let the elephant kick. When the elephant is done kicking, the good elephant trainer will go back to the elephant and patiently, kindly begin again to train the elephant. The elephant will learn. I hope when you have problems and fights in your relationships, you are all good elephant trainers.

Let the elephant kick. Let things work out. What you fight fights back. Relinquish control. All of these are ways of saying the same thing. You are responsible for your life, your feelings, your attitudes—and no one else's. You have no right to dictate another competent adult's life choices!

In the unfortunate case of an elder who is no longer competent to make decisions, your guidance will have to depend on past communication with that loved one. If the two of you had a solid communicative relationship before the elder became incompetent, and he or she expressed wishes and opinions to you, you should now follow them as closely as you can. If not, you will be forced to rely on your own judgment. Hopefully, you will have the help of family members and the medical profession in reaching solutions to the ongoing problems of your diminished elder.

KNOWING WHEN TO HELP AND WHEN NOT TO   When the need for elder care arises, often our first instinct is to rush in and take over. If it is an emergency situation, our instinct probably is correct. However, in most instances "Let me help you" is not the kindest, the most loving, or even the smartest thing we can offer. This is where judgment plays a key role.

As caregivers, we walk a very fine line between helping and

hurting the elders we love. We can do too much, help too much, be too protective—and end up hurting the very person whose life we are trying to improve. This is especially true if the elder is recovering from an illness and needs to relearn skills.

It's difficult to watch someone you love struggle to perform a simple task. You want to rush in and do it, to save him or her from the pain of stiff joints and the frustration of muscles that won't cooperate. To help seems the loving and compassionate thing to do; it appears cruel to simply stand by and watch. After all, when a child has difficulty performing a task, it is expected that we help. Consider this, however: Children are growing, developing beings. They feel no loss of freedom or control when you first tie their shoes, because they have never been told to do that—and can't, anyway. Later, when they have learned the procedure and you try to do it for them, you may well hear a determined "I can do it myself!"

Now look at the elders' situation. They know they used to tie their own shoes (and probably yours) without trouble, and in fact without having to think about it. As age creeps in, however, they have to concentrate on the job, and it takes longer—but they can still do it. If you help, what you have done is rob them of a bit of freedom and control, you have chipped away at their dignity and self-respect. Silently, you have told your elders that they are failing, unable to take care of ordinary tasks and, in a very real way, like helpless children again.

The judgment to help or not help isn't easy. It requires both an open mind and open eyes. Helping to tie the shoes might of course be seen as a kind act that saves the pain of arthritic fingers. But be aware that it might be seen instead as a condescending act that suggests to the elders that they're becoming more and more helpless.

Can You Accept Change?

Accepting changes is necessary, especially in a caregiving situation where anything and everything can change both suddenly and dramatically. Accepting change is especially difficult if you have a hard time accepting that you simply cannot be in control of anything or anyone but yourself.

Your elder may undergo a great many changes you will have to deal with in caregiving. Changes may be physical, mental or a combination of both and be the result of disease or an attitude shift brought about by the elder's assessment of their life. The cause is incidental to the fact that you must accept these changes and deal with their consequences while trying to ease the elder's situation.

If the root of the change lies in disease, it will help a great deal if you can mentally separate the elder from the disease that causes his or her problems. This is especially true if you are caring for someone in the final stages of a terminal illness. Be prepared to accept that the time might come when you can no longer handle this situation.

Changes, both mental and emotional, often occur as the elder looks back over (life assessment or life review) his or her life. Though we all tend to review and decide on possible changes for the future, an elder tends to view life in the context of its probable ending. A powerful interest in religion isn't unusual even among those who have never seemed particularly religious previously. The elder may begin to read religious books and suddenly seek out radio or television programs dealing with this topic. All this is fine, but it is also possible that the elder may decide to send out much more money than is available for making "love gifts," offerings or, in some cases of illness, healings.

Much the same situation can occur with family members. For a variety of reasons including guilt, atonement, ensuring love, etc., gifts to family members and friends may begin to flow like water. Part of your job as caregiver is to keep an eye on all things connected with your elder. This does not mean taking control of the affairs of someone because you disagree with some of her decisions or choices. However, if the elder has truly lost the capacity (psychologists, doctors and the courts will decide this), you may have no recourse but to serve as conservator (chapter 5).

At such a juncture, the elder probably needs more care than you can personally provide, and it's also time to consider placing him or her in a professional care facility.

Can You Accept the Inevitable?

Caregiving responsibilities have a tendency to engulf your entire life, but they shouldn't. Keeping the situation in perspective will help you to be relatively peaceful and guilt-free when the need for caregiving has ended. Achieving perspective requires acceptance of five important points.

Regardless of what you, the elder or the doctor do, the elder will, eventually, die. You will never like facing this fact, but you will need to come to terms with it, not only for yourself but for the sake of your elder.

The elder must adjust to the idea of death on a personal level. This means going from the abstract idea that death will come someday to the realization that death will come sooner rather than later. The elder will probably have an easier time accepting their demise (even if they are in good health) than you will. In the later stages of life, time is perceived in a much more finite way than when you are thirty-five or forty. If the elder has a terminal condition, acceptance of death is especially necessary. Discussing death promotes acceptance for everyone, especially for the elder and for you, the caregiver.

Are You Emotionally Well Balanced?

Caregivers have many responsibilities, not only to the elder and to family commitments, but to themselves—a responsibility to take care of their own needs. On the surface this may sound selfish when your concern is supposedly centered on an elder who needs so much care, and on a family as well. But it really isn't. Remember that the only way to have something to give to another is to first gather it yourself.

How can you help another to see joy when you are too

exhausted to see it yourself? When a loving elder says to you, "I feel like I'm such a burden," how can you think he or she will feel less guilt, or believe your protestations to the contrary, when you do nothing for yourself? The elder who sees you emptying yourself on his or her behalf and watches your life being hurt in the process might carry a load of guilt that will make life unbearable.

Consider now the case of Becky's father, who was dying. He had, at most, eighteen months left. She began spending every available moment with him. Her day began at 7:00 A.M., the same as her father's. She'd rush out to cook breakfast for him, leaving her husband to fix that for their child and see him off to school. She spent the day with her father, leaving only briefly to get her son from school. The moment her husband got home from work, she dropped the boy off and was back with her father again.

She knew that there wasn't much time left with Dad, but she went so far as to totally abandon her own family. Her father would chide her and say that she'd better go home. From a false sense of kindness, she refused. The result was a shaky marriage, an unhappy child and a father who felt so guilty that he one day confided to his son-in-law that his death would be a blessing for everyone.

SELF-ACCEPTANCE   Self-acceptance, which is difficult for many people at any time, is crucial for a caregiver, especially in the area of decision making. Even a decision based on the best information available, and on the elder's wishes, can prove wrong. It's easy for anyone to criticize such a move after it has been made. But there's no need for self-reproach. If someone tries to tell you after the fact that you were wrong, don't accept their guilt. Simply assert your position: "I did the best I could under the circumstances." You can also then ask, "Where were you when the decision needed to be made?"

Even when you're doing the best you can, with the best information and the best intentions, mistakes will be made. Just as often, and perhaps more often, a decision may seem to be a mistake when in fact it will prove correct. And sometimes you will never know one way or the other. As an extreme example, imagine that you are caring for an elder with a terminal disease. Treatments are no longer effective. Even the doctors recommend stopping. The elder dies. You feel guilty: Maybe if there'd been just one more treatment... if you hadn't all given up...

There will be many times when things aren't flowing as smoothly as you'd like. Tempers might flare. Someone (including you) may say something that really isn't meant. If a barb is aimed at you and sticks, try to understand why and deal with the temporary pain. Sometimes merely pretending that it never happened is the best way to handle it. If you're the one who broke loose, a simple apology is usually enough.

If you accept the situation of caring for an elder, learn also to accept what comes with it. And that includes both mistakes and things that *seem* like mistakes. No one is perfect. It's okay to forgive even yourself.

Can You Prioritize?

It's easy to get caught up in the endless round of chores that need to be done, especially if your elder is very ill. Sometimes we personally overburden ourselves with these, to avoid having to think about the seriousness of the situation. In doing so, however, the more important things can get lost. Try instead to concentrate on the things that are necessary to sustain quality life, and learn to cherish time.

If you are one of those people who have so much to get done that you end up scheduling everything, and worry about whether it will be accomplished according to schedule, and that if it isn't, this will put you so far behind that you'll never get caught up, *stop!* Take a deep breath. Relax.

There is a limited number of hours in a day. If you're trying to get twenty-eight hours of chores and other responsibilities done each day, no amount of scheduling is going to help. To get everything done that needs to be done, you have to prioritize: The most important things must come first. What you might find, however, is that what you think is most important is actually farther down the list.

Those things that are life-threatening have first priority. A fair second would be tasks that could become life-threatening if ignored. Third are the comforts that make life worth living. This category can easily begin to blur if you let it. It can range from relief of physical pain to the wide spectrum of human needs including love, care, dignity and much more.

The blurring continues into the fourth category of optional pleasures. Attending a child's school play or graduation, bowling, reading a book, watching a movie, sipping a beer or glass of wine while cuddling with your mate during a sunset—any of these things may seem frivolous on the surface but could be exactly what you need for putting the rest of your life straight amid all the turmoil.

When your caregiving situation has ended, you will look back at that afternoon when you and your elder sat in the garden going through an old photo album, or think of that feeling of communion you had while watching an old movie together. Those are the moments you'll remember—and, thinking of them, you'll feel their joy again. You will never regret not doing one more load of laundry.

It's not an easy balance to achieve. Doing it requires a dispassionate view that takes into account the feelings and needs of everyone affected. And do try to get those others involved. That will help you to determine the most important tasks, and will also help give them a better understanding of all the things that need to be done, as well as an understanding that things aren't going to be normal for a while.

One way to prioritize is to use index cards (or ordinary blank paper cut into three-inch squares). On each, write down one leisure activity you enjoy. Be specific whenever possible. If TV is a major activity, write down each program individually. On the bottom of each card place the letter W to indicate that you need to do the activity with someone (playing Scrabble, for instance), or A for an activity you prefer to do alone—such as reading. It will help you later if you take the time to write the contents of all the cards as a list on a piece of paper.

Spread all the cards out before you, face up. Choose the card with the one activity that is the least important to you and would be easiest to give up. Place it face up on the table. Now choose the card that is the next least important, and so on until you have ordered all the cards, each face up on the card beneath. The cards will then be in reverse order, with the most important on top and least important on the bottom. If you've been honest, that top card will be an activity that you consider to be of primary importance, and that you don't want to give up. Whatever else has to be eliminated, include this activity in your future scheduling.

The next step is to eliminate cards. The activity listed on the bottom card will be of least importance and will probably be something you can fairly easily do without for a while. So will many of the cards that follow.

Now is when that first list will come in handy. By making a second list of the remaining cards and comparing it to the first list, you will get a very good idea of just how easy it is to eliminate certain things, to organize others and to find some very nice ways in which you can share the time you *do* have.

Follow the same procedure, this time using chores as your subject. List every chore and errand that must be done by someone. On the bottom of the card write the letter M if *you* must do the chore. (Writing M—for "me"—means that absolutely no one can do the chore but you.) Write S on the card if someone else could do the chore. Spread these cards out and again begin choosing them in the order of importance.

One pitfall that caregivers experience is the trap of thinking, "No one can or will do it but me." In the beginning, it may seem that you can do it all. The reality is that you will get tired both physically and mentally. The more you can diversify the chore load, the more pleasurable caregiving will be for all those involved. Diversification helps prevent burnout and increases the length of time you can give care.

Take up the pile of chore cards marked M. Follow the

elimination procedures as outlined above. Which chore could you most easily assign to someone else? Write his or her name on the bottom of the card. (At this point writing someone's name is arbitrary. It does not mean that this person will automatically and absolutely handle this particular task.) Proceed to the next card.

Sometimes eliminating chores is harder than eliminating pleasurable activities. Responsibility plays an important part in our lives: It gives us purpose and sometimes defines our identity. If you find yourself unable to give up a chore, change your frame of mind by creating a game. Pretend you are stranded on a tropical island, so other people must take over your responsibilities. You must now assign every single chore to someone else. If you absolutely cannot think of one other person to take on this chore, place an H on the bottom of the card. This means that your only alternative to doing the chore is to hire someone to do it for you. With all this done, you can record the list of chores on a piece of paper. Write the assigned person's name (or "hire") after each chore.

All you've done so far is, again, arbitrary. Your goal is simply to clear your own head and then get a firm grasp on what *you* want and expect. This is not an absolute, and it's highly unlikely that things will turn out exactly your way.

The next step is to repeat this with anyone else directly involved (your spouse, the children, siblings, etc.). Each should make his or her own set of cards and from this a list of their own priorities. It's critical that you consider their needs and take them seriously. Now more than ever you need the support of everyone involved. Don't let that support evaporate because you haven't taken into account the importance of others.

A word of caution: Everyone's most important leisure activity is crucial and should be considered as sacrosanct as medicine required by a doctor to be taken at a specific time. Many caregivers make the mistake of thinking that enjoyment is the thing to give up. On the surface this may seem to be true, but the actual result of giving up this important bit of fun is burnout, anger and resentment.

Is Your Plan Realistic?

When you have done some soul-searching about the issues, you'll have a good idea of how far you are willing to go with caregiving. You will have thought about some of the problems you're likely to encounter and formed some tentative solutions.

It takes time to consider all the ramifications of caregiving. Don't expect instant unconditional support from your spouse. Instead, pick a time when there is little chance that you and your spouse will be interrupted, and state your concerns. Listen to the comments and answer the questions as honestly as possible. This is no time either to hedge or to bend the truth. If the initial reaction to your idea is less than positive, try to look at the objections without anger. Be ready to compromise—and always keep in mind that at least some of the objections might be valid.

A case in point is that of Julia, who'd had a long and satisfying marriage to Phil that resulted in two children. The kink had been an interfering mother-in-law, Caroline, who'd never quite accepted Julia. Phil knew the problem but generally ignored it to keep the peace. So did Julia—or rather did until Phil's father passed away and Caroline moved into a home just a few blocks away.

Phil was spending less and less time at home. There was always some little errand that Caroline needed him to do. She doted on the two grandchildren and continued to ridicule Julia. Instead of this being something Julia had to tolerate once in a while, it became daily. In fact, it got worse: Her own children began to echo their grandmother, with "Mom, why do you...?" and "Mom, why don't you...?" and "Grandma says...."

Caroline was diagnosed with Parkinson's. Her condition seemed to be slipping almost daily. Julia found herself wondering just how much of the slippage was the disease, and how much was yet another ploy on Caroline's part to grab attention. Almost instantly, though, she would suffer feelings of guilt for even having such thoughts.

As the disease progressed, the situation got worse—and it wasn't long before the children began to avoid Caroline. They understood that she was ill but didn't know why she did and said such strange, and sometimes cruel, things at times.

Phil wanted his mother to move in with them, since she needed almost constant care. He said that if they sold her house there would be money to pay the bills and that having Caroline in the spare bedroom would solve many problems. There was no real discussion. Julia agreed to avoid yet another of the growing number of arguments, to alleviate her feelings of guilt and also because she couldn't think of anything else to do.

The children became sullen. Her marriage was deteriorating. Julia was certain that everything now revolved around Caroline and Caroline's needs. She saw that her own life and her own family were falling apart. She felt helpless and lost. No one in the house was really talking to anyone else—but it wasn't as if communication had suddenly broken down. As a matter of fact, it had never really started in that household.

This case illustrates both the importance of working together at all times within a marriage and some reasons why you shouldn't enter into a potentially traumatic experience like caregiving without first thoroughly exploring it. Caregiving requires complete, open and honest communication, plus an understanding of what is to come—even what *might* come. Some research into the disease, and discussion of this, should also be a priority.

The following are a few of the areas that need to be discussed privately with your partner. Later, some of the topics need to be thrashed out with the rest of the family—and of course gone over with the elder. Use this list as a starting point and tailor the discussions to fit your situation, trying all the while to cover at least some of the what-ifs.

- How will caregiving affect your future as a couple?
- If you have children, how will they be affected?
- How will caregiving affect your finances?

- How will living arrangements be managed, both soon and in the future?
- How much time are you, personally, willing to give to elder care? Under what circumstances? With what limitations?
- Discuss viable ways to maintain the closeness of your marriage and family life.
- Pay special attention to any reservations either of you may have. Look for possible solutions.

Have You Considered the Children?

When you and your spouse have reached agreement about what you are willing to contribute to elder care, it is time to bring the children into the discussion. To what extent you take this depends on a number of factors, not the least of which is the age and maturity of the young ones. Talk with them openly and honestly about elder care and why you want to do it. Explain to them what their part in it would be, and ask if they are willing to participate. Gaining their cooperation is critical—and you're more likely to get it, and have it sustained, if the children understand the issues from the start.

It might seem that the kids won't be affected much. A teen who is expected to handle some of the chores obviously is, but what about the younger child? Here it's important to remember that when the parents are busy, they're not available for the youngsters, and that a nine-year-old may be involved in Little League. You haven't directly asked him to give it up, but if Mom and Dad are occupied, there's usually no one to take him—and the reality is that he has been deprived of what might be to him an activity every bit as important as your own "most important."

Even young children notice changes in adult behavior and are certainly aware of new living arrangements. And these things can be confusing when you don't understand them. But they can be just as confusing, or more so, when you have them explained to you in a way that is over your head. When you're facing the illness and eventual loss of a beloved elder, plus an increasing drain on your time, energy, budget and emotions, it's easy to forget that others besides the elder in your life need you. And the youngest children should be at the top of that list.

You may wonder why the elder has been pretty much left out of these early discussions. The primary reason was to allow you, your spouse and your children a chance to talk openly by yourselves without fear of hurting the elder's feelings. The secondary reason was that you're trying to find the answers needed to resolve certain problems in advance. When it comes time to talk with the elder, your preplanning will give that special person a variety of choices, some of which he or she may not have considered. Even if the elder already has a course of action in mind and rejects your ideas, you will have learned a great deal about yourself and the members of your family. It all takes a careful balance, and often a great deal of compassion.

THREE

Choosing a Living Arrangement

As you read through this chapter, keep your elder's situation in mind: Each case, like each elder, is different. It will be of considerable help to you if, before starting to read, you make a list of all your elder's known care needs, including medical. Also write down initial questions you may have concerning the necessary procedures for care. Add to the list all further needs and queries you think belong on it, as you read herein. Use the list as a reference when in contact with doctors, nurses and other medical or social service personnel. The extent of the list will of course be determined in large part by the number of "complications."

We never know how we will truly respond to any caregiving situation until we are in it. Some things that seem impossibly difficult may become routine, while other, more simple matters can turn out to be the most traumatic. Don't doubt your abilities without good reason. You are probably far more capable than you think you are.

Fortunately, there are a number of options available to those needing help in caregiving situations, and more will regularly become available as America continues to age. You will probably hear of at least some of them through friends and via the media. Learn to keep a notebook handy and jot down any such data that interests you. It could even prove to be vital information when you begin networking services and contacts—which *will* happen as you enter deeper into caregiving.

Assessing Caregiving Needs

There are three basic *levels* to caregiving. Each requires a different degree of involvement and commitment from the caregiver. As we discuss care levels and then options, use the notebook to record the types of problems and solutions that apply (or could soon apply) to your own situation. Check your phone book to locate addresses and numbers of the corresponding firms and associations in your area, and record them as well.

When you are analyzing your elder's care level, please remember that not all symptoms need be present and that an elder can have symptoms from more than one level. For example, someone suffering with severe arthritis (Level II) could need a lot of physical help and yet be totally functional mentally, or, conversely, he or she could be in good physical health but be unable to mentally relate to anyone else.

LEVEL I   People who need care at this level will probably require it in only a few areas. Basically, their minds are alert and otherwise functioning well. They are beginning to have some physical limitations but are still able to take care of themselves, live independently and meet their own basic needs. They may require occasional assistance because:

• Heavier cleaning chores, like washing windows and floors or yard work can't be performed.

• Balance may be somewhat impaired, and they may report occasional falls or stumbles—some resulting in bruises or abrasions.

• Vision or reflexes may be impaired to the point where they may not drive safely.

- Their diet is unbalanced due to lack of variety, or they are unwilling or unable to spend the required time in meal preparation.
- Bills are paid, but there are mathematical errors in their checkbooks.
- There is some confusion over a complicated medication routine.
- They may begin to withdraw socially.

Any or all of these conditions might be of a minor or sporadic nature. Care is therefore begun with just general helping. Running errands, assisting in some meal preparation, supplying homemade meals ready to reheat or handling the heavier household chores may solve most of the problems. If you cannot provide personal assistance, consider a daily meal service, such as Meals on Wheels, and perhaps a monthly yard or housecleaning service.

The errors in checkbook math problems can be solved easily enough with the aid of a simple calculator and/or a checkbook that makes a duplicate copy every time a check is written. Check the math in the checkbook, and reconcile statements, monthly.

The medication problem can be solved in several ways. If it becomes very complicated, a charting method (explained in chapter 10) can be employed.

The problem with lack of balance can be helped by the use of a cane or walker. A general mobility problem will involve the purchase of several aids, such as handrails for the bathroom, and a regular and thorough safety check of the home.

Withdrawing socially is a problem many elders have. It is important to discover the cause. It could be something as simple as lack of transportation or as serious as depression—which may require medical intervention.

LEVEL II   By Level II, affected people require more assistance, often in more areas. While still physically able to dress themselves, they may need help with such tasks as bathing. They can aid in preparing a meal, but either their efforts take longer or they become easily distracted. Disorientation can be a problem for them, even in familiar surroundings. They may have memory lapses, lose track of time, confuse appointments, and so on. Because of this and for other reasons, they frequently misuse medications. Their physical limitations increase, as does their need for emotional reassurance.

These problems obviously are more extreme versions of Level I. Those who wrestle with them require more supervision to handle daily living activities but still are too independent for a nursing home facility that is medically oriented. Possible solutions include live-in companions, group living, or moving in with an adult child. In some cases, using a combination of services such as an adult day-care meal service, telephone reassurance programs, and evening companions may alleviate the situation—especially if there is an elder spouse on the scene.

If the problems are mainly physical, an extensive remodeling of such elders' homes may be required. Depending on the circumstances, caregivers may have to give up, or cut back on, the hours usually spent in outside employment, in order to provide adequate care to their elders. Networking arrangements for shared care may also be an option.

LEVEL III   In this level the elder may have retained most of their mental faculties, yet require frequent physical care and/or can no longer handle basic living skills without help. These elders may even need help with eating or suffer from incontinence. Sometimes the opposite occurs: The body is in fairly good shape, but personality disorders have surfaced or cognitive reasoning abilities have been impaired. The last stages of most terminal illnesses usually necessitate Level III care. Depending on the illness and on how the medical program pertaining to it is directed, round-the-clock medical supervision may or may not be required.

Options

By now you should have a fairly good idea of what your elder will physically need for care. The hard part is balancing that with what he or she needs emotionally, mentally and spiritually to allow the remainder of his or her life to be lived out with dignity, independence and love, to the fullest extent possible.

Most elders will want to remain in control of their living accommodations. Many realize that they need some type of help but have only the vaguest idea of what is available to them. The following information deals with various programs and alternatives. (To prevent duplication of information, you will find more complete descriptions for medical aids, appliances and diet in chapter 7.) Use this chapter as a guide to researching options available in your area. Note ways in which they might be integrated into your elder's care situation. Later on, you will want to discuss these options with your family and, of course, your elder. If it is at all possible, the elder should make the final decision.

In considering housing, try to achieve a genuinely satisfactory balance between physical and emotional needs. Look for alternatives and compromises that allow emotional space for both the elder and the caregiver. Keep in mind the overall health of the elder when looking at the housing question. If his or her general condition is stable at Level I or II, then remodeling or ECHO housing (see chapter 4) may be of more benefit. For someone who needs Level III care, however, this choice is probably unsuitable.

The vast majority of elders want to remain as independent as possible, for as long as possible. They derive great comfort from being home, in familiar surroundings. Most have worked all their lives to have their home, and permanently leaving it—even when they know that is necessary—can be emotionally devastating. For some, leaving the family home is mentally equated with "I'm too old to handle life anymore. I'm useless. I might as well give up. There's nothing left for me."

Many very frail and chronically ill elders want to die at home, surrounded by comforting memories and where they feel safe. (Dealing with these issues and helping your elder to cope with them emotionally are covered in detail in other chapters.) There are many alternatives between "My elder shouldn't live alone anymore" and "I've got to find a nursing home." Consider the following approaches and aspects to some of your elder's problems. Some combination of these ideas may adapt well to your needs. The basic question is, "Where will the elder live?" Here you have three main choices.

First and probably best, at least for the elder, is for him or her to remain in the home he or she has come to know. The surroundings are familiar and probably filled with pleasant memories. Moving would probably mean selling the home. Being forced to sell the home and move can be devastating in itself, but it also highlights the fact that the person is aging and can no longer be self-sufficient. Usually an elder can accept assistance in the home easier than face the alternatives.

A second choice would be to have the elder live with you. The surroundings aren't as familiar but the people probably are. In making this choice, however, you have to be realistic. (The same is true in making any of the choices.) If you live in a one-bedroom apartment on the third floor of a building with no elevator and your elder requires Level III care, this choice would quickly prove to be impractical from a physical standpoint. Bear in mind, even if your living accommodations are or can be made adequate, a psychological problem may still arise, namely that the elder may feel he or she is imposing on you and/or your family.

A third option is for you to live with the elder. This could bring some serious problems, made worse if you have a family of your own (even if that "family" is only a spouse). Forcing your spouse and three children to give up their home and move into the elder's home can be damaging both psychologically and financially. Even if you're alone, this kind of move needs to be made cautiously. The financial aspects of having to sell (or even rent) your own home are bad enough. Psychologically, you will once again live under your elder's roof, and the old childhood relationship can quickly reassert itself.

Is the Elder's Home Suitable?

For any of these options, the home itself must be suitable. It's possible, even likely, that modifications to the home will be needed. Minor changes to a home usually aren't of much concern. If you have to build a complete extension, however, it will still be there once the caregiving has ended. So will the opening where a wall has been taken out. These factors have a definite financial impact. Modifying a spare room is generally fairly simple and inexpensive. But building an extension onto a house can cost thousands of dollars (and may not even be possible, depending on local ordinances, the layout of your property, etc.).

The details of actually making these sorts of changes to a home are covered in depth in chapter 9. For now, it is more important that you be made aware of other kinds of things you must consider if the elder is going to stay in his or her own home or move into yours, because these are important parts of assessing caregiving needs—and your ability to handle that.

- General safety is a primary factor, no matter where the elder stays. This includes his or her home, yours or a professional facility. Safety is also involved in many of the other factors listed below.
- Adequate lighting, inside and outside, is essential. It's not uncommon for a person to have failing eyesight with age. (Outdoor lighting also serves as added security.)
- Smoke alarms are a must, not only in every home but on every floor. If there aren't any, install them now, whether or not the elder will be living there.
- Handles and faucets may have to be changed or modified. Elders, especially those with arthritis, often have a difficult time with them. Locks often present the same kind of problems.

- The furniture in the home can present its own set of problems. Chairs that are fine for everyone else may be too low for someone with leg, hip or back problems. Tables may also be too high, or too low.

- Ramps may be needed at doorways, and not just for those using a wheelchair. Those who have difficulty walking could find the rise of an entrance painful. A ramp, which is fairly inexpensive and easy to build (see chapter 9), can help solve that problem, but it is a form of possibly restricted remodeling.

- Bathrooms can present enormous difficulties. They often are small, and get smaller when you have to be in there helping the elder. Modifications often are needed. Sometimes these can be so extensive that the effort becomes a major remodeling job.

- Slippery floors might exist throughout the house. Bathrooms are the most common example, with kitchens close behind. Stairs may be slippery and are also dangerous in and of themselves. Also to be considered are rugs, which can trip people and may also slide on the floor beneath.

- The number of cords and wires needed is likely to increase. There will be equipment that has to be plugged in, and perhaps a phone with a long cord installed. It's important that you find ways to get such things out of the way. Especially when someone who has difficulty walking and tends to shuffle can easily catch a foot and fall.

- Telephones provide communication with the outside world. This sounds trite, but if you are caring for an elder, you absolutely need to have good phone service close at hand. Suddenly facing an emergency and needing to call 911 is not the time to decide that a phone—or an additional one— should be installed. Also keep the elder in mind, particularly one generally confined to bed. A phone should be right there. Consider getting a cordless phone.

- Remodeling might be needed. This could be as simple as installing a peep hole in the entry door for security purposes or might involve tearing out walls, building extensions and the like. It's impossible to predict every possible home contingency and need—but you must try. This begins by accurately and honestly assessing the condition of the elder and continues into predicting how that will change in the course of the caregiving. In some cases, very little "home improvement" might be needed. In others, the extent and cost of the modifications would undoubtedly be such that you'll have to rule out caregiving at home before the fact.

Alternative Housing

Another method of accommodating an elder in your environment without extensive home remodeling is one of the previously cited ECHO units, also called a "granny flat" or an accessory apartment. The unit is a small, free-standing, removable housing module that would be positioned on the same lot as your single-family dwelling. The advantage of this type of housing is that since it has no permanent foundation, it is a temporary structure. (Depending on the length of time that the variance is in effect, *temporary* can mean *for years*.)

Cities and counties alike have their own specific zoning restrictions and guidelines outlining local and/or area requirements for this type of housing. The major regulatory concerns seem to be with property values, waste disposal and traffic patterns. (Some areas will accept modular or prefab housing but not even consider a mobile home.) If modular housing is a possibility, look into this option thoroughly, since a modular unit can be altered by the manufacturer to accommodate all the features needed. Check the appropriate city or county zoning department for guidelines, restrictions and variance procedures.

Day-Care Services

There are other forms of alternate care for seniors. Depending on the care level required, the elder might do well in a day-care environment. A day-care center is usually open during traditional business hours, enabling a caregiver to hold down an outside job. These centers are found in churches, storefronts and community centers. They may be sponsored by churches, subsidized by government or private foundations or run as a privately owned business. The staff can range from unskilled volunteers to trained nursing assistants, social workers, therapists and doctors.

The services each center offers also will vary. A few centers will offer physical therapy and rehabilitation, along with purely social interaction like games, exercise classes and even shopping or field trips. Transportation to and from the program is sometimes available either through the day-care facility itself or through a senior transportation program like Dial-A-Ride or the Red Cross. Normally, a senior must be ambulatory and able to handle bathroom needs without assistance in order to participate in the program.

Charges will usually be based on the type of services the center provides and how often the elder uses the program. If the elder is a legal dependent on your tax records, some of the day-care charges may be deductible if the center meets state and local regulations. Check with the IRS or your accountant.

For information on how to find a day-care center, contact church groups and county agencies, hospitals or any local Office on Aging. When looking for a day-care center, you can handle most of the basics by telephone. Always pay a visit to the center to assess the situation there personally. Make certain your elder visits, too. Many centers offer a "free" day during which your elder can get a feel for the place and decide if he or she likes it.

The following list of questions will help you to compare centers, and in particular their services. Use these as a checklist on your first visit.

- Is the center certified?
- Is the center recommended by your elder's physician or the local Office on Aging?
- Is the entrance well lighted and handicapped-accessible?
- Do staff members seem cheerful, helpful and competent?

- Is the environment cheerful?
- Is the temperature comfortable?
- Are there unpleasant noises or odors?
- Is the area clean?
- Is the furniture sturdy?
- Are there safety features in the bathroom, such as handrails and emergency call lights?
- Are the exits clearly marked?
- Is there a plan for emergency evacuation?
- Are there any medical or therapy services?
- What is the procedure if your elder has a medical emergency while at the center?
- Is the staff-to-elder ratio satisfactory?
- Do the other seniors seem to enjoy being there?
- Are they participating in the activities?
- Are there activities that your elder would enjoy?
- Does the center actually do the things planned according to its calendar of events?
- Is the food appetizing? Nutritious? Tasty? (Look at the menu for the week or month, and try to be around when the food is served.)
- Does the center make any accommodations for special dietary needs like low-salt, low-fat or diabetic restrictions?
- Check on the billing procedures. What is the cost of each service?
- Does the center offer refunds or credit if the elder doesn't attend due to illness?

Roommates and Companions

Some elderly find roommates through senior centers and/or church groups. These seniors band together to stay independent while sharing expenses. The 1990 statistics show that there has been a 57 percent increase in this type of arrangement since 1980. Unfortunately, in some locations zoning regulations restrict unrelated people from living together. Also, some governmental assistance programs may reduce payments to those who formerly lived alone when the guidelines include total household income as part of their computations for payment.

Paid companions are another way to handle care for the elderly. The length of their service can be for a few hours a day on several days, or something more like a live-in arrangement (with room and board a part of the salary). The cost of a suitable companion will depend on the amount of care required, how often that person is needed and his or her level of training.

The skill required in a companion is determined by the type of care your elder requires. Some companions are needed only to provide company and don't need particular skills. Others are asked to perform minor housekeeping chores or assist with some daily living skills, such as preparing a meal. More skilled companions may be nurses' aides (CNAs or Certified Nursing Assistants) able to give baths, turn a bedridden patient and so on. A licensed (LPN) or registered nurse (RN) may be required for respiratory care, injections or intravenous (IV) care.

If you think your elder needs a companion with medical training, be sure to check with the primary-care physician. That doctor should be able to supply a list of medical needs so that you can look for the companion with the most suitable training and background. The doctor can also provide an order or prescription for the service. (The doctor's order is required if the service is to be covered by Medicare or other insurance.)

Companions can be found through both newspaper advertising and agencies. Sometimes a doctor will immediately know of someone who does this type of work or can provide that information.

When you are interviewing a potential companion, pay attention to his or her personality as well as qualifications. The companion and the elder must be able to establish a rapport, because the better they get along, the easier everyone's life will be.

The following is a list of questions you might want to ask any potential companion or roommate. (Some of the questions apply more to a professional companion. Adjust the questions to the situation.)

- How long have you been a professional caregiver?
- Why do you prefer this type of work?
- Are you interested in any of the elder's hobbies?
- Do you have your own transportation, and are you able and willing to drive for the elder?
- Do you speak the same primary language as the elder?
- Do you have any physical limitations that would prevent you from physically caring for the elder? (This question is especially important if your elder will need a lot of physical care, such as lifting, or assistance into and out of chairs, etc.)
- Are you allergic to pets or smoke? (Ask only if these details are applicable to your elder's situation. But remember that this person could be a carrier of smoke or of pet smells or hairs. Thus, the matter could prove the reverse, especially if your elder is the one with breathing difficulties or allergic reactions.)
- Are you certified in CPR—or at least able to perform it?
- What is your philosophy on elder care?
- Are you willing to abide by the elder's wishes, even if they are contrary to your own inclinations?

Always ask for and check references, both professional and personal. This is a good practice even if you are only using an agency to locate a caregiver. If you are searching for a roommate, references are vitally important—because, unfortunately, elders are easy prey for many unscrupulous people. Extra caution is needed when a stranger will be sharing an elder's home, especially if that person was not recommended by someone whose judgment you trust implicitly.

If you want additional background information on an applicant, including a check for criminal convictions, you can contact a private investigative firm. You will need to supply the firm with not only the person's name, but also as much other pertinent information as possible. If you have copies of references, supply them to the agency as well. Background investigations can be done for as little as $150. The price varies depending on the agency and on how extensive a check you want. Most firms offer a free or low-cost consultation concerning your need and its expected cost.

The firm or investigator you select should be licensed and have the license (and other credentials, such as diplomas, awards, etc.) prominently displayed. Many firms are members of an association that permits them to check in more than one state. You can check the reputation of your chosen firm by asking it for references and by calling the Better Business Bureau. To locate a firm, check the Yellow Pages under *Detectives* or *Investigators, Private*.

Retirement Communities

Retirement communities are springing up everywhere. Generally they are designed for a leisure lifestyle for those fifty-five and older. Most offer single-family homes and/or town homes with a wide array of recreational facilities, usually including a clubhouse or recreation center, tennis courts, swimming pool and golf course. Some developers have really given serious thought to the needs of the elderly, designing homes that accommodate restricted lifestyles by means of lower cabinets, wider doorways and single-level units. In many cases, yard maintenance is included with the association fee. Prices for retirement community living vary greatly, so check more than one.

Life Care

A new type of retirement community, sometimes called life care, is available in several parts of the United States. This community offers graduated-care facilities. This is to say that, beginning with private homes or town homes for independent living, the senior can take advantage of all the amenities a typical retirement community offers. As health declines, the senior is moved to a group home on the same grounds. The group home usually has four private bedrooms and common living and kitchen areas. In this home, seniors receive assistance with daily living chores they are no longer able to perform independently. When even more medical supervision is required, the elder is moved to yet another facility onsite that functions much like a nursing home. A few of these facilities have their own medical staff and doctors. Some even have a private hospital or are affiliated with one.

The usual contract for a life-care facility is a lifetime contractual arrangement according to which the resident pays an entrance fee, which the government claims ranges between $20,000 and $200,000. There is also a monthly fee of between $500 and $2,000. The fees vary according to the size of the facility and the number of services provided. Many times, unfortunately, acute medical services are not covered.

In 1987 there were approximately 680 of these facilities with an average of 245 residents each. Only thirteen states regulate the care given, and the regulations vary in each state. As you might expect, a few problems have arisen with regard to some of the facilities. While they do assure daily care and health-care cost containment, their fees are not always realistic. Sometimes the fee is pegged too low and the firm eventually finds itself with financial resources inadequate to meet the residents' needs. Some firms immediately overcharge their residents for certain services. If your elder is interested in this type of living accommodation, be certain to ascertain what portion of the fees will be refundable if he or she decides to leave the community.

Board-and-Care Facilities

Board-and-care facilities are group residences wherein small numbers of people who need minimal help and support live together. Managers oversee operations and are available twenty-four hours a day. These facilities offer meals and social interaction with other residents, but usually very little in the way of therapy. The homes sometimes take elders for brief periods as well as for the longer term. The cost of living in these facilities varies—but it is not uncommon for an elder to turn over his or her entire Social Security check as payment. This will often have to be supplemented to pay the whole fee.

To find a board-and-care facility, contact your area Office on Aging or the Department of Health and Human Services, check the Yellow Pages of your phone book or ask such medical personnel as doctors, therapists and nurses.

Not all states regulate board-and-care facilities. If your state does, make certain that the facility you are interested in is licensed. Check with the state on the number of complaints against it and their resolution—because there have been a number of abuses reported about these places. You need to be sure that you're not forcing your loved one into a bad situation. As always, check out the facility personally. For a list of things to look for and questions to ask, read the following section on nursing homes.

Nursing Homes

Nursing homes differ from board-and-care facilities in the level of care given. A nursing home is required to give both intermediate care, which is usually short-term with limited medical assistance (such as in the case of a person recovering from a hip replacement who needs therapy), and skilled care, which is usually long-term and requires twenty-four-hour medical supervision.

There are vast differences among nursing home facilities. Some provide excellent care, while others offer only mediocre or even poor care. This why you must visit all facilities of interest, if possible with the elder in tow. But before you even begin your search, call the U.S. Department of Health and Human Services and request a copy of their *Guide to Choosing a Nursing Home*. (The questions at the end of this section were adapted from that public-domain publication.) This booklet explains many of the laws governing these homes, the patients' rights and many other important factors.

The cost of nursing home care may shock you: The average yearly cost is almost $30,000. Needless to say, financing this can be a severe hardship on most families. Be aware of your elder's Medicare and supplemental insurance policies. (Can the elder qualify for Medicaid? The hospital discharge planner or the nursing home's social worker can help you to find out, and if the answer is yes, that person can help get it.) Be aware that the elder must be placed in the section of the nursing home approved by Medicare, supplemental insurance or Medicaid in order for these programs or insurances to pay part or all of the costs.

There are other restrictions, too. You will probably be asked to sign a contract. Make sure you and your elder (if possible) understand all the legal points. It probably would be wise to have an attorney check and explain the contract.

Compile a list of referrals. Ask for recommendations from medical personnel, and especially your elder's physician. Check with your state for a list of approved, licensed nursing homes. Ask friends and clergy for referrals. And, as in similar instances, check your phone book. The elder's physician will explain the type of care needed and its expected duration. Use that information to reduce your list to those that can provide it and have an opening.

On your first visit, use the following checklist as a basis for comparing nursing homes and their services. Remember to compare facilities certified in the same category, because the homes can be certified in more than one category and have both intermediate and skilled patient sections within the same facility.

- Do the residents seem to enjoy being with the staff?
- Are most of the residents dressed for both the season and the time of day?
- Does the staff respond quickly to the patients' calls for assistance?
- Are the residents involved in a variety of activities, or is watching TV their main form of activity? Are activities tailored to individual needs?
- Does the home try to match roommates?

- Does the facility have a residents' council? Does the council influence decisions about and changes in residents' lifestyles?
- Does the facility have contact with community groups like pet therapy programs or the Boy or Girl Scouts?
- Are religious services available for the residents?
- Check a list of activities for the month. Ask residents if these tend to be enjoyable and how often special programs or activities are being provided.
- Ask residents if they are comfortable with their care.
- Time your visit(s) to include at least one meal. (Rate it as you would a similar one in a decent eatery.) Was it served in the dining room? Was the staff attentive to those who were having trouble feeding themselves? Were any allowances made for food preference? How were restricted or other special diets handled?
- Do various staff and specialists participate in evaluating each resident's needs and interests? How often is this checkup performed?
- Does either the patient or the patient's family participate in forming the care plan?
- Does the home offer programs to restore lost physical functioning, such as speech, physical or occupational therapy?
- Does the home offer any special-care services that meet your elder's needs (for example, special-care units for dementia, Alzheimer's or respiratory problems)?
- What is the home's policy regarding the use of physical restraints?
- What is the procedure if the patient needs hospitalization or has any kind of emergency?
- Look at the overall condition of the home. Is it clean? Cheerful? Free of odors?
- Are there outdoor areas for residents' use? Are they well maintained? Do the staffers help nonambulatory residents to use these areas?

- Does the home have handrails in the hallways?
- Look at a typical resident's room. Are there grab bars in the bathroom?
- Are residents allowed personal decorations? Do residents have secure and accessible areas for personal effects?
- Are there private areas for residents' visits with family, friends, clergy or physicians? Are visiting hours restricted? Is the home conveniently located for visits by family and friends?
- Does the nursing home have a good reputation in the community? A list of references? Does the local ombudsman visit the facility regularly? (Federal law requires each State Office on Aging to have an Office for the Long-Term Care Ombudsman. These offices provide help and information regarding long-term care facilities.)
- Is the home certified for Medicare? Medicaid?
- Are the resident (if possible) and the resident's family informed of any and all changes in charges or services? Are there any additional charges? If so, how are they paid? (Some homes have beauty or barber shops that require additional charges. Others charge for laundry and other personal services.)

A patient's Bill of Rights should be posted and adhered to.

1. The patient is to be fully informed, by a physician, of his or her medical condition.
2. The patient may participate in the planning of his or her medical treatment.
3. The patient is to be transferred or discharged for medical reasons only.
4. The patient is to be free from mental and physical abuse, and also from chemical and nonemergency physical restraints, except as authorized in writing by a physician for a specified and limited period of time or when necessary to

prevent the patient from injuring himself or herself or others.

5. The patient is to be treated with consideration, respect, and full recognition of his or her dignity and individuality, including privacy in treatment and care for his or her personal needs.

6. If married, the patient is to be assured privacy for visits by his or her spouse. If both are patients in the facility, they are to be permitted to share a room.

Hospice

Many people faced with a terminal illness choose to die at home. Making use of hospice services is an excellent and humane way for people to achieve their final goal in peace. The hospice philosophy embraces the patient's needs, rather than the illness, enabling the terminally ill person to live out the final months, weeks and days as fully as possible. The Yellow Pages will probably list several groups or organizations that offer hospice services in your area.

Hospice believes not only in pain control but also in easing distressing symptoms. In a hospital, painkillers are administered only when a patient requires them—and then the patient waits for them to work. The physician supervising hospice care uses painkillers to prevent the pain from even reemerging, by giving medication on a consistent basis and at levels needed to control it.

Hospice usually requires a physician's prognosis of six months or less of life. The patient cannot be involved in any type of aggressive therapy against an illness, such as radiation or chemotherapy for cancer. In other words, the prognosis must be that the patient is terminal and nothing can be done about it.

The array of personnel and services that hospice provides to the home is extensive. Personnel include doctors and nurses, social workers, therapists, clergy, and volunteers who do a number of helpful things—from sitting with the patient while the caregiver takes a break, to providing transportation for shopping and doctor's visits, to home tasks like cooking. Some even offer counseling regarding wills, financial matters, funeral arrangements and the family.

There are three basic types of hospice. Some hospice organizations offer more than one. There is *home care,* as described above; *in-hospital hospice care,* and *free-standing* hospice care, which is a residential setting for hospice patients. Those that have both free-standing and home care often move a patient into the free-standing program while the family takes a break from the duties of caregiving. Some patients remain at home until shortly before death and then are transferred to the facility. Others die at home. With hospice, the choice always belongs to the patient and his or her family.

Hospice cost is covered by Medicare and other types of insurance. Check with each individual hospice group for other arrangements. If there is a hospice near you it would be listed under *Hospice* in the Yellow Pages. Physicians and hospitals also give referrals to hospice organizations.

Living Together

The wide range of services offered to elders makes it more realistic for an elder to remain at home or to live with you or for you to live with the elder. The first choice is usually the best, but may not be possible.

The elder may suggest that he or she live with you, or vice versa. Think this choice through carefully. This is true whether you are married, single, have children or are childless. Either choice (the elder moving into your home or you moving into the elder's home) can have a major impact. The usual choice is to have the elder move in with you, at least in part because this tends to be less disruptive. But perhaps the elder's house is bigger or more easily adapted to the demands of this newly handicapped person, and at first it seems to make sense for everyone to move there. While that may be logical from an immediate standpoint, the decision can prove an emotional catastrophe.

Take a look into the case of Elaine and her mother, Katherine.

They had always been extremely close—more like best friends than mother and daughter. When Elaine married Barry, Katherine embraced him like the son she never had. Far from being an interfering mother-in-law, she was always warm, generous and a genuine friend to both. This was quite a contrast to Elaine and Barry's relationship with Elaine's father, Robert, which at best would be considered antagonistic. His critical and overbearing attitude prevented any real closeness.

When Katherine was stricken with Chronic Obstructive Pulmonary Disease (COPD), Elaine and Barry did all they could to take up the slack with daily visits, running errands and helping with most of the chores. As Katherine's condition worsened and she was on oxygen continuously, Robert decided to institutionalize her. If there was one thing Katherine feared, it was to be put away. She wanted to be with her family and surrounded by the things she loved.

Robert would not consider moving with Katherine into Elaine's and Barry's home. It would be overcrowded, and they all would have to give up too many things. Therefore, if Katherine was to stay out of a nursing facility, Elaine and Barry would have to sell or store their possessions and move in with Robert and Katherine.

Elaine gave up her job to assume full-time care of her mother and run the house. Even though they paid half of the household bills plus their personal expenses, Robert still complained about how he was being taken advantage of. Elaine soon felt like a drudge with no space to call her own. She and Barry had no privacy and no input into the house rules. "It was like being a child all over again. It didn't matter that I was more than forty years old. Knowing it was my father's house and my father's rules made it incredibly difficult to feel like a woman or an adult. Looking back, I think it would have been different if they had lived with us. I would have felt more of a right to say no."

Sometimes the caregiver and the caregiver's spouse can feel like they are children again, even in their own home. That may sound improbable on the surface, but there are valid reasons for this feeling. When you review your past, you remember being a child and the process of maturing into an adult. Think of your parents: You never saw them as children or watched them grow into adulthood. Instead, in your eyes they were always strong, in control and usually right. They had power over you and what you could or could not do. In a very real sense, your key to happiness was pleasing your parents. They were the givers of rewards and punishments.

Later, as you grew, you learned to withhold certain information about your activities when you knew they would not approve. This was a way to maintain a relationship without confrontation. Rather than assert your independence and insist on the respect due to a conscientious adult, you simply became an older child. While this circumstance is not necessarily bad, it can be a difficult situation when it comes to caregiving. If your father still thinks of you as a child, it will be hard for him to take your advice and probably difficult for you to assert your opinion. When you feel like a child inside, it feels wrong to insist on your rights as an adult, including the right to your own life.

Dad and Mom may be the nicest people on earth, but they have their own way of doing things. You and your spouse *also* have your own way of doing things. If your parents come to live with you, you'll find yourself doing some things their way and compromising on even more. After years of being together with him or her as lover, spouse and friend, your reversion to childlike behavior around your parents may confuse and even anger your mate.

Lack of privacy and major changes in rules can be a huge problem. Perhaps the kids have gotten older and you and your spouse once more have treasured Sunday mornings together. You lounge in bathrobes and linger over coffee as you chat, cuddle and perhaps read parts of the paper together. This behavior is shocking to Mom, who believes Sunday mornings are to be spent in church. Frankly, she's quite embarrassed to find you in your bedroom attire. While this may sound absurd in your present situation, the point is that when your freedom is curtailed in your own home, resentment and tension build—fast.

Values often differ from one generation to another. This reality can become a big bone of contention, especially when criticism of a spouse or child is involved: "Son, in my day a father didn't let his boy wear a pigtail or an earring" and "I would never have dreamed of asking my husband to help get dinner" are invitations to dogfights. When criticism of *any* type comes up, it must be handled delicately if harmony is to be maintained in the home.

Think about how you will deal with this type of situation. Will you uphold your spouse's position or your child's prerogatives? Will you ignore the problem and hope it goes away? (It won't.) Will you assume that your parents' criticisms are automatically valid? You probably know your parents' opinions and beliefs and can make an educated guess as to what traits or habits of yours will be acceptable to them—and which of theirs are likely to cause problems. While you cannot preplan for every situation, these are the kinds of issues you need to think about and then discuss with your spouse as soon as possible after you sense their importance.

You and your spouse should of course discuss, privately and regularly, how you will maintain your marriage. If you are considering a "live together" situation, remember that having another adult in the house can be very trying. Mom may be your parent, but she is your spouse's in-law. Even if all three of you like each other, your spouse doesn't have the same relationship or history with her that you have. Besides, liking someone, even when you see each other frequently, is not the same as living with that person. If you are to keep your marriage intact, you will indeed need to schedule some private time for you and your spouse.

The following are a few of the areas that need to be talked over between you and your partner. (Later, to be sure, some of the topics will need to be thrashed out with the rest of the family, including the elder.) Use this list as a starting point. Tailor the discussion to fit your situation now, and try to cover some of the what-ifs.

- What are the living arrangements to be, starting now and in the future?

- How much time is each of you willing to give to elder care? Under what circumstances?
- How can the two of you maintain the closeness of your marriage and family life?
- If you have children, will the elder have the power to grant permission or administer discipline to the children? Under what circumstances?

Any reservations? Possible solutions?

When you and your spouse have reached agreement about what you are willing to contribute to elder care, it is time to bring the children into the discussion. Talk with them openly and honestly about such care, stressing why you want to do it. Explain to them what their part in it would be and ask if they are willing to cooperate. Gaining their cooperation is critical, and you're more likely to get it and have it sustained if the children understand the issue.

Setting ground rules with your elder is also a necessity. As discussed elsewhere, it is important that the senior be part of the family rather than a burden, but it is equally important that you have time for other activities in your life. Many of the initial ground rules will depend on the present mental and physical capabilities of your elder, and in all probability the rules will change over time. That's one reason why good communication is important.

Moving into someone else's home means getting used to a new routine, new ground rules. It also means that no matter how much you're loved, when push comes to shove, it is someone else's home, and ultimately that other's rules apply.

Imagine yourself as a guest in someone's home. You try to anticipate what your host requires of you. What time are you expected to retire for the night? Is 7:00 A.M. too early to make a cup of coffee? You look for signs that you may be intruding. What do you do if a minor argument ensues between your host and hostess?

Naturally, as your elder and your family adjust to the caregiving arrangement, other situations will crop up. An elder may interfere in discussions between you and your spouse or may disapprove of your parenting skills. That senior may also assume that you will include him or her in all of your activities. If he or she lives pretty much independently yet requires your assistance, you might be in for spending every weekend paired off with a second partner. Discuss these matters when they first come up.

Do not allow yourself to be maneuvered into an intolerable situation that will eventually explode into a destructive argument between either you and your elder or you and your spouse. Do not try to parent your parent. Listen to the needs, and encourage him or her to talk about what will afford comfort. At the same time, do not revert to the child role. You are an adult with a life and responsibilities of your own. State them and stick by them.

Consider writing out some rules so that your elder knows what is expected. The list may include chores, meal times, family times and weekend routines, indicating when the elder is expected or invited to participate and when the elder is not. The more familiar the elder is with your schedule and routine, the easier it is for that loved one to adapt and contribute.

What about setting some rules for yourself? You need to maintain a balance in your life. If you find yourself giving up every activity you value, you'll soon find yourself resenting the situation and the elder alike. It is destructive to sacrifice your life for another person.

You need to schedule time for yourself alone, and with others minus your elder. This form of respite is necessary to keep your perspective. (It is also one of the needs most caregivers overlook.) A regular routine that allows for your rest and relaxation is as important as anything you can do for your elder. It is your first line of defense against burnout and helps keep your relationships with others running more smoothly.

Think about your life as it is today. How do you *really* spend your time? Make a list detailing the time you spend sleeping, working, running errands, doing chores and pursuing leisure activities. If you spend seven hours sleeping and nine hours working (including travel time), that means you only have eight hours per day left to get everything else done. You can safely assume, we assure you, that you will spend twice the amount of time on caregiving that you estimate, regardless of the elder's mental condition. So— where will you get that time?

As hard as some of us have tried, we cannot create more time. And we can't save it. What we can do is use to our best advantage the time we have. Being rested and happy, feeling in control of our lives, is to our best advantage. Most people are vague when it comes to defining what gives them the most pleasure. Consequently they have a nagging suspicion that others are happier than they are. They feel they are missing out on something, but they're never sure of what it is. If you have not yet done the self-testing described in chapter 2, do so now. That simple test will help you to set up a caregiving plan that everyone concerned can live with!

FOUR

Assessing the Financial Impact of Caregiving

The vast majority of elders want to remain as independent as possible, for as long as possible. They derive great comfort from being home, in familiar surroundings. Most have worked all their lives to have their home and leaving it, even when they know it is necessary, can be emotionally devastating. For some, leaving the family home is mentally equated with: "I'm too old to handle life anymore." "I'm useless, I might as well give up." "There's nothing left for me."

For the elder who may be facing impending physical limitations, living expenses can escalate due to special needs. As discussed in chapter 3, there are four main options for living arrangements. Each brings its own set of costs.

The first three involve "staying at home," so to speak. The home used is your own (he or she moves in with you) or that of the elder (either the elder stays there or you move in). Regardless, there could be the cost of remodeling. Just how much remodeling depends on the home, on the medical condition and on the prognosis for the future. If the elder's problems are mainly physical, an extensive remodeling of the elder's home (or yours) may be required, and the financial expenditures can be very high. On the other hand, it might only be necessary to install a handrail in the hallway. Consider not only whether you and your elder can afford the needed remodeling, but also whether or not the remodeling will change the house rather permanently, which might decrease the home's market value.

One method of accommodating an elder in *your* environment without extensive remodeling is the Elder Cottage Housing Opportunity (ECHO), unit a small, free standing, *removable* housing unit that would be positioned on the same lot as your single family dwelling, but without the need of more permanent changes.

The cost of nursing home care may shock you. The average yearly cost is almost $30,000. Board-and-care or group homes can be almost as costly, depending on the services and accommodations. Financing this can be a severe hardship on most families. Be aware of your elder's Medicare and supplemental insurance policies. Can the elder qualify for Medicaid? The hospital discharge planner or the nursing home's social worker can help you work out the details. The elder must be placed in the section of the nursing home approved by Medicare, a supplemental insurance or Medicaid in order for these programs and insurances to pay part or all of the costs. There are other restrictions, too, and you will be asked to sign a contract. Make sure you and your elder (if possible) understand all the legal points. It would be wise to have an attorney explain and check the contract.

Discussing costs of care with your elder can be difficult, especially if your family is not used to communicating on this subject. However, the realities of it *must* be discussed. The elder needs to feel like a contributing member of the family, not a burden that you must support, and is important to his or her continuing to have a feeling of self worth.

It's impossible to determine what financial impact caregiving will have in your particular situation. The variables are almost infinite. These include not only your elder's financial resources (and yours), but the physical conditions, the level of care required, the length of time caregiving is needed and many other factors that vary from situation to situation. Even the geographical location will be a factor in the cost and availability of some services.

It's sometimes difficult to practically and coldly assess the financial situation when it comes to caring for a loved one. However, doing so, and doing so honestly, is critical. To begin estimating your possible costs, the first step will be to make a list of all the things your elder needs help with and the length of time you expect the help to be needed. Keep in mind that the situation is almost certain to change.

As mentioned in chapter 3, caring for a Level I elder usually means helping out now and then. The costs involved, however, might surprise you. (Imagine running an extra twenty errands each week.) Complicating it may be the loss of income—yours and/or the elder's. There is also the possibility that you won't be able to handle everything personally and will have to hire help.

The situation is likely to progress into Level II and possibly Level III. As it does, the costs go up even more. You are probably more capable than you might imagine, but everyone has limitations. Those include practical limitations, such as needing a particular skill or training, and personal, such as time to keep your own life intact. Professional help becomes more necessary and even essential. Although insurance and other programs can help, they won't remove the entire load. (It's important to find out, ahead of time, what is available and how much financial relief it will provide.)

Throughout, additional expenses are likely to be incurred for specialized equipment and appliances, food supplements, specific diet limitations, medications, therapies, increased medical visits, increased utility bills, hiring skilled help and finally, perhaps, admittance to a care facility. Transportation is another expense many don't consider. It can add up fast, especially if emergency or other special transportation becomes necessary (such as for someone in a wheelchair). Having a bus available doesn't do much good if a person who has a hard time walking from one room to the next would have to walk three blocks to the nearest bus stop and then climb steep steps to get into the bus. Taxis can be a solution but become expensive if used often. Services such as a Dial-a-Ride may be available.

Family Help?

When you take on the role of caregiver, you will spend more than money. You will spend your time—something you can never replace. You may have to reduce the number of hours you spend at your job, or give it up entirely. Either results in diminished income.

Perhaps you have siblings or other relatives who have agreed to help. They may or may not follow through. If they don't, you will either have to make up their contribution yourself or find some other means. Even if they hold up their end of the agreement, it may not be as much help as you originally anticipated. Regardless, expect that your own end as primary caregiver, financial and time, will be more than expected.

If the elder wants the estate split equally, you might want to suggest the estate is divided after the primary caregiver has been reimbursed for the money spent on the elder's behalf. In this way, simple record-keeping can substantiate your claim. Buy a simple notebook and list each expenditure by date and item. Keep the receipt (note what it is for) with a canceled check attached if possible. Drop the receipt into a manila envelope.

Keep a small notebook with a record of your mileage on the elder's behalf. This might include medical appointments, trips to the senior center, etc. Don't be surprised to find these little extras and the mileage add up to thousands of dollars—dollars you may need to pay for your children's college education or your own retirement.

Ideally, all of this will be taken into account by the elder when the will and other financial matters are updated. Many times the elder is not made fully aware of the financial impact of caregiving and what it means to your own situation. It's common for the elder's estate to be divided equally among the heirs, which doesn't take into account that you've had to cut into your own savings.

Changes to make things more equitable should also be made known to others if they are aware of previous arrangements. Too many times family members have heaped praise on a caregiver for all the wonderful care an elder received only to resort to anger and accusations the moment the funeral is over, and a portion of the estate has been set aside to help the caregiver recoup the losses.

Chances are good that you, and the others, will be uncomfortable discussing the financial aspects of caregiving. It seems cold. The loved one is sick and perhaps getting sicker. The need to provide care emphasizes the reality that this person may not be around much longer. This may *seem* to be the worst possible time to be talking about money. Unfortunately, it's a necessity. The time to work out the details is before it becomes needed, or even a crisis. Perhaps worst of all is to wait until it's time to settle the estate because by then it's too late.

Property

Real property (homes, cars, boats, etc.) often represents a sizable amount of money. The largest investment most people have is their home. Under certain circumstances, it can also become the biggest liability. For example, the home might be older and in a state of disrepair. Or perhaps the amount owed on the home makes the amount of equity low. An even more common situation is having a large mortgage payment due at a time when medical costs alone are taking more than the elder's total income.

Statistics were gathered in 1985 concerning the living accommodations of seniors (those aged sixty-five and older). These remain essentially the same ten years later. Of those who still had mortgages on their homes, 21 percent were spending at least half of their income on housing costs (less than 7 percent of those under sixty-five did). Another 8 percent also spent 50 percent of their income on housing even though they did not have a mortgage. For seniors, the median amount of income spent was 28 percent with a mortgage and 18 percent without a mortgage. Mortgages aside, other costs of home owning must also be considered—taxes, insurance and upkeep.

Most seniors have owned their home for years. Approximately two-thirds of the elder population live in houses that are more than forty years old, some built before World War II. Granted, the age of a house doesn't always indicate the condition it is in, but older homes tend to need more frequent repair. Upkeep can be costly when insulation, plumbing, electrical and roofing problems occur. Complicating matters, a home that has served very well for decades may not be quite so suitable—and could even be dangerous—for the elderly. This could mean the necessity of making costly alterations to the home.

The physical layout and structural condition of the house must be considered when alterations become necessary due to a permanent, or even temporary, physical condition. A two-story home that has been a source of pride and comfort to a young family may create an impossible living situation for someone who can no longer climb stairs.

Making structural changes to a rented property requires permission from the owner. In virtually every case you can't legally make even minor structural changes to a rented property without permission, let alone tear down a wall or build an extension. Keep in mind that many of the alterations you'd make, even with permission, will be at your own or the elder's expense but will become the property of the owner.

Homeowners have an advantage over renters. Physical changes to the structure might cause a difference in the property value (up or down), but at least the choice is there for a property owner. In some cases alterations are an investment that increase the value of the home. In other cases, the alterations will have to be "undone" afterwards, which further increases the cost of caregiving (or decreases the home's value). All of this can not only affect the overall expenses of caregiving but can also cause a change in the home's equity.

USING EQUITY When a homeowner makes a monthly payment on a mortgage some of the money goes to pay off the interest on the loan and some of the money goes toward actual ownership of the property. The degree of ownership that accrues over the years is called *equity*, and it can be used in several ways.

The equity in the home is an asset that can be drawn upon in times of financial crisis. (Renters are faced with increasing rent, while a house payment usually remains the same over the course of the loan.)

Discuss the options with your attorney or financial counselor to find ways to utilize the home to ease financial burdens. Outright sale, second mortgages and refinancing are a few familiar options. There is also a "reversible mortgage," an arrangement in which a lending institution pays the homeowner a monthly sum based on the equity in the home, with the money plus interest repaid from the sale of the home at the end of the loan or upon the owner's death. A lending institution or financial professional in your area will know the availability of these types of loans and their qualifications. (A relatively new alternative is somewhat similar but doesn't involve property. In this the owner "sells" the proceeds of a life insurance policy, with the "purchaser" then being responsible for the bills.)

Taxes

As a caregiver, you may have to help your elder file tax returns each year or file a return on behalf of an incompetent elder. Tax problems continue, and sometimes become worse, after the beloved elder has passed away. While facing your grief you will also be facing inheritance tax, executor income and liability, and more. You, or someone else, could be responsible for filing final tax returns.

If someone is hired to give care, taxes must be withheld from each paycheck and paid to the proper agency. The person must also be given a statement of withholding by January 31 of the following year.

Your caregiving may also affect your own taxes. If your parent or another relative lives with you, and you contribute more than half of the money necessary for their support, that person may be claimed as a deduction. If the money needed for the elder's support is a group effort by the family, any member contributing

10 percent may claim the entire deduction, but only one family member can claim the deduction for the elder in any year.

Dealing with the tax laws can be difficult, confusing and time-consuming. Consult your local IRS office, accountant and/or tax attorney for the most current information.

Social Security Benefits

Social Security benefits are available to those who have paid into the system. Reduced benefits can begin as early as age sixty-two, with full benefits beginning at age sixty-five. To receive payments, your elder must apply by phone or in person to the office at least three months before the payments are to begin. Addresses and phone numbers are under *United States Government* in the phone book.

The amount of the monetary benefits will vary, depending on how much the person earned while working within the system. Payments can be made to your elder either by direct deposit to their bank account or by having a monthly check mailed to them.

If your elder is no longer able to handle his or her finances, contact the Social Security Office to apply for *representative payee* status. This term describes someone who is acting as an agent for someone who is receiving benefits. Pamphlets describing the representative payee procedure and Social Security qualifications and benefits are available from the office.

Medical Insurance

MEDICARE   Medicare is the medical insurance with Social Security, and both are usually applied for at the same time. It is available in parts A and B (doctors and hospitals, respectively). There is a yearly deductible if hospitalization is required and a monthly fee that is deducted from the Social Security check.

The fee deducted from the Social Security check for insurance is considered income for the elder for tax purposes. This must be declared when filing income tax returns. A statement of Social

Security income is sent to the recipient by the government once per year for this purpose.

Do not rely on Medicare to pay all your elder's medical expenses. First, Medicare is coinsurance, which means that the insured person pays some of every bill. Medicare pays 80 percent of "allowable" charges and this according to their schedule of costs. For example, if Medicare allows $100 for a service, they will pay $80, you will pay $20. If the service is billed to you at $150, Medicare will still pay $80, and you will pay $70. Second, Medicare does not pay for all types of medical treatment or medications. Some of these aren't "approved," which means that you are responsible for the entire bill.

If you will be filing Medicare claim forms on behalf of your elder, or will be submitting claims to a supplemental insurance company, *keep copies of everything!* Bills will arrive at separate times, which can make it difficult to keep track of what has been paid. Claims tend to cross payments in the mail; forms can be filled out incorrectly. Some doctors will bill Medicare for you; some will bill both Medicare and supplemental insurance; others won't bill either. Check with each doctor about billing procedures. Adapt the following instructions (based on you having to handle all billing yourself) to your needs.

1. Photocopy every medical bill twice.
2. Photocopy every Medicare statement twice.
3. Photocopy every completed Medicare form twice.
4. Fill out a claim form (one form for each bill).
5. Attach a copy of bill to the form (especially if you are mailing more than one form in an envelope).
6. Mail with first-class postage.
7. Attach remaining photocopies to the bill and file.

When the bill is paid by Medicare, you will receive notification stating what was paid and how much was paid. If the money was to come to you instead of directly to the doctor, you will also receive a check.

Sometimes a claim will be denied. Don't panic. It could be a clerical error or a wrong code. The first step is to read the explanation portion of the form to find out why it was denied. If you still don't understand, or if you believe the claim should have been paid, call the Social Security office.

The second step is to call the doctor's office and ask for the billing department. They can double-check the diagnosis and treatment code. They will either correct the error with the Social Security Office or provide you with a new form to attach to the bill. Resubmit the bill, following the same procedure as before.

SUPPLEMENTAL HEALTH INSURANCE   Health insurance is a major issue for everyone, but it is even more vital for seniors. There are dozens of plans and options available. Be sure you compare the plans carefully.

Supplemental insurance is available for those who have Medicare parts A and B. This insurance pays the Medicare deductible for hospitalization and the 20 percent of Medicare's allowable charge that you would pay without the insurance. Usually these policies are based on Medicare coverage, so if Medicare doesn't cover something, the basic policy won't either. However, many of these companies are offering rider policies that give other options such as chiropractic and extended-care-facility coverage. Again, the type of policy and its benefits and costs vary from company to company, so compare carefully.

When filing a supplemental insurance claim, be sure to do all of the following:

1. Fill out the claim form.
2. Attach a copy of the doctor's bill.
3. Attach a copy of the Medicare payment statement.
4. Mail with first-class postage.

When supplemental insurance pays a claim, they will send you a check, or a check and statement. Photocopy the check if you don't receive a statement. Put this statement or copy with the doctor's bill and Medicare copies. Attach a note that gives the total amount of the bill, the amount paid by Medicare, the amount paid by supplemental insurance and any balance paid by you or the elder.

Attach the canceled check or receipt for the balance. File the completed transaction under *Paid Medical* so it will be easier for you to locate documentation for tax purposes. If a question arises about payment of the bill, or someone questions the claim, it is easy to trace who paid what if you have good documentation and extra photocopies.

MEDICAID   Medicaid is medical insurance for those who do not qualify for Medicare. Many people who do not receive Social Security payments but do receive Supplemental Security Income (SSI) qualify. Medicaid is available for the disabled, regardless of age. The program is a combination of state and federal aid and is usually administered by the state's welfare department, though the program itself is not welfare. Specific qualifications for this program are clearly defined, but financial guidelines change from year to year. Generally, a qualifying person may have a house, a car (up to a specified value), a prepaid funeral plan and burial plot and a minimal amount of cash. The cash amount varies. For further details check with your local Social Security Office or state's welfare office.

HMOS   Health Maintenance Organizations (HMOs) are available in many portions of the United States, mostly west of the Mississippi. These organizations have their own doctors, laboratories and, in some cases, hospitals. They provide total medical care for a monthly fee. Prescriptions are usually heavily discounted. In the case of an elder who is eligible for Medicare parts A and B, many of these organizations offer a "senior" version of the plan. The senior assigns the organization his or her medical coverage from Medicare and agrees to pay a small charge for each doctor visit and somewhat higher charges, depending on the HMO selected, for hospital visits and emergency room treatment. The organization in turn accepts these copayments from the senior and the Medicare payment as "payment in full." Not all treatments are covered, and the patient must use the HMO's doctor(s).

Hospice Care   Hospice is a special service for people who have a prognosis of six months or less to live. It is important to realize that Medicare and some insurance plans cover the cost of an approved hospice service. This can be a financial lifesaver when you consider that at-home nursing and doctor visits, equipment and medication are totally covered in most cases. (See chapter 3 for a more detailed discussion of hospice care.)

Senior Discounts

Discounts are available to seniors from many different companies. Banks, pharmacies, department stores, restaurants, travel agencies, transportation firms, theaters, concerts, museums, hotels and motels are among the many businesses that offer discounted prices. Many require only proof of age; others request an application. In many areas it is also possible for needy elders to get a discount from utility companies and even on rent.

For many companies, this is a plan for getting business. For the senior, it can mean substantial savings. A discount of 10 percent on an occasional prescription won't mean much, but an elderly patient might need hundreds of dollars in medications every month. It adds up quickly. With a little shopping around, you can find a combination of lower normal price and larger senior discounts.

Food Stamps and Food Assistance Programs

Food stamps are available to qualified elders who live independently or in certain home-care situations. The stamps are used like money for the purchase of food and help to extend a limited food budget. The program is sponsored by the U.S. Department of Agriculture but is usually administered by a state welfare agency. Contact them for information about the program and eligibility requirements.

In many communities, other food assistance programs are available. Often these are administered by private organizations and churches. If a church is the sponsor, the help given is usually nondenominational. Some groups charge a nominal fee and give many times that amount in food. Others take volunteer service to the organization as payment, alone or in combination with money. To find out if these groups exist in your area, contact churches, the welfare office, the Chamber of Commerce or town government offices.

Funeral Arrangements

It's not easy to discuss funeral arrangements. Facing the inevitability of death, whether impending due to a terminal illness or in the distant future, is a highly emotional issue. To both you and your elder it can seem that you are planning for the worst before it has happened. However, it's not unusual that doing so can actually ease the mind of the elder. If this is true, even if it's uncomfortable for you, it's important that you listen, and help where possible.

If your elder seems reluctant to discuss the arrangements, you will have to take the initiative. Chapter 7 on "Intervention" can provide a good starting place. You may also find help through a clergyman or trusted friend. Chapter 12, "Communication," deals with the emotional issues that may surface while making these decisions. For now we will look at those things involving legal or financial obligations.

Funerals can range from simple memorial services to elaborate and religious ceremonies. Costs can vary widely, from less than $1,000 to many thousands of dollars. The earlier you plan these services, the more input your elder can have. Preplanning will help curb the last-minute impulsiveness and confusion that happen when people try to make decisions during times of emotional crisis. Take time to plan, and you'll find it much easier to reach a decision where everyone's needs, emotional and financial, balance.

Before you begin the search for a funeral home, it is a good idea to talk about the type of service that the elder wants. The type of service requested will affect the cost. One example is using the funeral home's chapel as opposed to a church. You will be charged for the use of the funeral home's chapel, while a church may have only a nominal fee or none at all. However, using a church involves additional transportation costs. Bear in mind that in many cases there are psychological advantages to using a church rather than a funeral home's chapel. For some, a funeral home's chapel is just that, part of a funeral home, whereas a church has a more spiritual atmosphere.

Costs are a big factor in funeral choices. Under Federal Trade Commission rules, a funeral home must provide you with a list of services, equipment and facilities, and a list of charges for each. All expenses should be discussed with the funeral director before a funeral home is selected. This may seem like price shopping—which is exactly what it is, in a way. But funeral homes provide essential services, and comparing those services and their costs is the best way to decide which provider to use.

As you are discussing these matters, make notes of the elder's plans and wishes. These will help you when you are selecting a funeral home. Once the choice has been made, leave a copy of the paper with the funeral home and place the original with other important papers so it is easily found when needed.

Be aware of your elder's status as a veteran and involvement with various lodges and associations. Some of these organizations may help with expenses or will influence the type of ceremony your elder requests. This participation can affect the price of your arrangements.

When you are discussing funeral arrangements, your basic options are the following, although almost any variation can be accommodated by most funeral homes:

- Traditional funeral with or without viewing, formal service and graveside service
- Memorial service
- Graveside service with or without a memorial service

- Immediate burial, no service
- Cremation, no service
- Cremation with service in which the urn is placed in a mausoleum
- Cremation with memorial
- Cremation and burial at sea
- Cremation with formal service, and shorter service at a mausoleum

The cost of the funeral will vary, depending on the type of service and funeral requested. If arranged separately, florists, clergy, musicians, choir or soloist and those who provide motor escorts will also expect payment. For a nominal charge, the funeral home can obtain a death certificate for you. (Death certificates are discussed later in chapter 5.)

A cemetery plot can range from a few hundred dollars to thousands. Mausoleum crypts for above-ground burial can also cost over a thousand dollars. The least expensive choice is usually cremation.

Grave markers are often purchased through the cemetery. Those cemeteries that provide ongoing or perpetual care usually have specific requirements for the markers.

Paying for a funeral, burial and related costs can be a drain on resources and may even require a personal loan to be taken out. Surveys indicate that although 90 percent of adults know about prepaid funeral plans, only about 20 percent participate in them. The prearranged funeral plan offers some valuable benefits: The kind of service desired has been guaranteed by contract, paid contracts don't burden the surviving family members financially, and fewer decisions need to be made at a time when emotional stress is high.

There are two types of prearranged funeral contracts, funded and nonfunded. The funded type is commonly handled either by insurance or a savings trust. An insurance policy or burial policy can be written to cover the exact cost of services once the fees have been determined. The funeral home will honor the policy, and provide the specific services contracted for without additional cost, regardless of when the policy is needed. The policy can be purchased through a funeral home or independently. Once the complete cost of the services has been determined, a savings trust account can be opened in the amount of the projected sum with the funeral home listed as the beneficiary. The interest that accumulates to the account should help offset most inflationary increases.

Nonfunded plans are those where arrangements have been made but financing is delayed until needed. Some people plan to use their life insurance to pay for their funeral; others designate funds from different sources and investments to offset this cost.

A funeral home representative can give you specific information on these types of plans and their costs. Keep a copy of the plan or the insurance policy, and the funeral arrangements, with other important papers. Make sure that you, the funeral home and the elder's attorney all have copies.

Death Benefits

When there is a dependent child or a remaining spouse, Social Security pays a death benefit of $255 to the survivor(s). Other death benefits may be available from a number of sources. It is imperative that these people be notified as soon as possible.

Remember to keep copies of all correspondence and benefit statements. You will need these later for tax purposes. The following are examples of letters you can use to check on these benefits.

To Social Security or the Railroad

Addressee name   Date
Address

To whom it may concern:

Please send me any forms or list of documents you may require so that I may make an application for Social Security (or railroad) benefits to which I am entitled in connection with the death of my (relationship), (full name: first, middle, last), Social Security (number), who died on (month, day, year).

Sincerely,

Your signature
Your full name (printed)
Your address and phone number

TO THE VETERANS' ADMINISTRATION

Addressee name   Date
Address

To whom it may concern:

My (relationship), (full name: first, middle, last), (service number), died on (month, day, year). He/she served in the U.S. (branch) from (month, year) to (month, year). The government insurance policy number is (list number or unknown). The VA claim number is (list number or unknown).

Please let me know if further documentation or information is required to make a claim. Please advise me as to any other benefits to which I may be entitled.

Sincerely,

Your signature
Your full name (printed)
Your address and phone number

TO INSURANCE COMPANIES

Addressee name   Date
Address

To whom it may concern:

My (relationship), (full name: first, middle, last), died on (month, day, year). I am designated beneficiary on policy (number).

Please send me the necessary forms and a list of the documentation that you require in making a claim. Please check your records for any other policies my (relationship) may have had with your firm.

Sincerely,

Your signature
Your full name (printed)
Your address and phone number

TO EMPLOYER OR EMPLOYER RETIREMENT ASSOCIATION

Addressee name   Date
Address

To whom it may concern:

My (relationship), (full name: first, middle, last), (ID number if any), died (month, day, year). Please send me any information relating to any benefits to which I am entitled, along with the forms and list of documentation I will need to apply for them.

Sincerely,

Your signature
Your full name (printed)
Your address and phone number

FIVE

Legal Matters

As discussed in the last chapter, many families find it difficult to talk about the financial and legal aspects of living and dying. In our society it somehow seems crass to discuss money, wills, bequests, medical insurances and funeral arrangements. Yet as sensitive as these issues can be, they must be discussed if you are to be responsible for your elder's care. The potential problems are bad enough under the best circumstances. Trying to handle the situation without knowing the details, and your loved one's wishes, only makes things worse. If you have siblings, in-laws or others who are expecting to be involved in your elder's finances, the possibilities for misunderstandings can increase dramatically and can even cause rifts that last for years.

An all too typical case might involve a brother and sister who got along for decades, held each other closely and with love at the funeral, then ended up not speaking to each other for years afterwards because each wanted a certain set of dishes.

The best time to initiate this type of discussion is when the elder is healthy. Waiting until the need is urgent can be devastating, especially if the elder is not capable of expressing wishes or revealing the location of necessary documents.

Many elders are eager to have the financial and legal aspects settled so they can get on with their lives without the worry of dealing with those matters in the future. Others may be quite reticent about their legal arrangements and financial situation. There are a number of reasons for this attitude: For example, a fear of becoming a burden to the children can prevent an elder from discussing the problem; for others, the making of a will brings with it an unwelcome sense of finality. There is also the possibility that the person may get the idea that your main concern is "How much do *I* get from the deal?" Coupled with this is perhaps your own fear—often falsely based—that your loved one might get this idea.

As important as inheritance issues might be, they are usually only a small part of the overall legal situation: dealing with government agencies such as Social Security, making funeral arrangements, handling death benefits, filing death certificates, dealing with insurance companies, etc., etc., etc. However complicated you think it might be, double that. Then add in the fact that waiting until the last minute means that you'll be dealing with all those details, likely with insufficient information, at a time when you are suffering from grief and possibly have no legal right to handle things. It's important to begin before the elder passes away.

Finding sources of assistance shouldn't be started *after* the need for help is overwhelming. Getting organized ahead of time means considerably less stress later. You don't want to be dealing with a funeral, probate and a stack of bills while digging through stacks of paper to find deeds, lists of assets, insurance policies and other documentation. As hard and cold as it might sound, the time to gather and organize the details is before the crisis, before the grief and while the elder is still sound of mind and body. Waiting is an invitation to disaster.

Although there are many similarities, the exact details will be different for each person. Virtually everyone will have to make some contact with Social Security, but the forms needed will differ, as will the local phone number and address to be contacted for these. Taxes involve contact with both federal and state offices, with the federal system being divided into regions, so an address and phone number valid for California filers won't be for those in Florida. Telephone numbers and addresses for government agencies are easily found in your local phone book, most of which have sections set aside (often in blue) for local, county, state and federal offices.

Beyond this are the more personal needs. Where did the elder work before retirement? For how long? Was there a pension plan? Did it have death benefits? Did or does the individual belong to a group, association, union, lodge, or other organization that might offer assistance or benefits? Was he or she a part of the military? Are there spousal benefits that either start or stop with death?

What insurance policies are in force, and where are they? It's not uncommon for a policy to have been purchased, stuck into a filing cabinet and then forgotten. Even if not forgotten, if the only one who knows where it's kept it is the elder who has just passed away, your task may be digging through files, or even shoeboxes stuffed with paper, to find it.

What about personal possessions? The elder may have certain items of property that have a value others may not recognize. It's not all that unusual for priceless heirlooms to be sold for pennies at an estate sale simply because no one knew that the slightly cracked vase was actually from the Ming dynasty and not from the corner thrift store.

There is no way to totally separate financial matters from legal ones. Bear in mind that the two are often very nearly the same. A will, for example, is a legal document that deals largely or even exclusively with the dispersal of financial assets. Medicare, Medicaid, Supplemental Insurance, Death Benefits and virtually all the rest also involve both "legalese" and financial impact. When you become a caregiver you take on *both* financial and legal responsibilities, and these will continue after the death of the beloved elder. But do you have the legal right to act on his or her behalf?

To answer this and other questions, you may well need help from a lawyer, an accountant, or other professionals. There are a number of ways to locate them. Ask friends and business associates for recommendations. Check the Yellow Pages. Call hospitals, associations and referral services. The research librarian with the adult reference section of your public library can help you find local and national sources of help. Some senior centers and organizations also recommend professionals who do this work for elders at reduced rates or even base their charges on ability to pay.

Remember, when choosing a professional, ask the appropriate questions *before* an appointment is made. Briefly outline the situation and the type of services needed, then ask about consultation fees, applicable charges and what the average bill is for this type of work. If you don't do this, it's all too easy to find yourself owing large bills for services that don't serve.

The following is a general discussion of issues that must be considered when dealing with your elder's financial and legal matters. Remember that it is always a wise idea to have things in writing and signed. This prevents problems and lessens the caregiver's load when an emergency or question arises in the future.

Wills

A will is a legal statement that defines a person's wishes to be carried out after death. Often it concentrates on the distribution of belongings, such as cash, real estate, stocks, bonds, personal possessions, etc. It may also formally and legally forgive debts, name an executor (male) or executrix (female) to be responsible to carry out those wishes and a number of other things that will vary from person to person. (For example, it could contain personal messages to loved ones, or might set up conditions for inheritance.) The law on what makes a will valid varies from state to state. Some stages will accept a handwritten will under certain conditions; others accept forms (sometimes called do-it-yourself will kits, available where office supplies are sold and even in stationery stores) as valid.

Regardless of what your state allows, the safest option is to select an attorney to draw up a formal will. This becomes more important if there are many people involved, or if there is the chance that someone, including the government, might question the competency of the elder making the will. When there is a lot of property to be handled, this should be your *only* choice.

Attorneys, like doctors, tend to specialize, so make certain the person selected knows current state and federal real estate and tax laws as well as current applicable court cases. The right person will be able to develop a financial plan and a will that will meet the elder's wishes now and in the future.

To save time and money when consulting an attorney, have a complete list of the elder's holdings. This should give a full, legal description of each piece of property, its worth, how it is owned (joint tenancy, community property, etc., discussed later in this section) and who the property will be left to. The more complete the list is, the less time and money you will spend at the attorney's office. Discussing how the property is owned will give the attorney an opportunity to show you how you can disperse funds, property and other assets with minimal tax liability and, in some situations, avoid probate entirely.

The attorney will help you determine which assets should be handled formally through the more permanent will, and which should be handled informally through a list that will be an adjunct to the will. That list saves having to revise the will continuously as property is dispersed before death or the designated recipient changes.

Part of a typical list may look like this:

Rental property at 1911 E. Smith; own 25% in common with brother, Samuel; appraised value $15,000; to daughter, Alice.

1993 Pontiac LeMans; community property; to wife, Emily.

1853 pocket watch; gold with diamonds; appraised value, $2,975; to son, Daniel.

Legal Instruments

Tenancy in common is an arrangement in which a person owns an asset along with any number of other people. The portion each owns (not necessarily equal shares) is part of that person's estate and may be passed (willed) to another person.

Joint tenancy ownership is usually held between two people and allows the survivor to claim sole ownership in the event of the death of the other owner. Property held in joint tenancy does not have to pass through a will or probate.

Community property is an asset of a marital relationship. Not all states have community property laws. When community property laws are in effect, a married person can generally dispose of only your half of any given asset through a will. Once an asset is listed as community property, a change to a different form of ownership will require the consent of both spouses. An attorney may recommend another form of ownership or another way of handling finances that offers more tax advantages, depending on the senior's estate.

A *Trust* can be drawn naming a person, institute or even a pet as trustee. The trustee's obligations are clearly defined. Although there are many different kinds of trust, the one of concern here is often called a living trust. With it the elder's assets are put under the control of the trustee so that the elder's needs and obligations can be met. After the death of the elder, the trust often serves as a sort of will and directs how the balance of the trust assets will be used or distributed. This trust can be set up to be revocable or irrevocable. The first allows the elder to change the trustee, modify the trust or cancel it entirely. The second makes this much more difficult (almost impossible). This is usually done if there is the chance that the elder might become mentally unsound and change the trust, dangerously, on a whim or after being talked into it by someone. Either way, the trust can be set up only if the elder is of sound mind. It requires the services of an attorney and may also require official recording to become operative.

Guardianship or *conservatorship* papers must be drawn up by an attorney and can be completed in advance and filed with the court for the time of need. The elder names a person to act on his or her behalf if the elder becomes mentally incapacitated or unable to communicate. In that event the court appoints a guardian or conservator, usually the person requested, who then has the power to act for the elder. If the elder does not prepare the petition in advance, the court can appoint someone it feels will best serve in this capacity.

Power of attorney is similar to a Guardianship. (The attorney can explain the differences in your particular case, and which is better.) It is a legal document enabling one person to act in legal matters on another's behalf. It may be restricted to specific authority, such as opening checking or savings accounts, or selling or acquiring property. Or a power of attorney may be unlimited, authorizing someone to handle all affairs, including medical care that the elder will receive. The validity of this document is dependent on the maker's competency, and its authorization ends with the maker's death. In many instances, it is a good idea for spouses to have each other's power of attorney so that they have the authority to make necessary decisions.

A standard power of attorney is available at many stationery stores. The document will need to be notarized and recorded. Because of the amount of power this document gives over another's life, and the legal ramifications, an attorney should always be consulted before anyone gives or receives a power of attorney.

Living will (or right-to-die declaration, or durable power of attorney for health-care decisions) refers to a document that makes a person's wishes regarding medical treatments known. Sometimes this document is used to designate a specific person to make health-care decisions on behalf of an elder who cannot make or communicate for them.

These documents are not legally binding in every state but do carry moral and ethical weight. The person issuing the living will can *add* specific instructions and directions to it. The document should be signed, dated and witnessed by two other persons. It is a good idea to have the elder sign and date the document annually so that there is no question that these are ongoing directions. Make several copies of the living will. Give one to the physician, hospital, to several family members and to the caretaker. Keep the original with other important papers like wills, insurance, etc. As with any legal document, it is a good idea to have a living will checked by an attorney to make sure it complies with the law in your state.

Voting

Some elderly find it difficult or even impossible to get around. This doesn't mean that they have to be denied the right to vote.

Voting by mail is allowed. Voter registration is handled by your county registrar. This office, listed under "County Government" in the phone book, will give you the needed information for voting by mail and the deadlines that will have to be met. If your elder cannot write, a son or daughter is allowed to register and sign for the parent. Discuss this with the registrar's office.

Personal Identification

Everyone needs personal identification. Usually a driver's license is accepted, but when the elder no longer drives, another form of ID is used. County offices, police departments or the department of motor vehicles/driver's licensing bureaus have photo ID cards available. Usually the charge is nominal though some states issue these cards free of charge.

If your elder becomes disoriented or is prone to "wander," a simple ID bracelet or small disc on a necklace-type chain (engraved with their name, plus your name and phone number) can aid them.

Personal identification becomes particularly important if there is a potentially dangerous medical condition. If this is the case, a Medic-Alert bracelet or necklace should always be worn. During its 38 years in business, this organization has been credited with saving many lives by providing medical information/history in emergency situations to hospitals and medical personnel. The bracelets are inscribed with the person's medical condition and allergies on the back side. The emergency phone number will allow medical personal to access all medical information about the person in seconds.

The initial cost of the bracelet or necklace varies on the style and material used (stainless steel, sterling silver, etc.). This cost includes the first year of service. After the first year, a fee of $15 per year (at press time) is charged. The elder can update the information as often as needed.

For more information contact: Medic-Alert, 2323 Colorado Ave., Turlock, CA 95381-1009, Phone 1-800-423-6333.

Notification of Death

Lists should be made of all the people who need to be notified immediately upon the elder's death. Keep the list with the elder's important papers. Copies should be with at least two other family members, including yourself. Be sure an address and phone number follows each name. List the names of clergymen, physician(s), hospice service if used, attorney, insurance agent, and funeral home. List all family and friends who need immediate notification.

In the days that follow a death, banks, business firms and creditors will need to be notified. Some accounts will have to be closed or a spouse's name cleared from it. List all of them along with contact names, addresses and telephone numbers. Many of them will require a death certificate.

Upon death the Social Security Administration should be called at once. You will send written notification when you receive the death certificate. You can find the telephone number in the *U.S. Government* section of the phone book under *Health and Human Services*. If the person was alive on the fourth day of the month, the benefit money for that month does not have to be returned. If the person died during the first three days of the month, the money must be returned. If the check is for both the deceased person and the spouse, a portion of the money will have to be returned. The Social Security Office will tell you how much needs to be returned. If the recipient was using direct deposit, the bank will have to be notified to stop the check or return the appropriate amount of the deposit.

DEATH CERTIFICATE   The death certificate and copies can be arranged for with a funeral home. There is a nominal charge for this. It is a good idea to purchase at least two. One will be stamped "For Official Use Only." This one is to be sent to the Social Security Administration with written notification to cancel benefits for this person. Keep the other death certificate for your records. You may have to order additional copies, but sometimes insurance companies, employers, retirement affiliations and so on will accept a photocopy. (Ask, don't assume.) They are also available from the county recorder's office. Either the funeral home or the recorder will ask for certain information for a death certificate. The information you provide must be accurate. Claims, benefits and other legal procedures will make use of this document. The following information will be needed:

- Full name of the deceased (first, middle, last)
- Social Security number
- Current/last residence (street, city, county and state)
- Birthdate
- Birthplace (city, state, sometimes county)
- Employer (if any)
- Date retired (if any)
- Spouse's name (first, middle, (maiden), last) (if any)
- Father's name (first, middle, last)
- Father's birthplace
- Mother's maiden name (first, middle, last)
- Mother's birthplace
- For railroad employees: company name, address and dates employed
- For military veterans: branch of service, dates and service serial number

SIX

The Family Meeting

As has been mentioned many times before in this book, caregiving involves people other than the elder. Obviously there are the doctors, nurses, medical technicians, social service workers, attorneys, accountants and others. Closer to home is the primary caregiver, the caregiver's immediate family, the elder's family (including the spouse) and sometimes friends and neighbors.

What this means is that more than one person is affected by the decisions being made. They deserve and need to be involved. The closer they are to the situation— the more they are affected— the more important it becomes to include them. As one example, if the decision is to have the elder move into your home, it shouldn't be your decision alone. The elder has to want the same thing. Your spouse and possibly the children must also be included.

All this begins *before* the decisions are made, not afterward. This means that you should assess the overall situation thoroughly and as honestly as you can, and then call a family meeting.

The purpose of a family meeting is to establish everyone's position in relation to the elder's care need. It is *not* to decide the elder's future. The two exceptions are if (1) the elder is in medical crisis and cannot make decisions, or (2) you have been advised by medical or judicial authorities that the elder is in need of immediate intervention. Other than these two emergency situations, the first meeting should be considered as one in which possibilities and care options are to be explored.

It's important that at least the first meeting be with your immediate family *only*, especially if you intend to open your home to caregiving (although most experts say that your children should be left out of the meeting and told later of the decisions). This isn't a move to keep the elder (or anyone else, for that matter) out of the decision-making process. The goal is to create a time when everyone can speak openly and honestly, without pressure and without the fear of hurting the elder's feelings. The basic questions to be answered are "Do we want to do this?" and "To what extent?" (The latter includes "For how long?")

Depending on the circumstances, a second family meeting might be needed, this time one that involves other members of the family who are affected. This potentially includes anyone who might become involved. In fact, "family" must be defined more broadly at this point. The elder may have one or more very close friends—actually closer to the elder than anyone in the family. Don't shut them out simply because they're not related by blood.

In any case, it's critical that you work out what can be done, and what can't, before bringing the options to the elder in need of care. If you let your emotions take charge and offer your elderly mother the spare bedroom in your home, then find out that the situations is such that this won't be possible, there may be hurt feelings all around.

Once you have all the facts (or as many as can be gathered or predicted), and assuming that the elder is lucid, the options can be given to the person most affected by the situation, namely the elder. Don't forget that he or she may reject what you consider to be perfect solutions. Your job then is to find out why. There may be valid reasons. Perhaps you can maybe compromise or you may be facing a whole new problem.

Be Honest

Someone directly (or indirectly) involved may have a reason to be reluctant to become a caregiver. In Betty's case, she dearly loved her father-in-law, Michael. In contrast, she had gone through years of verbal abuse from her mother-in-law, Sylvia. Nothing Betty did was quite right. In the guise of helping, Sylvia was constantly saying things like, "Wouldn't it be better if you...".

Betty and her husband, Frank, had gone on a two-week vacation. They left their keys with Michael and Sylvia so their house and pets would be cared for. When they got back they found that some of the living room furniture had been replaced and that the entire kitchen had been rearranged. Sylvia's response was, "Don't you think it's better this way? I do." In addition, Betty saw that their mail had been opened. ("I was just trying to help.")

Later, when Michael suffered a stroke and needed care, Betty wanted very much to help him. She was a registered nurse and had the qualifications. But the distance between Betty and Sylvia had continued to grow. It was hard enough on Betty to visit their home. She knew it would be impossible to let Michael and Sylvia move in.

It was hard enough on Betty to visit their home, especially since Sylvia's criticisms extended to Betty's professional advice. She knew it would be impossible to let Michael and Sylvia move in as Frank wanted. She also was not willing to give up her position as head of nursing at the local hospital. It wasn't lack of caring or willingness to help on Betty's part: She had simply been driven to the limit and couldn't work with Sylvia.

The situation deteriorated further when Sylvia managed to convince Frank that Betty was at fault. One thing that made it possible for Sylvia to do this was Betty's reluctance to fully communicate the depth of her feelings and her reasons for them. She felt Frank had enough to deal with without hearing a litany of complaints about his mother. She was dishonest by omission, and it strained her marriage to the breaking point.

The Family As a Team

Whether or not your family can form an effective team depends on many factors. The better your communication skills, the more easily you will arrive at workable group decisions for care. If your family has a history of helping its members in various ways, there is a good chance of strong participation in a caregiving situation. Hopefully there is also a good deal of sensitivity and empathy, which will help you know when intervention is necessary.

Suppose your family doesn't resemble the Waltons. In today's society, very few families have this type of lifestyle. Does this mean that caregiving isn't a viable option? Not at all. It simply means that you may have to look elsewhere for additional support in the areas where you receive none from your family. (It's important to note, however, that you shouldn't simply *assume* that the family will reject the idea of caregiving on the basis that they've never done it before.)

You're not alone in this need. Many caregivers have to deal with other family members whose interest and participation in the situation ranges from smothering to total disinterest. An extremely frustrating situation exists when a family member is hardly being affected at all, and who isn't so much as offering to help, is critical of your efforts.

In some families old power struggles or sibling rivalries will resurface. Or a sibling's relationship with a parent that has been strained over the years comes out. Distance can be another factor. So can an uncooperative spouse (yours of the elder's) or employer. Some may refuse to deal with the situation at all.

When elder care becomes an issue, turmoil is likely to ensue. Every family is different, of course, but the result is the same. Everyone's life will change. Many people, regardless of their age, do not welcome change. Emotions go to war with logic, and the various positions and attitudes can be very hard to reconcile.

The Agenda

To get the most out of a family meeting, it helps to be thoroughly prepared. Preparation includes reaching an agreement with your spouse as to the level of participation you are willing to undertake, becoming familiar with the financial and legal ramifications of caregiving in your elder's particular situation, understanding your elder's current medical condition (diagnosis) and what it is likely to become (prognosis), and any other facts that might apply. Make a list of your elder's current needs. Check into available services that correspond. When you have all the facts and information, strongly consider writing out an agenda for the meeting.

Cold and heartless? Too businesslike? There is a big advantage to writing down an agenda. It keeps the meeting focused on the subject. If the meeting gets too far off track in a nonproductive way, simply remind everyone of the meeting's purpose and the agenda. Referring to the agenda will also make certain every important topic gets covered.

The underlying cause of the meeting is highly emotional in nature. You're trying to make decisions concerning the life and future of a loved one. The meeting itself, however, is about the decisions. This must be handled in a logical, rather then emotional, manner. Some of the things you should cover include these:

- An outline of the elder's needs with a projection of what those needs are likely to be in the near future (include all aspects of the needs: medical, financial, care services, resources and the possible solutions to help the elder)
- How long the care situation, and the responsibility, is likely to last
- Who agrees to be primary caregiver
- Who agrees to provide what specific help (often financial)
- How the immediate situation could be handled and the options available
- How future needs are to be handled and the options available

If your family situation is particularly tangled or there is a serious problem with communication, you might want to have the meeting conducted by the elder's attorney, doctor, clergy or social worker. This solution is particularly effective in situations where power struggles are likely to occur, because the "outsider" usually appears to be an authority figure.

Consider a Written Agreement

Draft an agreement covering everyone's promised contributions and responsibilities and the plan of care. Why a written agreement? After all, this is family.

That's exactly why: Because it *is* family.

Most families establish patterns of behavior for each member of the unit. One sibling becomes the achiever or "doer." Another may develop a way of sliding out responsibilities. Still another may fall somewhere between. Each sibling has a separate and distinct relationship with the elder, with you and with each of the other siblings. When things are formalized through an agreement, everyone's responsibilities are clear.

This is especially important if the care of an elder appears to be long-term. After the initial elder-care crisis has passed, life for everyone settles into a routine. As individuals become involved in their own lives again, it is easy to miss an obligation to the elder, to cancel a visit or to become increasingly late with a financial contribution. A written agreement helps keep obligations clear and prevents someone using "I didn't agree to do that" as an excuse.

This doesn't mean that you're trying to create a legal and binding contract. Only rarely is such a thing needed. Your goal is simply to define, in writing, who has agreed to what. Rather than causing problems, this can prevent them.

The suggested agreement is not difficult or complicated. It can cover anything from simple financial contributions to complete living arrangements. The sample given below covers a typical live-in elder-care situation involving three siblings.

Janet agrees to be the primary caregiver for Father. He will live in her home, and she will provide food, do laundry and assist with daily living chores. She agrees to pay for 20 percent of care expenses for those things not covered by Father's assets or insurance.

Bill (who lives in the same town) agrees to handle transportation for medical appointments, keep financial records, including insurance billing, and contribute 20 percent of care expenses for those things not covered by Father's assets or insurance. He also agrees to assume total personal care of father for forty-eight hours during the third weekend of every month and for seven consecutive days once every four months.

Barbara (who lives out of state) agrees to visit Father at Janet's house or have Father visit her for seven consecutive days once a year, when she will provide total care. She agrees to call Father twice per month. Barbara will contribute 60 percent to care expenses incurred that are not covered by Father's assets or insurance.

Remember that the purpose of the agreement is fairness. Help for you, the primary caregiver, is very important and needs to be included. As an elder-care situation progresses, it is easy to lose your personal life as you find yourself doing more and more. If you have never been in a care situation, it is typical that you will underestimate the amount of time you will spend caring for your elder. In fact, it isn't unusual to be unaware of the increase in caregiving time you expend, especially if the situation changes gradually. That's one reason it is important to garner all the help possible in the beginning. It's much easier to get people, including family members, into the routine of helping when the need is not so crucial than to thrust them into a situation where they feel overwhelmed.

Notice in the above agreement that Barbara lives out of town. In effect her caregiving is "long-distance," but it is just as valuable to the elder. There are many things Barbara can do to contribute to the happiness and well-being of the elder. By agreeing to call at least twice each month, contact is maintained. It's enhanced by the promised visits. The larger share of the financial burden is again due to fairness. Janet and Bill are handling most of the actual work.

The Long-Distance Caregiver

Not all caregivers are able to participate in daily care of their elder. Many times an elder-care situation will arise when an adult child is pursuing a career in another town or state. It is not uncommon to be giving care to an elder and then find that a spouse's parent also needs attention. Beyond this, not everyone is emotionally suited to caregiving; some simply cannot handle the mental, emotional or financial strain.

For whatever reason, someone's inability to make a commitment to giving personal care on a daily basis does not make that person's concerns or feelings for the elder any less real. There are a variety of ways long-distance caregivers can participate in caregiving and enhance the quality of life the elder experiences.

- Stay in touch. Call or write often. Visit whenever you can, even it is only for a day or two. (Be aware, however, that when visiting you might be causing an additional financial and emotional strain).
- Send letters, articles that would interest the elder, photographs and drawings by the grandchildren.
- Give the elder a cassette recorder and send tapes. Get other family members, especially your spouse and children, to participate. If the elder has friends in your area, encourage them to send tapes as well. The tape recorder can be a wonderful way for the elder to respond to you as well, especially if the elder has difficulty writing.
- Many people have camcorders and access to a VCR. If this is true for you, consider making recordings of the area, holidays and special events to send to the elder.
- If you live nearby, make a definite commitment to visit and spend time with your elder or vice versa. If another sibling is the primary caregiver, consider using this time to give him or her a break, too. If you live at a distance and the elder's health permits, invite the elder for an extended period, perhaps a week or two.
- Whenever possible, involve your elder in a family project. Recording family history and anecdotes on the tape recorder, sharing long-distance quilting projects and playing chess through the mail are just three of the possibilities.

It is also possible to be a *primary* caregiver if you live at a distance from the elder. Roy, an only child, lives in South

Carolina. His widowed mother, Florence, lived alone in Arlington, Virginia, at the time of her stroke. When the initial medical crisis had passed, Roy moved Florence into a skilled nursing facility in Arlington. Roy says, "I'm really pleased with the way this worked out. At first I thought I'd have Mom transported back to South Carolina and hire care for her here. That probably would have been easier for me, but I don't think it would have been best for her. In Arlington she has friends that drop by to see her. The doctor she's had for years works closely with the nursing home. Both are important things she wouldn't have here. So once a month, I take a Friday off work and drive to Arlington. I take care of bills, do some errands for her, talk with the medial staff and spend time with her. Saturday we go to brunch and spend the afternoon doing something fun. I usually drive back Saturday night or Sunday morning. I have found that because I'm away from home, I concentrate on Mom instead of overscheduling my weekends with things that have to be done."

A problem in being at a distance is that you sometimes don't know what is going on. The usual situation is that other members of the family who are closer, or perhaps a close friend, will serve as your eyes and ears. When this isn't possible, consider contacting the elder's attorney or doctor, who may be able to recommend someone to handle communication.

The National Association of Professional Geriatric Caregivers is a registry of professionals across the country. They offer a variety of services to the public (for a fee) including checking on the elder, keeping you informed and even making sure that the elder's bills are being paid. This group is listed in the Resources section of this book.

Family Problems

Joseph's mother, Doris, was diagnosed with multiple sclerosis at the age of fifty-three. At first the symptoms of the disease were sporadic, and Doris could care for herself with very little help. Shortly after her sixtieth birthday, she had a really bad bout with

it. Complicating matters, she got pneumonia and was hospitalized. Her prognosis wasn't good. She had permanent breathing
difficulties because the spinal curvature was making it difficult for
the lungs to properly inflate and she would be subject to continual
respiratory infections. The spinal curvature had progressed to the
point that the doctor felt a walker was permanently needed for
balance. He further suggested that Doris have at-home care or
move to a facility since her condition was past the point where she
could safely do many physical tasks without assistance. Fortunately, her mind was still as sharp as ever.

Joseph was the middle child of three brothers. Both the
brothers and their families lived closer to Doris, but neither would
help. The eldest brother, Jackson, said he wouldn't know here to
begin and it would be too hard on his own family and business.
Michael, the youngest, whose wife was a nurse, said he and
Margaret liked their life as it was and she didn't want to take care
of Doris. Her attitude was "If I wanted to take care of someone, I'd
have kids." In short, the two brothers and their families refused to
help in any way. As for financial assistance, there were a few vague
comments about helping out occasionally, but the help didn't
materialize.

Joseph's wife, Linda, had been raised in a large family with lots
of aunts, uncles, cousins and grandparents around all the time.
Whenever anybody needed help, everyone pitched in. For them,
and for her, it was just how things were. She couldn't understand
the attitude of Joseph's brothers. Linda had gotten along well with
Doris, as had Joseph. Their decision was mutual and easy. Doris
moved in with them.

Over the next five years Michael and Jackson rarely called and
even more rarely visited. Doris would sometimes drop into a
depression, wondering what she'd done wrong to make two of her
sons so abandon her. When they did make contact, they were
constantly challenging Joseph about the money being spent.

Then Doris's insurance ran out. Joseph had to come up with an
extra $10,000 to pay for her care. He called his brothers, both of
whom were financially successful. Despite their earlier promise to

help with the bills, they refused. Mike's excuse was "Margaret insisted on a vacation. We just got back from three weeks in Tahiti. There's no way we can afford to send you some money right now."

Not long after this conversation Doris passed away. Within a matter of days Joseph was confronted by his two brothers, who volunteered to fly up and help dispose of Doris's possessions. The end result was a rift between Joseph and his brothers that still remains.

There had been warning signs of Jackson and Michael's disinterest, but neither Joseph nor Linda was prepared for their almost total abandonment of Doris. Joseph had always explained his family as independent and undemonstrative, the exact opposite of Linda's.

He learned what *you* must learn. There is virtually no way to force someone to take unwanted responsibility, and certainly no way to force a show of love and compassion. This might have come out in a family meeting. The result could have been realizing up front what to expect—or could have been a commitment on the part of the two brothers that would have prevented the problems from occurring.

Sometimes a general "air clearing" is all that's needed to put old sibling rivalries aside. More extreme situations require the services of a family counselor. It is not unusual to find two or three siblings out of four agreeing to help while one or two refuse to participate equally. If this is your situation and all attempts at healing the breach have failed, you'll have to accept it and move on. There is simply no point in continually upsetting yourself over a situation you cannot change.

Be prepared for rejection, negative feelings, anger and even greed. But also be prepared to learn that you've misjudged a relative or friend. The family meeting, and the crisis itself, can be a time to patch old wounds and bring the family back together. Don't be surprised if you find that a decade-old squabble started with something none of those involved even remember.

Try to maintain a positive attitude. This isn't always easy at the time but makes things much easier in the long run. And if someone is truly unresponsive, or even abusive, let it go. You have a more important job to do at the moment.

Every family is different. Hopefully the family meeting will show you exactly how much help you can expect to receive and how the help can best be utilized for the elder's well-being. You should come away with a much better understanding of what you face.

The next chapter will show you how to put that help to use through intervention.

SEVEN

Intervention

In the ideal situation, the elder who needs help requests it. More commonly, an adult child perceives the elder's need and has to find a way to bring up the problem and to help find a solution that the elder will accept. Nearly as often, the elder has made, or is about to make, a bad decision and the caregiver has to step in. This is called intervention.

We have been taught to be hesitant when it comes to interfering in someone's life. From childhood we remember our lessons of "It's none of your business." We are also used to our elders being in control. We remember them as the ones in charge.

It's difficult when the time comes when *we* have to be in charge. Part of us says to back away, yet at the same time we feel an urge to protect the beloved elder. So we reluctantly decide to intervene, knowing that bringing up these problems is delicate and even traumatic.

Warning

You've gathered the facts. You know the elder's medical condition and what caregiving is going to entail, at least for the time being. You have carefully researched the options for care services. You've had the family meeting and reached an agreement. You are ready to present all these plans and options to the elder.

What are you expecting to happen? Are you anticipating that your elder will welcome these suggestions? Do you think your ideas might meet with some resistance? Or even anger and hostility? Resentment? Fear? Outright refusal? Why? You're only trying to help, right?

Before you go rushing in, stop. Take a deep breath. Think about what is really happening.

You see the situation your elder is in. You're worried and you want to help. You want to protect your loved one, perhaps even from himself or herself. You see what you are doing as an act of love and compassion. It probably is.

However, if you simply take over the situation and solve the problem for a competent elder without the elder's permission or input, it is an act of control. You are then, in essence, parenting your parent. Unless your elder is incapable of judging or caring for himself or herself, parenting your parent is demeaning, demoralizing, destructive and simply cruel! It's also completely unnecessary.

Never forget that caregiving means giving care.

Look at the situation through your elder's eyes. For fifty years or more, your elder has made decisions. Many are small decisions like what to wear. There have also been big decisions like how to finance a home, provide for retirement and raise the children. There have been life-altering decisions like marriage or changing careers. Parents remember being responsible for the decisions they made not only in their own lives but for the decisions they made for their children—like you.

Certainly they made mistakes. That's part of being human. Some of the decisions, small and large, were the wrong decisions. If this is bothering you, ask yourself honestly if you've ever made a mistake. Of course you have.

Do you remember the times you thought your parents' decisions were too harsh? The times you couldn't wait to be older so you could make your own decisions? You're an adult now, with years of experience making your own decisions and accepting responsibilities. What would you do, what would you feel, if suddenly someone simply took over your life and made all your decisions for you?

At seventy-eight, Mrs. Jefferies lived alone and enjoyed an

active social life. Though she was in good health, she was not as steady on her feet as she once was. Her arthritis acted up. Climbing the stairs in her two-story home was becoming a chore. More and more often she spent the night on the couch in the living room. Mrs. Jefferies didn't want to give up her independence, but she came to agree that her daughter's concerns for her safety had some validity.

"I know I'm having a few problems," Mrs. Jefferies said, "but don't we all? Maybe I do have a few days when just opening a can of soup seems like too much bother. But I'm not that bad off. Why, just last week I went with the Senior Citizens' Tour Group to the zoo and then over to the mall for lunch and an afternoon of shopping.

"Then two nights ago I fell again. I was afraid for a while that I wouldn't be able to get back up. I did, but I've got this huge bruise all down my right side and on my leg. Now I'm worried about my daughter finding out. She's been after me to move into a retirement home or in with her and her family.

"That time might come. I'm not as insensible as my daughter sometimes thinks. I'll be okay on my own for a while longer yet. It's not as though I'm really sick or something, and I'm not that old, either. I like my privacy, and I don't want anybody telling me what to do. I'm not a child to be fussed at and watched over.

"I changed her diapers. It's not time yet for her to be thinking about changing mine." The result of the daughter's well-intentioned actions caused a rift between the two. Mrs. Jefferies hid the bruises and began to hide even more. To the daughter this was "proof" that her mother really did belong in a facility. Communication broke down. Both were miserable.

Is Intervention Really Necessary?

Convincing the elder to accept help may be your most difficult task. Why should this be so difficult? Your love, concern and logic have told you help is necessary; surely the elder can see this, too?

Try this experiment. On a sheet of paper, make a list of all the things you do without the help of others. Pay special attention to those things you take special pride in. This might be your career skills, your appearance, your abilities as a cook, community or volunteer work, gardening or any number of other things.

Close your eyes. Imagine losing those skills. Imagine, for example, that you've always received great praise for your painting, and now you can barely hold a brush. Or that one of the highlights of your day was to take a walk early in the morning, and now it's painful just to go from the living room to the kitchen.

To some degree, we all identify who we are with what we do. The loss of skills is frightening, even terrifying. When you are scared, it is a very small mental step from not being able to perform a task to total dependency. And to depression. Remember that in many cases the person faces the knowledge that those skills will never return. It's not like suffering from a broken bone in an accident that will heal.

How would you replace the loss of your cherished skills? How would you compensate? How long would you deny or hide their loss? What would you say to yourself and others to get yourself through the loss?

Answering the questions on paper will help you to understand what your elder might be feeling. It can also help you to prepare answers for the opposition you may encounter. When you understand what your elder is experiencing, you will also understand why it takes time in many instances for the elder to accept help—even yours.

Another feeling that sometimes accompanies loss of skills is shame. Many elders will see a friend slipping and deny that it could ever happen to them. They feel shame when it does, as though they have been betrayed by the body's natural aging process. They don't want anyone else to know of their need. It feels somehow demeaning to need help with something they have always done for themselves.

To admit need, to acknowledge a lessening of capabilities, to confront the unpalatable fact that one is growing not older but old, is a confrontation with one's own mortality.

When most people think of dying, it is in an abstract "someday" sense. When an elder of seventy-five or eighty contemplates the end of life, "someday" is sooner rather than later. Facing this issue is something many people put off as long as possible, especially if they have a great fear of dying. For many, an even greater fear is that of becoming helpless.

Manipulation by the Elder

Shame may make some elders resort to conscious or unconscious manipulation. "If you insist I need help with the heavy cleaning, okay. But you have to be the one to do it. I can't bear the thought of strangers in my home." Or "You've the only one who knows how I like the laundry done. People you hire just don't care. They won't do it the way it's supposed to be done."

Why will an elder use manipulation of this type? One of the strongest reasons is to hide the infirmity or need from outsiders, which will prevent the elder from becoming an object of pity. You may try to convince the elder that he or she will not be the object of pity or comparison, or will not be treated like a child, but it is unlikely you will ever succeed. Why? Don't you feel sorry for someone in worse shape than you? Do you think that your elder, over a long life, has not pitied someone, perhaps some older person who was no longer able to function independently?

Another reason for manipulation is the need for reassurance. An elder needs to feel loved and wanted, as we all do. Usually, how deserving of love we feel is dependent on our self-esteem. After all, we are "good" people. We help others, do thoughtful things and are productive members of the community.

An elder who no longer views himself or herself in this light has taken a very hard blow to self-esteem. It's hard to see yourself as a person worthy of love when your view of your own worthiness has been diminished. It's hard to see yourself as anything but a burden when you require more and more care. So the thought process becomes "No one loves a burden, and I have become a burden."

Following this thought process is a need for reassurance. In the last twenty years we have all heard of "Ask for what you want and need," as part of our psychologically oriented culture. Unfortunately, this kind of straightforward verbal transaction is not something our elders were taught. In fact, expressing needs and feelings was not encouraged for either sex of our elder's generation—men in particular, who have been drilled and drilled with what it means to "be a man." Is it any wonder they would have trouble expressing the need to have someone tell them they are loved and wanted? Instead, to meet the need to feel love, they will consciously or unconsciously manipulate people and situations. To do everything possible to meet a need, to fill a void, is simply human nature.

Helping the Elder to Accept Change

Changing situations become hard to accept and deal with as we get older, because the status quo forms a focal point for a narrowing reality. Self-directed routine and familiar surroundings bring a measure of psychological security. Many people, especially elders, tend to withdraw when faced with situations they don't feel capable of coping with. Many would rather do without than make a change that would better their lives, because they are not certain they can cope with the ramifications of change. The more simultaneous changes there are, the more there is to cope with. It may be more difficult for your elder to agree to your personal intervention and then lose it after weeks (which feels like rejection) than it would be to accept a stranger's help in the beginning.

Getting someone to accept change is not always easy, though there are ways to make change more acceptable, even attractive.

Always try to present any needed change in the most positive light possible. This is done by focusing on the beneficial aspects of the solution instead of the disruption to routine caused by making the change. When you talk about the solution, show enthusiasm. Getting an elder excited about the possibility of making a beneficial change is about half the battle in having that change actually work. Because enthusiasm is contagious, hearing you speak positively and in an upbeat manner about a change makes it easier for the elder to see it in a positive light.

As a warning: Be prepared for your enthusiasm to be met with coldness. Most people resist change. An idea that seems wonderful to you may be nothing more than "proof" to the elder of being no longer useful or wanted.

Also be aware that your enthusiasm should be genuine. If it's not, examine your intentions more carefully. If you don't feel enthusiasm for a solution you're suggesting, maybe the solution isn't so great after all.

Refrain from using negative manipulation to get the elder to fall in with your plans. This creates resentment and lessens the chance of the proposed solution working. "If you loved me, you'd stop driving." "If you want to make me happy, you'd do what I'm asking," "You're making me miserable because you won't let me help." These are all examples of negative manipulation.

Intervention is meant to benefit the person being helped. Being negative almost never accomplishes this goal.

Presenting the Elder With Choices and Solutions

No one can predict how an elder will react to intervention. Do not make blanket statements or promises using "always" or "never." "Mom would never agree to outside help." "I'll never put Mom in a nursing home." All situations are subject to change and usually without notice. People do change their minds. Locking yourself into absolute statements will limit your ability to solve problems and limit your elder's ability to accept changes. Blanket statements also increase your guilt load when unforeseen circumstances force you to go back on your word.

Every day you have dozens of choices. Having choices helps you feel in control of your life. Your elder feels the same way. First discover the cause of the problem. Then try to present more than one solution to it.

For example, let's say you are having a difficult time getting the elder to eat a balanced diet. The cause could be anything from lack of interest in food or not having the energy to cook to being unable to shop for foods that are appealing or not wanting to eat alone. Depending on the cause, there are a number of possible solutions. The following are only a few of them:

- Prepare several meals in advance for reheating in the microwave or oven.
- Form a luncheon group from the elder's friends and rotate lunch sites.
- Take advantage of senior citizen discounts and two-for-one offers at restaurants.
- Add a liquid food supplement to the diet (with the doctor's approval).
- Choose a home meal delivery service like Meals on Wheels, or find a senior center that serves a nutritious noon meal.

Suppose your father needs help with lawn care and maintenance around the house. You might try to get him to accept help by saying, "Dad, how would you like to teach your grandson Timmy all about yard care? He wants to start a lawn service after school to earn some extra money." Or "There's a family I know of that's starting their own business doing home maintenance. Do you think there's some work around here we could give them?" Or "Dad, I've hired a great new lawn service. What do you think about giving them a try around here? Then you'd have more time to spend in the workshop."

Choose the approach that is most consistent with your elder's personality. If the elder is family-oriented, teaching a grandchild the tradition of gardening could work well (assuming that the grandson is willing, and knows that *he* is to do most of the actual work). If they are the type of person who believes in lending a helping hand, the answer could be to ask the elder to help a new small business or to use an organization that is teaching job skills, such as to troubled teens. You could also try paying for the service yourself and giving it to the elder as a gift for a birthday, holiday or anniversary.

When purchasing services, consider a three-month trial. Psychological studies indicate it takes about ninety days for new behavior to become a new habit. Three months will give the elder adequate time to adjust and enjoy the new service. Be aware, however, that after three months the service either must be paid again or will stop.

In all the examples, the idea of accepting the intervention is presented in a positive manner. At no time should the caregiver say anything judgmental that would make the elder feel defensive or useless, such as "Dad, you know you can't handle the lawn care anymore."

The Importance of Good Timing

When possible, try to tackle one problem at a time, taking the most critical problem first. There are three primary reasons for this strategy.

First, when one problem is successfully solved, you can point to the success as an encouragement to make other beneficial changes. Second, if you try to change everything at once you increase stress levels, since dealing with change is stressful for anyone. Third, in pointing out so many areas in which you feel the elder needs help, you are undermining the elder's self-confidence, saying in effect, "You are failing. Look at how much help you need."

Choose the time to intervene, Intervention is not a spur-of-the-moment thing. It requires advance planning. Not only do you need the facts to back up your plan but you need the time to discuss the subject at length with the elder. The elder needs to be in a communicative mood and as free from outside stress as possible.

Talk. . . and Listen!

When you discuss a problem, listen to the elder. Listening is work! It means you have to drop all your own ideas and notions so that you are honestly hearing what the elder is saying. It means that you are making the effort to understand needs and emotions from *the other person's* perspective. If you don't it's not intervention but interference.

The elder may have thought of other solutions and may also have objections to your solutions. You may think that having the elder move in with you is the best idea. Your elder may prefer the companionship of others the same age on a daily basis and opt for a care facility. Conversely, you have available a wonderful, affordable facility only to find that your elder always assumed you'd live together if the need ever arose.

Modifying your solution may be the answer, but you'll never know if there is another way to handle the problem unless you listen. If at all possible, try the elder's solution first. This allows the elder to keep some self-esteem and goes a long way toward establishing a good, cooperative, working relationship between the two of you.

Stay flexible. Sometimes a change of schedule is all that's needed to make a situation work better. "Mom, why don't we do the grocery shopping on Wednesday instead of Saturday? That way we have one less chore on Saturday, and we can take our time."

Remember that the basis for all intervention is love and honesty—on both sides. Don't be manipulated into situations you can't tolerate. If an elder wants to live with you or have you personally handle a chore, and you simply *cannot* comply, you'll have to be honest and say so. Never, never volunteer a solution you're not fully prepared to accept.

When you feel you've reached an agreement, end the discussion with a positive recap. "Dad, let's make sure I've got this right. I'm going to tell Timmy you agreed to teach him how to care for the lawn and the gardens. You want him to come over at ten o'clock Saturday mornings, right?" A positive recap reinforces the elder's agreement to the intervention and helps prevent misunderstandings.

Intervention and Dependence

The interventions we have discussed are easily applicable to Level I caregiving, where you have the time to introduce changes in a more or less leisurely manner. Sometimes, as in the case of an injury or surgery, many things change at once, at least temporarily. In this case, discuss the situation with the elder and make the needed changes, but always reassure the elder that these changes are temporary and that there is time to think about other more permanent arrangements if they are needed.

In this case, discuss the situation with the elder and try to follow any suggestions he or she may have. Changes necessitated by illness or accident may not be exactly what the elder wants, so be certain to reassure him or her that the changes or arrangements are of a temporary nature until a better plan for more permanent arrangements, if needed, can be formed. If the elder has been previously self-sufficient, the sudden need for care can be met with resistance. Still, you must discuss the arrangements with the elder and make whatever compromises are possible. To do otherwise is to assume control, which can cause even more problems.

Sometimes when an elder is recovering, the physical healing can be the least of the problem. An elder can become overly dependent on a caregiver and hinder recovery. The pattern for this is very insidious.

When the accident or illness first happens, the elder is physically weak, perhaps disoriented, and needs a lot of physical care while adjusting to new circumstances. Many times the psychological damage the elder sustains is worse than the physical problem. Even though the person may be recovering physically, fear and worry can become constant mental companions. "What if I fall and break something else?" "What if I have another heart attack?" "This therapy is so hard. It hurts. I can't do it. I don't think I'll ever get better." The attitude problem is underscored by age. Elders rarely have the physical recuperative powers of someone younger, so recovery takes longer.

We all take risks every day. Many times the risk factor doesn't even enter our conscious thought. When you want to chat with you next-door neighbor, you go. You don't think about the process of getting there. Your elder thinks about getting up and managing to get to the door, looks at the seemingly vast distance (maybe 150 feet) to the neighbor's house, perhaps considers having to negotiate a few steps up to the front porch, walk into the house and settle in for a cup of coffee and a chat—then, a short time later, the whole process has to be repeated to get home. Is it worth the risk of falling to chat over a cup of coffee? The elder may reason that it is so much safer to use the telephone.

The physical body does not recover without exercise. Elders who do not perform the tasks they are capable of handling will soon lose the ability of being able to perform them at all. In that case the dependency on the caregiver will become heavier.

The physical aspects are obvious. There are also psychological aspects to increasing dependency. Either of you, or both, may become resentful. Elders who become more dependent are reminded of their incapacity and their increasing reliance on someone else. For caregivers the job of giving care is more of a burden. This resentment can lead to new and deeper problems.

There are a few things you can do to prevent or reduce dependency:

- Encourage activity along with adequate rest periods and wholesome nutrition.
- Encourage gentle exercise. If therapy has been ordered, make certain you understand the procedures and coach the elder through the process. If an exercise program is needed, ask the doctor to recommend a physical therapist who will evaluate the elder's range of motion and demonstrate proper stretching and isometric exercises to improve fitness. Participate in the exercises with your elder. This accomplishes three things.

First, you know the exercises have been done. Second, it's easier to exercise with someone than alone, so your elder may be more willing to undertake an exercise program if you join in. Third, you will benefit by ridding yourself of excess tension even through a simple light exercise program.

- Have the elder participate in household chores. This is important especially if the elder lives with you. Chores are a necessary part of family life. To feel wanted and accepted, an elder must participate in as many aspects of family living as possible.

- Encourage independence by reducing unnecessary assistance. This is especially important if an elder is recovering from an accident or illness. If the elder is not succeeding or cooperating as predicted, doctors or therapists can offer a number of techniques to help. Also, because they are perceived as authority figures, it may be easier for an elder to grasp the importance of therapy when they explain it, even though you may have said the very same thing.

Helping the Elder Accept Relocation

When elders have reached Level III care, it is necessary for them to have a supervised environment. If they cannot receive this in their own surrounding, there are only two options left. The choice is to move into someone else's home (usually an adult child's) or to become a resident of a care facility (or a hospice facility if the elder's condition is terminal).

Why is it so hard to get Mom or Dad to accept having to move? The question implies that the sole problem is one of relocation. It isn't. You are dealing with another situation that is at least as important as the move. Consider what has led to the decision to move in the first place. Illness? Accident? Lessening of the ability to function independently? Whatever the cause, your elder is not looking at the move so much as at the reason and the feeling behind it. Many times an elder will be able to use the familiar surroundings of home to adapt to diminished physical and mental capabilities. If severe mental impairment is an issue, the elder may not be able to prepare for a move because he or she is unable to think about it.

Sometimes the best decision is to help the elder find a care facility. Society seems to blame the caregiver when this becomes necessary, as though the caregiver is somehow inadequate. If you find yourself faced with this situation, turn your back on the critics. They obviously haven't been in your position. Sometimes the most loving thing you can do is placement.

The elder can also place enormous guilt trips on the caregiver, saying anything from "You don't love me anymore," to, "After all I've done for you!" If your elder begins to harass you with guilt, the only thing you can do is keep repeating both to the elder and to yourself in a calm manner, "You know I love you. You also know the old situation was not working out. You simply weren't getting the care you need. I know you are not happy with the situation, but please try to remember that I do love you."

If it is possible, have the elder visit the proposed facilities and make the selection. Some of the facilities will allow the elder to stay for the day and get to know the staff and residents. Spending time at the facility before the formal move-in can help the elder feel more comfortable about the move.

Signs the Elder May Be Seeking Intervention

Sometimes an elder will send signals that intervention is wanted or would be accepted. These signals can be conscious or unconscious, verbal or nonverbal. Be alert to changes in your elder's attitude and behavior. Among others, the following may be significant:

- The elder asks for safety devices to be installed.
- The elder inquires about community services.
- The elder talks of a friend needing services or help.
- The elder asks your opinion of a new product that was advertised.

• The elder openly discusses concern for the future.

• The elder wants to talk about hypothetical situations such as "What would you do if I decided to sell the house?"

• The elder accepts your offers of assistance faster or more often than usual.

• The elder gives various family members different pieces of information or conflicting stories.

• The elder's eating, sleeping or grooming habits suddenly change.

• The elder's short-term memory seems impaired: forgetting medication, appointments, events, paying bills, burning food, etc.

• The elder refuses to see a medical professional, is reluctant to talk about a doctor's visit or asks you not to tell anyone about a medical appointment.

• The elder undergoes noticeable personality changes.

• The elder makes accusations like "You don't care about what happens to me" or "You'd be happy to be rid of me."

• The elder exhibits unexplained bruising, limping, or painful mobility—possible results of a fall.

Techniques for Discussing Intervention

Adapt the following techniques to fit your and your elder's personality and situation:

Concerned approach. "Dad, I've really been worried about your plan to paint the house. The idea of your getting up on ladders really scares me. Can we talk about it?"

Questioning approach. "Mom, have you thought about getting a Meals on Wheels service?"

Favor approach. "Dad, would you do me a favor and have Timmy cut the lawn? He really needs to learn some responsibility."

Friend approach. "How does your friend Erma like the senior-care center she's going to?"

Gift approach. "You know how you're always saying that you don't want any birthday present because you have enough stuff? Well, this year we want to give you either a year of weekly housecleaning services or a year of yard maintenance. Which do you think you'd like better?"

Mediator approach. "I've been reading about the new tax laws, and they really are confusing. I think we should check things out with your attorney and make sure you are prepared. Would you like me to call and make the appointment?"

Warning approach. "We've been putting off talking about your plans for the future. Let's think about some options, and when we get together next Saturday we'll talk, okay?"

DON'TS FOR INTERVENTION   Don't parent your parent by assuming control and making decisions when your elder is capable of deciding for himself or herself.

Don't underestimate your elder's abilities.

Don't make blanket statements or promises such as "I'll never put you in a care facility" or "I promise I'll call every weekend."

Don't think that words are enough. Show your love through hugs, pats on the back and caring actions.

Don't expect that your elder will always tell you when something is wrong. Learn to read moods and actions.

Don't expect your elder to respond to anything medical in a predictable manner. Be observant. A book or a doctor can only instruct you in the "typical" way a person with a particular personality or condition will react. There are as many variations as there are elders.

Don't offer help unless it is really needed.

Don't allow your elder to become overly dependent on you.

Don't let your elder dictate your life.

DOS FOR INTERVENTION   Do give reassurance and encouragement both verbally and with physical touch. Use "positive reinforcement" by complimenting accomplishments.

Do try to discuss the problem and come to a resolution. When you think agreement has been reached, summarize the agreement in one or two sentences. Example: "Okay, Mom. We agree that I'll call Meals on Wheels tomorrow and arrange for meals to be delivered to you, right?"

Do present the need for help in the most positive light possible.

Do consider alternatives, including a change of schedule if that will solve the problem. "Mom, I know you've been preparing wonderful dinners for years, but why not consider eating the big meal of the day at noon at the senior center? That way our Sunday dinners together will be even more special. What do you think?"

Do keep an open mind. There is no need for you to come up with all of the solutions. Your elder may have workable solutions, too. Stay flexible. Though not every possible solution will work, one of them will. Compromise will become a way of life.

Do listen. Paraphrase what your elder has said to you to make certain you have understood.

Do assist your elder in making decisions by gathering information and finding services.

Do encourage your elder to try new things.

Do help your elder to maintain social contacts.

Do be honest about your feelings and concerns for your elder and his or her behavior.

Do take the initiative to learn all you can about your elder's needs and medical problems.

Do be observant. Watching how your elder reacts when worried or fearful or simply not feeling well will sometimes tell you more than a conversation will reveal.

Do celebrate the moment. Victories in elder care can be rare and hard-won. If your elder manages to walk across the room unaided after having had a broken leg, or has withdrawn from the world and now expresses an interest in going out, celebrate the victory. Brag about it. Reward the behavior and encourage more of it.

Do encourage your elder to talk and to express emotions. Facilitate the healing of relationships.

Do help your elder to accomplish goals.

Do separate your elder from your elder's illness in your mind. Caring for an elder, regardless if sick or well, will increase your chore load, but doing all the chores in the world will not give your elder what is most needed: loving human contact. Take the time to hold hands, share a sunset, give a hug and kiss goodnight. This sharing and touching is important to all people, ill or not, regardless of age. Love and affection is a basic human need.

Other Kinds of Intervention

There are times when other kinds of intervention are needed. The goal, *always*, is to help the person. The risk, *always*, is going too far or too soon, especially when you feel you are protecting the elder.

Many kinds of protective intervention aren't pleasant. A relative may be trying to take advantage of the elder. A sham artist may have come by and convinced the elder that the roof or driveway needs to be redone. A doctor may have suggested a treatment that is useless or risky.

Other times intervention will involve handling details, such as dealing with an insurance company or government agency.

Your main job as caregiver is to remain as aware as possible. If you don't, situations will arise and escalate. Intervention then becomes much more difficult. Imagine, for example, that the elder has accepted a live-in companion who has been there for two months before you find out. Just stepping through the door and sniffing, you realize that the situation is bad and is getting worse. Perhaps you even notice that some valuable objects are missing.

The time to intervene is when intervention is needed, not after the situation has become a crisis. Once again, however, this must be carefully balanced with calmness, common sense and virtually always with the permission and knowledge of the elder.

To repeat what was said early in this chapter, the job of the caregiver is to give care. The purpose of intervention is to make this possible. Except in extreme cases, it is *not* to take control.

EIGHT

Dealing With Medical Personnel

Many people hold the medical profession, doctors in particular, in awe. As lay persons, we generally understand very little of medicine. We tend to think that a doctor can fix anything but the most deadly forms of disease, and even then we expect breakthrough treatments and experimental cures. As a whole this profession deserves our respect and admiration because of the amazing work its members do to improve our lives.

When medical professionals are considered individually, you will find a mix of good and bad, of competent and incompetent, just as you will in any job. The question is: How do you find good, competent medical care for your elder, or assess the medical care the elder is currently receiving?

In a medical situation you will probably deal most often with your elder's primary-care physician, a family physician, general practitioner or internist. This doctor will treat all age groups from infancy through geriatric patients (elders) and may even do minor surgeries. A primary-care physician must be versatile and have excellent diagnostic capabilities. During the course of a day, this MD may see a child with a raging fever, an adult with unexplained headaches, someone with severe stomach pains, an accident victim and an elder with chest pains or a sudden onset of shakiness. If the diagnosis indicates a problem outside the primary physician's ability to treat, a recommendation to a specialist will be given.

The recommendation doesn't end the primary-care physician's function. A concerned doctor will follow up on the treatment the patient received at the hands of specialists and coordinate all treatments. (Don't rely on this, however. It's up to you to make sure that the communication is complete.)

The doctor also needs to be able to effectively communicate with the patients on their level. This takes time and compassion. Any doctor can toss medical terms around until the language doesn't even resemble English. You need a doctor who will put the medical condition and its treatment in terms that are easily understood.

A compassionate doctor will explain each and every step and phase of an illness, treatment or recovery. This information is necessary if you are to evaluate your ability to care for an elder or need to arrange care. Knowing in advance what is likely to occur helps both you and the elder to be at least somewhat emotionally prepared.

This doctor also listens. Every patient is a unique case. Changes in lifestyle, unexpected reactions to medication, unexplained vague symptoms of "just not feeling as good as I used to": All are pieces of a puzzle that a good doctor uses to help the patient regain health.

An excellent physician is one who treats the whole patient— one who considers the patient's mental and emotional needs as well as physical ones. This often takes extra time, as well as lots of patience and understanding. Unfortunately not all physicians are willing.

The patient may simply need to talk for a few minutes about a frustration that may seem unimportant on the surface. That excellent physician will know that those complaints sometimes explain things that would otherwise escape overall diagnosis. These doctors understand that the patient's emotional status can be the real cause of what seems to be physical.

As a caregiver you need to be able to form a working relationship with this professional so that you feel free to relate all areas of the elder's situation and condition. Working as a team, you and the physician will provide optimum care for your elder.

Case Study: Working With Doctors

It was time for Helen's annual physical. She had been feeling a little run-down lately and asked her daughter, Marie, to drive her to the appointment with Dr. Brown.

"Mom is a shy person," said Marie, "not one to volunteer information. So I was happy to go along if only to meet the doctor she had been seeing for years and make certain she told him about her lack of energy and appetite."

The nurse came in and took Helen's blood pressure and pulse, asked some preliminary questions and requested a urine sample. Dr. Brown came in, read what the nurse had written, listened to Helen's heart and lungs, then asked, "How are you doing?"

Helen said she was tired but otherwise felt fine. The doctor glanced at her chart and said, "Well, you're seventy-seven. You're no spring chicken. Just rest and eat right."

He ordered the standard blood test and a mammogram and was gone in ten minutes.

Dr. Brown's nurse called about two weeks later and said everything was okay except that Helen had three red blood cells in her urine—but not to worry. It was within acceptable limits and was probably just a low-grade infection that would clear itself up.

Helen continued to feel run-down. Marie finally convinced her to see another doctor who was part of a group practice. An immediate problem arose. Not all doctors even within the group accept the same insurance. In this case, the doctor didn't work with Helen's insurance, but another one in the same practice did. An appointment was made with this alternate physician, Dr. Rivera.

The nurse came in and did the same preliminaries. When Dr. Rivera arrived, he chatted with Helen for a few moments before beginning the exam. He did everything Dr. Brown had done, then proceeded with a breast exam and a pap smear. He checked the ears, nose and throat and tested reflexes. When he got to the toes, he took one look, frowned and said, "That's a fungal infection, and you need to see a podiatrist to have it looked after properly."

Helen and Marie were surprised, because in all the medical exams Helen had before, nothing had ever been said about her feet.

Then Dr. Rivera took the time to really talk with Helen. He found out about her love of walking and that she was too tired most of the time to do it anymore. This concerned him because Helen had gone from walking three miles a day to getting worn out from a simple trip to the grocery store two blocks away.

Helen said she wasn't really worried because, to quote the earlier doctor, "I'm seventy-seven and thought it was natural not to be a spring chicken."

Dr. Rivera joked with her about wanting a few more tests just to be sure she had progressed normally from a spring chicken to a summer chicken, then ordered blood and urine tests. The nurse called the following week and requested that Helen come in for a follow-up visit.

Dr. Rivera had her records from Dr. Brown and the results from his own tests. Everything seemed normal. There were no traces of infection, but there was still a minute quantity of blood in her urine. He ordered a third urine test, which again showed trace amounts of blood.

Dr. Rivera referred Helen to a urologist. The urologist looked at the tests and said that such a small number of red blood cells was probably nothing to worry about. Helen would have left thinking everything was okay and that everyone was making a big fuss over nothing, but Marie told him that Dr. Rivera wanted Helen's bladder visually examined by the urologist using instruments that would allow the urologist to actually see inside the bladder. Fortunately, Marie had listened closely when Dr. Rivera explained the procedure he wanted performed and was able to repeat exactly what had been said. The urologist was hearing Dr. Rivera's reasons

and request for a particular exam for the first time. This is not
unusual. In a referral situation, many times one doctor's office
staff calls another doctor's staff to arrange an appointment or
simply asks the patient to set his or her appointment with the
referral doctor. Even with fax capabilities, information and
requests can go astray. The urologist wanted another urine test,
which he checked on the spot, before he agreed to do the visual.

After the visual exam, he talked to both Helen and Marie and
said that Dr. Rivera was absolutely right. Something was wrong.
The urologist had discovered a small nodule, about the size of the
tip of your little finger, inside the bladder. From its appearance he
was almost certain it was cancer, but too small to be shedding cells
into the urine at a detectable level.

Helen was scheduled for outpatient laser surgery three days
later. She went into the hospital at 7:00 A.M. and was released at
11:00 that same morning with a catheter. That afternoon Dr.
Rivera, not the urologist, called with the biopsy results. It was
cancer, but the urologist had assured him that it had not invaded
the bladder wall and that he was certain all of it was gone.

The complaint and symptoms were there. At least in part due
to Dr. Brown's comments, Helen was ready to dismiss them; she
was getting older. Marie was lucky enough to contact a second
physician who followed through. She was also wise enough to not
be so intimidated as to trust that the doctors had been in
communication. They hadn't. Dr. Rivera wanted the specialist to
perform a thorough exam, not just more tests. The urologist
wouldn't have known that if it hadn't been for Marie.

Helen's cancer was so small that it was easy to miss. Because she
and Marie worked *with* the doctors, it was caught in time. Marie
didn't challenge the first doctor's expertise, she merely sought a
second opinion. When she got that from Dr. Rivera, she followed
his recommendation and didn't let the urologist intimidate her
into ignoring what the second had said. The specialist might have
found that the second doctor's suspicions weren't correct. Marie,
and Helen, might not have known until too late if Marie had
relied on the doctors being in firm communication.

Evaluating the Physician

Use the following suggestions when evaluating a doctor:

1. Get as many recommendations as possible from friends and family. Ask them about the doctor's attitude. Does the doctor listen to their problems and answer their questions fully? Do they feel comfortable with the doctor's attitude and treatment?

2. Call a referral service (usually listed in the Yellow Pages under *Physician Referral Service*). Get their recommendations based on your needs.

3. Call the doctor's office and question the office manager. Explain that you are looking for a particular kind of doctor for your elder. Many managers will tell you about the doctor and what types of patients he or she specializes in or sees the most. The manager can also tell you which insurance the doctor accepts and which hospitals and clinics he or she is affiliated with.

4. When you have narrowed your list of doctors, contact the State Board of Medical Examiners. This board will tell you if the doctor has had any action taken against him or her. Locate this board in the White Pages of the phone book under the heading of *State Government*.

5. Make an appointment with the doctor for an interview. Make certain the elder is there along with you. The purpose of the appointment is to get acquainted. How does the elder feel about the doctor? Do they talk easily? Does the doctor answer questions in language you can both understand? Does the doctor inspire trust? Does the doctor understand the elder's viewpoint on various things such as surgery, blood transfusions, "heroic measures" or life support systems? (Some may be a violation of the elder's religious beliefs.) Will the doctor agree to abide by the elder's wishes in these matters? Do you think there is a good chance you and the elder will be able to work with and rely upon this individual?

Be aware of the general atmosphere of the office. Is it warm and friendly? How are the people? Are they helpful or stressed out and presenting a curt manner? This is a doctor's office and a place of business, but if the people you will be working with don't show a warm, compassionate manner, chances are the disease an elder has may be treated but the emotional and mental aspects of the patient's health may be given less importance than they deserve.

You will probably have to pay for the appointment, just as you do at other businesses that charge a consultation fee. The fee may or may not be the same as a regular office visit and may not be covered by insurance.

Some people balk at the idea of interviewing a doctor or resent the time it takes. However, most people shop around until they find a mechanic or hairstylist that they trust. Why would they take less care when their own well-being, their family's or their elder's is at stake?

The Hospital

Selection of a hospital is usually dependent on two things. One is whether the hospital takes your elder's insurance or is willing to accommodate other payment arrangements made in advance. The other is if your elder's selected doctor has practicing privileges there. The first is financial. The second becomes a factor in selecting a doctor.

It might seem that a licensed doctor would be able to use any hospital. This is not the case. In order to be able to practice at a hospital, a doctor must be accepted by that hospital's board before being able to admit and treat patients there.

If the patient is admitted to a hospital where the doctor doesn't have practicing privileges, have the admitting doctor call the elder's own doctor. Chances are the elder's doctor will be able to petition the hospital for temporary privileges, consult with the admitting doctor on this case or arrange to have the elder change hospitals once the condition is stable. Don't expect it to go so easily. Take the time to know what to expect.

Hospitals themselves vary in quality and services, which is one reason why doctors may spend a lot of time selecting the hospital(s) they are affiliated with. Usually their selection is founded on the types of facilities that will be afforded their patients. If a doctor has a heavy pediatrics practice, a hospital with good general care and an outstanding pediatrics wing might be selected over a hospital with good general care and a top-notch coronary-care unit.

Informed Consent

When anyone uses a hospital for emergency treatment or tests, the legally and financially responsible person (elder, caregiver with guardianship or conservatorship, court-appointed responsibilities, or other person with these court-appointed responsibilities) will be asked to sign an Informed Consent form that gives permission for the facility to treat the person. This form covers general care. In the case of surgery, another Informed Consent form is presented that specifically lists the surgery. Signing an Informed Consent form means that the surgery or other procedure was explained, including the risks, and that the person signing agrees to have the treatment performed.

It is ultimately more convenient for the medical and administrative staff if the form is simply signed by the appropriate person. What you may not be told is that it is perfectly legal to make notations or exclusions on this form. (For reasons of clarity, the word "you" in this section will now represent the person responsible for signing this form and agreeing to medical procedures.)

For example, you can sign to have a breast biopsy done but not a mastectomy, or you can agree to a biopsy but state that the family must be told before a mastectomy is done. You can refuse to have a blood transfusion or refuse to accept any blood except that which is your own or from specified people. (You must make arrangements for this type of blood donation in advance. The doctor will tell you how this is done.)

Good communication is vital. Your doctor needs to be told of these stipulations when you are discussing the surgery because in many cases stipulations do increase the risk factor in the treatment. However, simply discussing them is not enough; they must still be put in writing in the "Informed Consent" form.

Anne's mother, Louise, noticed a mole on her right ankle that changed color from brown to black. The doctor found that the mole was cancerous and subsequently removed it. A year later the cancer recurred at the same site. The cancer was removed again. When the cancer appeared for the third time, the surgeon advised that, although he would try again to remove all the cancer, amputation of the foot below the cancerous site might be necessary.

Louise was emphatically against any procedure that would "take what God gave." She would let him operate on the cancerous site, but there would be no amputation. The doctor explained the immense dangers of leaving the foot on if the cancer was well progressed. Louise still refused amputation. When the nurse brought the consent forms, she wrote out clearly on the form that she would not permit amputation.

Louise knew the dangers. So did Anne. Both knew that melanoma is often swift and deadly. Delayed surgery (including amputation) can force even more extensive procedures or can mean that the condition has become inoperable. Fortunately, the surgery worked. It could have come out otherwise.

Whenever you are faced with surgery discuss it thoroughly with the doctor. You may be scared and uncertain, but your "gut" or your head will often tell you what is best for you right then. There are many situations, however, when you must simply give your informed consent and pray for the best. Heart attacks may require immediate surgery. Don't wait until you have all your affairs tied up in a neat little bundle. Same for strokes. Serious injuries from car accidents, falls, and other bad happenstances may also require deferring the best judgment of the medical professionals.

Medical Lawsuits

With rare exception, the doctor is on the patient's side and is doing everything possible to save lives and make things right. If there is good communication among doctor, patient and care-giver, everything that can be done will be done within the restrictions you've all agreed upon beforehand.

Especially in an emergency situation, sometimes things go terribly, tragically wrong. At times, if it's someone's fault, there is a right to legal redress. Other times it's just an ordinary risk. Anesthesia is a good example. There is a small chance that any patient will die from a reaction to general anesthesia. The human body reacts differently in each situation, and once in a great while, someone dies. It is no one's fault.

Complicating this is uncertainty. There have been times when an anesthesiologist was found to have been drinking or was otherwise impaired. The cause of death is no longer as sure. Could it have been just an unfortunate reaction, or was it something that could have been prevented?

These days many people are "banking" their own blood when an operation is expected. More and more popular is a stipulation on the Informed Consent form that names certain people as donors. This is due at least in part to the number of cases in which a person gets a blood transfusion and ends up with a fatal disease such as AIDS.

In such a case, it's not always easy to determine fault. It's unlikely to be the attending physician or surgical staff. It may or may not be the hospital and/or the blood bank that supplied the blood. It would certainly start with the blood donor, but even that assumes that the donor knew about having the disease.

Still, a loved one has died, or has been injured. You may find yourself in need of consultation with an attorney, preferably one who specializes in such cases. Be aware, however, that while most lawyers are honest (as are most doctors), there are some who are more interested in the amount they can get in a settlement than in serving justice. The doctor may be perfectly innocent, with the lawyer knowing that settlement is often the easier route.

These days especially, it's easy to assume the worst. You might be too ready to sue, and possibly to sue the wrong people, due to distrust of doctors. Or you might be too willing to accept the situation because of a distrust of lawyers. Neither response is correct.

Home From the Hospital

Hospital and medical treatments have changed a great deal in the last two decades. If you haven't been personally involved with a newly released patient before, you may be in for quite a shock.

A seventy-six-year-old woman broke her leg. Her son was assured that the hospital staff would put the leg in sturdy cast. Not only was this a reasonable assumption, he'd let them know clearly that she broke her leg in the first place because she was having a problem with balance. He also told the emergency room physician that his mother couldn't balance well enough to use crutches and needed a wheelchair.

Instead they put her leg in an immobilizer, which is a stiffened fabric held together by adjustable Velcro fasteners. The staff showed him how to position the appliance for stability and comfort. They told the woman to not put any weight on the leg, to keep it elevated and to see her doctor in three days. Then they handed her a pair of crutches.

Her son was a little surprised at this. The staff told him that this was standard procedure for a broken leg and insisted she try to use the crutches. After three attempts, during which she fell into the physician's arms, he finally wrote a prescription for a wheelchair rental and warned them that it probably wouldn't be covered by Medicare because it was outside the standard treatment guidelines.

Her primary-care doctor did manage to get the wheelchair covered by insurance by citing another medical cause as the reason for the inability to use crutches. In the meantime they had rented the needed chair.

Why all the fuss over something as simple as a wheelchair? In short, there has been abuse of moneys allocated for Medicare and Medicaid. To combat the problem, the government, under the auspices of Medicare and Medicaid, set up a group of regulations

called DRGs (diagnostically related groups). This group of standardized regulations established which treatment, including
equipment, was authorized for a particular illness or condition,
how much Medicare would allow as payment for each service by a
doctor, nurse or therapist, and how much they would reimburse
the hospital for a patient's stay.

For example, for each patient who is admitted to a hospital for
total knee replacement surgery, the hospital is reimbursed X
amount of dollars. If complications occur, the patient is given
another standardized diagnosis, and another X amount of dollars is
allotted to the hospital for that patient.

As you can imagine, if a patient can come into a hospital, have
surgery done and promptly go home, then the hospital stands to
make money or at least operate within its budget. If, on the other
hand, the patient comes in, has surgery and then languishes about
for an extended recovery time, then the hospital loses money.
From this method of operation, our society has now come to the
"quicker and sicker" method of sending people home from the
hospital.

For younger, generally healthier patients, this isn't necessarily
bad. Women who have given birth are released in a matter of days
rather than a week or more. Not only are costs reduced, it has
been found that in many cases the patient recovers better and
faster at home. An unfortunate side effect has been that sometimes a patient in more serious circumstances is released too soon
and/or without adequate care, equipment, supplies or even medication. What this means for you as a caregiver is that you may find
yourself taking care of an elder who has just been released from
the hospital in a much lessened state of recovery than you might
expect.

In the old days a person going in for knee replacement surgery
would probably be admitted to the hospital about noon on, say,
Thursday. A nurse would take the patient's medical history and
list food and medication allergies so that any significant health
problems could be noted for the nursing staff. Baseline vital signs
(blood pressure, temperature, pulse and respiration) would have

been taken and recorded. A phlebotomist would draw blood. Supper would be served. After supper the anesthesiologist would drop by to talk about what type of anesthesia would be used and what the patient could expect when waking up after surgery. The doctor would drop by to answer any last-minute questions. If the patient had family members there, they were also informed about what could be expected from the surgery, the recovery and when the patient would be able to go home. Once the patient was well informed about the surgical events to follow, the nurse would drop by with an Informed Consent form to be signed. Then the nursing staff would clear the patient's bowel for the next day's surgery.

After surgery, the patient would be kept on injectable medications for pain control for at least one or two days (depending on the procedure) and then weaned down to oral medication. By Monday, the patient would begin physical therapy and have several days of this while in the hospital.

Once the patient was up and about, the catheter was removed, the IVs were out, the bowels were back in working order, a normal diet was resumed and the baseline vitals were back within normal limits—once everyone was comfortable that the patient would be safely functional at home with the minimal assistance from the family—the patient went home. The scenario accounted for about five or six days.

Today a knee replacement patient sees the physician on, say, Friday to receive final instructions and pick up a bowel preparation kit, then goes to an outpatient laboratory for preliminary blood work and possibly a chest X ray. Over the weekend the patient follows instructions and uses the kit. On Monday, the patient enters the hospital and has surgery. Barring complications, the patient leaves on Wednesday, about forty-eight hours after entering.

If the patient is younger or is very spry and wants to get up and about quickly, you are a caregiver with an "easy" patient on your hands. You will probably have to serve meals, give pain medications as needed, help with sponge baths, assist the patient to the bathroom and generally help until the staples (stitches are no longer generally used) are removed and the person is able to handle things independently. You may have to provide transportation to the doctor's office and to therapy. Taking care of an elder in this condition is about the same as taking care of a sick child. But what if something goes wrong?

Case Study:
Complications During At-Home Recovery

Cindy, a registered nurse who specializes in home health care, tells the case study of Ivy, an eighty-four-year-old woman who developed a lump in her breast. Ivy complained to her doctor earlier in the week of tenderness in her breast and of stiffness in her left arm. She was admitted to the hospital Friday morning, at which time she signed an Informed Consent form for a breast biopsy and a total mastectomy if it was needed.

The biopsy was positive for cancer of the breast. Several of the lymph nodes were also positive, showing that the cancer had begun to spread. A total mastectomy, in which the entire breast and some lymph nodes were removed, was performed.

Ivy was sent home Saturday morning. Her surgeon did not discharge her personally as it was not "his weekend to be on call." The hospital's discharge planner told her that she would be seen at home twice a day by an RN. So Ivy went home to be cared for by her seventy-six-year-old sister and her sister's husband (also elderly). A niece who lived near the trio volunteered to help out.

Cindy said, "I was paged with this referral midday on Saturday. The only information I was given was that the patient needed a mastectomy dressing changed twice a day. I had no idea that the patient had surgery on Friday until I reached the family by phone to arrange a visit. The sister was beside herself with fear.

"The family was panicky because the patient was sent home so quickly. Ivy was freshly 'post-op' and had been sent home in her original bandages with a drain tube in place. It was brimming with bloody drainage. Ibuprofen was given for pain control. Ivy was contorted with pain when I arrived. Although Ibuprofen is a wonderful drug, it's just not strong enough to control the pain a person has after having major surgery.

"I got on the phone to the doctor on call and got some strong pain medication ordered, got clarification on how the dressing was to be changed and how the drainage tube was to be handled. The niece was back at the house with the needed medication in fifteen minutes.

"Once Ivy was medicated and comfortable, I began to change the dressing and show the family how to care for the drainage tube. Slowly but surely, panic gave way to knowledge. I really admired their grit and determination in the face of a scary situation."

Many of these problems could have been avoided. In the first place, both Ivy and her family believed the lump was probably nothing and the biopsy would prove it. They were in no way prepared for a mastectomy. The sister and her husband thought they would be informed before the procedure was performed, but Ivy had signed the consent form herself.

These people were lucky that an excellent RN (Cindy) received the assignment. Although she didn't realize that the surgery had taken place just the day before, she called the family immediately to arrange an appointment that would be convenient for them. After learning what was going on, she rescheduled her other appointments so she could get to Ivy quickly, and once there she knew who to call to put things right.

Be aware that you may not be so lucky. It's critical that you do everything possible to stay informed, and that you never agree to anything until you are certain that you fully understand the situation. This would have made all the difference in this case. The family agreed to accept Ivy's release without knowing what they'd be in for in a few hours after the anesthesia wore off.

When you have been told that you will receive home health-care services, such as a visiting RN, get the contact number. And keep it in a prominent place! That way, if a problem arises, you have somewhere to turn. The time to track down a desperately needed phone number isn't at 2:00 A.M. in the middle of a crisis.

Of course, most of the problems in Ivy's case wouldn't have happened if her family had maintained a good working relationship with Ivy's primary-care physician. No doctor, no matter how terrific, is a mind reader. If you don't understand something, ask questions! Keep asking until you do understand! If you need help with care or are having other problems, don't be afraid to talk to the doctor.

Throughout, try to keep in mind that people in the medical profession are people. They get tired, need time off, make mistakes, forget things now and then... same as all of us. Add in the equally human factor that someone in a particular job tends to forget that those outside that field don't automatically know what is "common knowledge" to the professional.

Therapy

Sometimes a patient will require physical, occupational or speech therapy and will be given a daily program to follow at home. If you are going to be supervising these therapies, make certain you clearly understand what is to be done and how to do it. Observe the therapy session the elder goes through. Take notes. Have the therapist observe you directing the elder. If necessary to obtain clear instructions, ask the therapist if you can use a camcorder to tape the session. With a tape and a VCR, both you and the elder can have a visual record of the procedures involved for the therapies.

The Caregiver's Relationship With Medical Personnel

In all your dealings with doctors, nurses, therapists and hospitals, you are a customer. If you are honestly convinced that you are not getting the treatment you need for your elder, find someone else. In dealing with these professionals you should expect (and deserve) the following:

1. Respect. You and your elder should be treated with respect, and no one's dignity should be violated with derogatory comments or even being treated as ignorant.

2. Everything about the condition, its treatment and prognosis, should be fully explained to you in language you can understand.

3. All questions should be answered in language you can understand.

4. Your phone calls concerning medical questions should be returned promptly. (Keep in mind, however, that you're not the doctor's only patient, and that the doctor is only human. *Never* claim an emergency that isn't one!)

5. Getting a second opinion by a specialist should be encouraged by the doctor in any situation in which the condition is potentially life-threatening (cancer, heart disease, etc.) and/or when multiple treatment options and/or surgery are recommended.

6. You and your elder should be full participants in health care. Your wishes concerning blood transfusions, organ donations or transplants, "heroic" life-saving measures, living wills and so on should be respected by all medial personnel and accepted without undue pressure or coercion. (Explaining the consequences of these actions is *not* coercion—it is a medical responsibility.)

Remember, good medical care is a two-way street. You and your elder have responsibilities, too. Medical personnel have the right to expect certain behavior from you:

1. Show respect. Regardless of the circumstances or what you may be feeling, there is no excuse for verbally abusing anyone.

2. Before you can speak to the doctor, you will have to deal with the office manger or the receptionist. Explain your problem clearly and calmly. If you genuinely think the situation is an emergency, say so. *Never* claim an emergency when one doesn't exist. Do not demand to speak to the doctor immediately if it is a simple question that does not pertain to a life-threatening situation.

3. When you are running late or need to cancel an appointment, give as much notice as possible. Not only is this practice common courtesy, it helps the entire staff to function more efficiently, which keeps the waiting time to a minimum. (If every patient did this, your own waiting time would be reduced.)

4. Have patience. Medical emergencies don't happen according to anyone's schedule. The doctor may be running late not because the staff overbooks but because another patient had an emergency. A good doctor will squeeze a patient into a fully booked day when it's an emergency, but the greatest physician can't be at the office taking care of patients while also being in the operating room saving a life. This is a fact you will appreciate when your elder's health is the emergency.

5. Be forthcoming with information. If the elder is having difficulty following the doctor's orders, explain why. If there is a problem with a nurse, therapist or another doctor that the elder is seeing, tell your primary-care physician. Calmly! Your primary-care physician should be concerned with all aspects of care. Many times the doctor can solve the problem where you've had no luck.

6. Discuss the elder's lifestyle and habits with the doctor. You'd be surprised what is important. Insomnia can be caused by the elder taking too many naps in the afternoon, or fewer naps that are too long. Even medication can be interfered with by lifestyle.

7. Take responsibility for health care by making certain the primary doctor is aware of every medication (even over-the-counter remedies like cough syrup and aspirin) the elder is taking and why. If one doctor orders a course of therapy or medication that seems contrary to what your primary physician has told you, inform the primary physician. In both of these situations the primary-care physician is (or should be) thoroughly familiar with your elder's history and is in the best position to judge his or her overall care. Let the course of action rest with him or her.

8. Keep a *written* up-to-date medical history on the elder. Begin with early diseases, surgeries and pregnancies if applicable. List the date and any pertinent information, such as complications,

that the elder can remember. List the treating doctor's name, address and phone number. Include medication history in the summary. Note any allergic reactions to food, medications or substances. Keep track of where and when tests and X rays were done. Keep a copy of the history in the car with you. This information may be needed by emergency room personnel. It is difficult to remember everything a doctor should know when you are in the middle of a crisis. A copy of this information also goes to each doctor. Update the copy to the primary-care physician as needed.

9. Medical personnel deserve to be treated with compassion and understanding. Doctors and nurses are advised in school to keep an emotional distance from their patients. They are taught this in hopes of preventing or at least delaying burnout. This and normal human nature can make medical professionals seem distant at times. Even so, people usually enter this profession out of caring for others. They often fight valiantly to help end pain and suffering, to control diseases and to improve the quality of life for a patient while knowing that even with all their training and education they will eventually lose the fight to death. These are people with jobs that make heavy demands, and many times they can't even discuss the problem because of patient confidentiality.

Was the doctor a little distant today? It might be that yet another battle was lost and a longtime patient just died.

Was the doctor irritated to find out you haven't been following the treatment plan? How would you feel if you'd spent your life in a particular field, offered sound advice and then had it ignored by someone who'd read an article in a magazine (if that much)?

It truly is a two-way street. Cooperation goes in more than one direction. You hired the doctor for his or her expertise and training. You have the right to expect certain things from your "employee." At the same time, you *did* hire this person because of superior knowledge. While you have the right, and even the duty, to ask questions, you must either accept and follow the doctor's expertise—or find another "employee." (Bear in mind that a doctor who follows *your* advice all the time isn't likely to be the one you need.)

NINE

Setting Up the Home for Caregiving

In chapter 3 the importance of getting a handle on the needs of caregiving was addressed. Of large importance was the topic of housing, with the concentration on discovering and exploring your options in various conditions. This chapter assumes that you've decided that caregiving in the home is a viable choice. The goal now is to provide practical guidance in making adaptations to the home.

Much of the information in this chapter involves the fine points that you will need to deal with once any needed remodeling has been accomplished, and the little things you might otherwise learn the hard way. A few of them can save a life. Most simply make the job more pleasant and easier to handle.

If the family and the elder have decided to try living together, there are some guidelines that will make it easier to adapt to the situation. Be certain you discuss all the points fully and reach agreement before the move:

- Have you made sure the elder's living environment is safe?
- Have you discussed the situation with your immediate family? Your siblings? The doctors? With friends and neighbors who have expressed an interest in helping?
- Have you researched the community services available to you?

- Have you set ground rules for the new living arrangements? Have you discussed the ground rules with the elder? With everyone else who is directly or indirectly involved?
- Have you made an alternative plan in case you are unable to give care for a period of time?
- Are you satisfied that others, in the role of secondary caregivers, will live up to their responsibilities and their specific commitments?
- Do you have all the legal, medical and financial matters under control?
- Have you discussed the daily routine with your elder? Have you both expressed your feelings and listened to each other?
- Have you ensured some time for yourself so that your independence and privacy remain intact?

The elder needs to feel as much a part of the family as possible. There are some things that you can resolve with the elder in advance of the move that will make the arrangement more comfortable for all of you.

- Will the person have his or her own room? What is the possibility of redecorating using some of the person's own things and favorite colors?
- If the person must share a room, is there space for both people to have some privacy and a place for their belongings? Sharing usually isn't a good idea, because minor personality conflicts and habits can flare to huge proportions when two generations are forced to share a greatly reduced space.
- Look at the rest of the house. Will the elder feel welcome or like an intruder? Could Dad's favorite chair be located in the family's main activity area? Could Mom's cooking utensils have their own space in your kitchen? Is there room for your elder's hobbies?
- If the elder is incapacitated, have you made allowances for medical equipment?
- Think about lifestyles. How much time will you and your elder spend together? How much time will all the family

spend together? The family, the elder and you will all need time for normal life activities free from the guilt and resentment this type of living arrangement or caregiving situation can entail. How will your elder spend the day? Consider your family's employment and school schedules.

- What will the elder pay for? What will your siblings or other family members pay for? What financial commitments are you and your spouse willing to make? How will you handle the situation if no one contributes financially?

- Will the elder have any responsibilities for maintaining the household? Be sure to consider your elder's capabilities and encourage as much participation as possible. Treating someone like an invalid unnecessarily will damage the person's self-worth and diminish the feeling of usefulness and purpose. It is possible to kill with kindness.

- Will your elder have the power to grant permission to any children living in the household? To discipline them? Under what circumstances?

- How will you maintain your marriage? You and your spouse should discuss this privately.

If the elder is to continue living at home, or move to the caregiver's home, a certain amount of safety proofing may be needed. Depending on the elder's ability to balance, susceptibility to falls, ability to reach, visual capabilities and so on, a number of aids can be purchased or made. Some are general, others are more specific.

Exactly which of the tips you employ, which you do not and which you modify to suit will depend once again on the particular situation.

General Safety

Many elders appear to be easy targets for various crimes. "Don't open the door to strangers" is the advice given to children. It applies to elders, too. The porch area of a home needs to be well lighted. A door viewer, sometimes called a peephole, needs to be installed. This allows a person to see the area around the front door without opening it. If the home already has this device, check it for height; people lose height as they age, and a viewer that is too high for the elder to use does no good.

An elder who has vision problems may not be able to use a door viewer at all because the image visible through it is much smaller than life-size. If this is your elder's case, consider installing a small pane of unbreakable glass as a viewing port.

Doorknobs and Locks

Doorknobs can be difficult for some elders, such as those with arthritis, to operate, and a person who can't open a door can become trapped. Replace typical doorknobs with lever-type handles.

If your elder feels the psychological need for a locked door, you shouldn't deny it unless there are compelling reasons. You must balance being able to get to an elder who has fallen (for example) with that person's right to privacy. The compromise is to use a lock that can be *unlocked* from outside if necessary. This usually means little more than removing hook-latch locks and replacing them with another type, such as those within the doorknob.

On a larger, and possibly more important level, the entrance doors to the home may need to be locked when there is no one around but the elder. If the locks are difficult to operate, he or she could become trapped in the home. This can be disastrous in an emergency, such as a fire. The solution might mean physically modifying the lock handle. Often it is enough to simply make sure that the locks, knobs and so on are all in good working order.

A similar situation arises if the elder has developed the tendency to go out of the house in a daze; this can happen, for instance, with diseases such as Alzheimer's. In some ways it's like having a very young child who wanders outside, but with the reasons being quite different. Locks used to confine may become necessary, but this must be handled carefully. The inability to get out presents a potential danger, which you must weigh against the danger (not inconvenience) of having the elder leave without you knowing.

Lighting

Install outdoor lighting around the perimeter of the home, including walkways and porches. Not only does this make good safety sense, it discourages burglars.

Install night lights, especially in bedrooms, bathrooms and halls. Waking or moving around in complete darkness, even if you've totally familiar with the room, can be disorienting. Leave the lights burning continuously. (These lights consume very little energy).

Other lighting throughout the home needs to be checked. Are the bulbs strong enough to provide the proper amount of illumination? Are there enough lights, and in the right places, or do you need additional wall outlets? Can the elder operate the switches easily? (See "Standard Wall Switches" later in this chapter.)

If wall outlets are not available, they can be easily installed. If you are good with tools and can follow simple directions, you can pick up a book detailing this and other simple repairs at your local hardware shop, bookstore or library. An alternative is to hire a handyman or electrician to do the job.

Bathrooms

Bathrooms can present major safety problems. Install grab bars (*not* heavy-duty towel bars) near the commode and in the shower or tub area. Make certain that the bars are securely fastened to the wall studs. If you need to drill through tile or fiberglass, your local hardware store can supply instructions and the proper drill bit.

Slippery surfaces, like the floor of the shower or tub or of the bathroom itself, can be very dangerous. In the tub or shower use a rubberized bath mat that is in good condition, or attach rubberized appliqués to the bottom surface. You might consider installing wall-to-wall carpeting. At the very least, use a nonskid bath mat.

Both can be found made of material that easily handles water. Bear in mind, however, that using this kind of carpet increases the need for effective ventilation so that the water can evaporate.

For those who love showers but cannot stand for the length of time needed to take one, get a shower chair and a hand-held personal shower. (See "New Bathrooms" in this chapter for more about this device.)

Being unable to control water in a sink, shower or tub can present a variety of safety problems, including the chance of being scalded by water that is too hot. Because traditional faucet handles can be difficult to turn, replace them with easy-grip pull-push knobs or lever-type handles. It's a good idea to make sure that faucets have labels for Hot and Cold, even if the arrangement follows the standard of having Hot on the left. This advice applies to kitchen faucets as well. As an additional precaution, strongly consider adjusting the thermostat on the water heater to a lower temperature.

Because the bathroom presents a number of dangers, consider installing some kind of signaling device for the elder. This can be tricky because the elder may be in any of several places. Having a button on the wall won't help much for an elder who can't get out of the tub.

One solution is to install an intercom so that you can hear everything that goes on in the bathroom while the elder is there and unattended. More complicated is to have the signal button attached to the end of a wire that goes to the signaling device. If this is your choice, it's important that the system use battery power only to prevent shock or electrocution.

Smoke Alarms

Smoke alarms are a necessity. There are two types. One is wired directly into the home's electrical system. It may or may not have a back-up battery (in case of a power failure). Another type is powered solely by a battery. Regardless, the unit should be checked at least once a month to make certain that it is functioning.

The prices for the alarms begin at about $10. For the battery type, installation usually takes only a few minutes and is done with a couple of screws. Make certain that the alarm you purchase has an extremely loud continuous buzz, because it may have to wake someone who is hearing-impaired. A good idea is to place an alarm in the hall outside the elder's bedroom and another in the kitchen area. If the home has more than one story, make sure alarms are on every level.

More extensive systems monitor for the possibility of fire and also serve as burglar alarms. You can even modify such a system to signal you if an elder who needs to be watched has gotten out of bed or, worse, has left the house.

Slippery Floors

Tile or polished wooden floors can be beautiful and hazardous, especially to those with balance problems or who are prone to falling. Cover the walking areas with nonskid (rubberized back) area rugs or runners. Attach them securely to the floor with nails, tacks or screws or by gluing Velcro strips to the floor and sewing them to the rug. Be sure all edges are secure. If the room is carpeted and area rugs have been used on top of the carpeting, Velcro can be stapled, sewn, nailed or tacked into place, depending on the carpet style and the surface underneath.

As discussed above, don't forget the floors in the bathroom. These can become especially slippery due to being wet.

Cords and Wires

Electrical cords, including extension cords, are often needed to operate lights, radios, televisions, special health care equipment and other appliances. They are also easy to trip over. Make sure this type of wiring is secured to baseboards with staples or tape. If the wiring absolutely must cross flooring, make sure it is taped down and covered with carpeting or a rug. You are trying to eliminate any unexpected unevenness in the walking path. Elders, especially those with physical impairments like arthritis or recovering stroke victims, do not lift their feet as high as normal when walking; some tend to shuffle, and others appear to walk with a normal stride but scrape the surface with the tip or entire sole of their shoe.

Furniture

Many elders refuse to use a cane in the house. Instead they touch, sometimes grab, pieces of furniture for support or balance when crossing a room. If the piece of furniture is strong enough to do the job of support, like the back of a sofa, there's not much problem. On the other hand, if it is a light chair or something low like a coffee table, the danger of falling increases. The problem is further compounded if the elder is suffering from failing eyesight.

Consider installing railings in travel areas. Be aware, however, that these must be sturdy enough to hold a person's weight. If the rails themselves and their mountings aren't strong, you're building a false sense of security that can cause problems rather than prevent them.

Elders often develop the habit of using table tops and chair arms for additional support when sitting down or getting up. For this reason, avoid using drop-leaf tables and armless, swivel or rocking chairs. Solid tables and sturdy armchairs are preferred.

In addition, some sofas and chairs are too low for an elder to rise from without a great deal of effort. One solution is to set them on, or even attach them to, a sturdy wooden platform that raises the furniture to a more convenient height.

Tables and desks are normally about thirty inches in height and will accommodate most wheelchairs. If you find drawers or panels are interfering with comfortable use, try putting concrete or wooden blocks under the legs. Make sure the legs are secured to the blocks.

Ramps

There is usually a four- to six-inch step that must be negotiated to either enter or leave a home. Other homes have a sunken living room or den. Many older homes are two-story. For a typical person, these don't represent obstacles. For someone having problems with a knee, hip or back, that six-inch step can be agony. If you're weak or in a wheelchair, it can be insurmountable.

For an exterior step, build a ramp from plywood and brace it with two-by-fours. The top of the ramp should be slightly narrower than the doorway and attached in such a manner that it will not move. Outside the doorway, the ramp should be about four feet wide. Make sure the ramp is long enough to permit a gentle rise—about one foot long for every inch in height. The ramp can be painted to match the house trim if you wish.

The same height-versus-length rules apply for a single interior step. And again, the ramp should be four feet wide to accommodate a wheelchair. Consider adding a side railing if the person does not use a walker. Such a railing might be essential if the person is in a wheelchair that has to be collapsed and moved through a doorway.

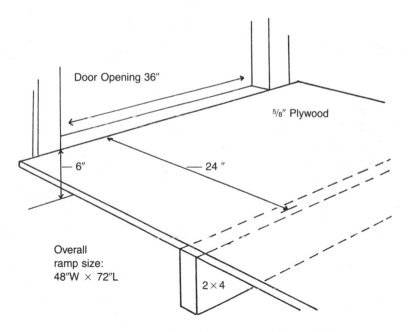

Fig. 9-1: A ramp will help the elder get in and out of the house.

Inside or out, you can use carpeting to cover the ramp. If you prefer to stain or paint the ramp, add nonskid rubber strips to the ramp for safety.

Remodeling

If the elder is planning on staying in his or her own home, but has physical limitations or the prognosis of physical limitations, remodeling may be your answer. Some of the ideas, like making ramps, are easy and inexpensive. Others may require professional services. Often there will be a balance between the cost of remodeling to make the home suitable and the comparative cost of selecting different housing. (Don't forget to add in the psychological "costs" of removing the elder from familiar surroundings.)

As discussed earlier, it's important that you be realistic. A home that has been perfect for decades may suddenly be totally unsuitable. This is particularly true when the home has more than one floor. It's not uncommon for the living room and kitchen to be on one floor, with the bedroom(s) and only bathroom on the other. Going up and down the stairs can become painful, dangerous or even impossible for an elder with arthritis or one who is wheelchair-bound.

Another factor in this is more long-term. Physical changes to the home may increase, or decrease, its value. If the home is rented, there is the additional complication in that you cannot legally modify the structure without permission.

When estimating the cost of remodeling, think about function and practicality. The elder's bedroom should be large enough for two people to move around easily *after* the furniture is in place. If you furnish the room with simple basics—single bed, night stand, dresser, lever operated recliner, TV and stand, and perhaps a small bookcase for mementos—it may seem that a room size of ten by twelve feet would be adequate. For normal living purposes it is. However, when you add in two people (one assisting the other into bed) the space is quite cramped. The space will be further restricted if the elder eventually needs a wheelchair, bedside commode, trapeze, electric hospital bed, oxygen equipment and other hospital supplies.

Remodeling plans begin, then, with what rooms are available. If the only room available is an eight-by-ten-foot spare bedroom, the remodeling needs will be more extensive than they would be if a larger room is available. If there are no spare rooms at all, you may find yourself having to build an extension onto the home. If the only suitable living space available is on one floor and the only bathroom is on another, once again the remodeling needs become more complicated, and more expensive. At other times, however, remodeling can be as simple as building ramps where there are small rises, or (as above) changing doorknobs.

Check with your accountant about the deductions that may apply and possible methods of financing for remodeling projects. Remember that remodeling your home is considered a home improvement in most instances and could actually improve the value of your home.

MULTI-STORY REMODELING   There are two ways to handle a multi-story home. One is to close off all but the ground floor and rearrange most of the elder's needed possessions into this area. Some remodeling of the primary area may be necessary to make this option comfortable for the elder.

The second option is to purchase or rent a stairside elevator. Normally this can be installed in a few hours with no major structural change or additional wiring. Check with the equipment provider for specifics. Sometimes insurance will cover the cost of a stairside elevator if it is prescribed by a doctor or therapist. Check with the doctor and insurance company to see if the elder qualifies.

NEW BATHROOMS   Add a bathroom built with caregiving needs in mind to your remodeling plans if possible, because bathrooms are the biggest trouble spot when giving care. Doorways need to be wide enough for a wheelchair to pass through without trapping fingers or banging elbows. Inside the bathroom, there needs to be enough room for the wheelchair to turn around. Easy access to the commode is necessary. The elder must be able to reach grab bars and/or a commode chair accessory easily. Remember, there will be more than one person in the bathroom if you are assisting with the bath or shower. For safety's sake, you have to have enough room to position yourself properly to help. Putting the commode in a little separate room of its own is the current trend, but it doesn't work very well because it creates cramped quarters.

Most showers are small and enclosed, have a lip on the bottom and are accessed by a rigid door. Think about getting the door open, a wheelchair in front of it, and the person transferred into the shower, possibly into a chair inside the shower. You'll wish that you could be in two places at once (both inside and outside the shower), while simultaneously realizing that you yourself are getting in the way. Now try to imagine assisting with the shower itself. The smaller the shower space, the worse this becomes.

If you are having a bathroom added, leave a shower space three feet wide and five feet long. Have the floor in this area slope to the center to facilitate water drainage. Add rubber strips or rubberized appliqués to prevent slipping. Do not add the traditional lip that separates a shower floor from the rest of the bathroom floor, because you want to be able to roll the wheelchair directly and safely into the shower area. If the lip is there, you have to raise the front of the chair over the lip and gently put it on the other side. This is not easy under the best of circumstances and can be painful to the chair's occupant, especially one with a spinal injury or broken bone. Getting the wheelchair into the shower will make transfer to a shower chair much easier. To enclose the shower, add a spring-loaded curtain rod and a plastic shower curtain.

For the most convenience, install a personal showerhead. This device is a hand-held showerhead on the end of a flexible tube. Being able to precisely direct the water flow is almost like being able to move the shower rather than the person. If you choose the kind that offers a range of water intensities, you'll find the pulse setting offers relief and stimulation to sore body parts.

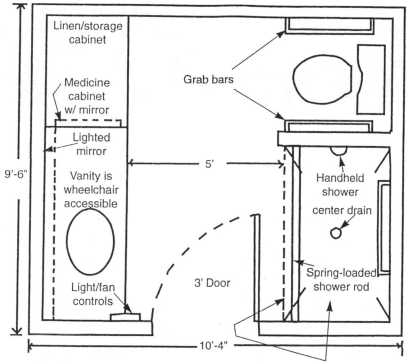

Linen/storage cabinet

Medicine cabinet w/ mirror

Grab bars

Lighted mirror

Vanity is wheelchair accessible

Light/fan controls

9'-6"

5'

Handheld shower

center drain

Spring-loaded shower rod

3' Door

10'-4"

3' x 5' tiled shower stall with center slope to drain.
No lip between stall and main floor (dotted line).

Fig. 9-2: An example bathroom floor plan.

Emergency!

When an emergency arises, people remember to call 911 or their emergency number but in their panic often forget their address or phone number. It is true that most emergency 911 systems have a way to trace the call, but it's foolish to risk a life on it. The system might not be functioning, your home might be in a remote area or not have a street address, or the person making the emergency call might be a visitor. Under the best of circumstances, having the system trace your location takes time, and those few minutes can mean the difference between life and death for your loved one.

One of the first steps in preparing your home is something you should have done long ago. Post the needed information beside *every* telephone, preferably in plain view but at least easily accessible. Most of the time the information will all fit on a single index card, but be sure that you write large and legibly enough for the information to be read easily.

Phone number
Address
Nearest main cross streets
Directions
Your work number
Your spouse's work number
Your primary physician and number—for each person in the
    household, if different
Name and location of preferred hospital(s)

The need for most of the information is obvious. The phone number and address are crucial. Often knowing the nearest major intersection will guide help to you faster. This and directions become especially important if the home is located in a remote or rural area or on a cul-de-sac or is hard to find for any reason at all.

Phone numbers where you can be reached are important when someone else is taking care of things. This includes others in your immediate family. In an emergency people have been known to forget their *own* phone numbers. This is not the time to be paging through the directory. When you go somewhere other than work, don't forget to leave a slip of paper with the number(s) where you can be reached at least by the main phone, and consider putting copies by every phone. An emergency can just as easily happen while you're out to dinner as while you're at the office.

In a severe emergency the patient will be transported to the nearest suitable facility. This may or may not be the hospital on your list. Once stable, the patient can be transferred. This can be important if the nearest facility doesn't accept your insurance or isn't affiliated with your chosen physician.

Information Center   An extension of this basic information is a more complete "information center." This is one of the most important adjuncts to caregiving. It keeps all the information needed for contacting medical personnel in one place, whether for day-to-day caregiving or in the event of an emergency. Everything you need will be at your fingertips. It will also be readily available for emergency personnel.

The kitchen is a good place to locate the center because it is usually the most accessible and frequently used room in the home. The center itself contains five key elements: (1) a telephone; (2) a message board for emergency numbers; (3) a similar board for the medication schedule; (4) a month-long calendar with spaces for each day that are large enough to keep track of the elder's health-care appointments; and (5) shelf or part of a counter where the elder's written medical history, the drug book and the charting book are kept.

Everyone involved with elder care should be aware of the information center and trained in its use. This includes the elder, primary caregiver, all household members, anyone caring for the elder even on a limited basis and the home health practitioner. Even a small child should be able to point out where the center is (and be trained to not touch anything connected with it).

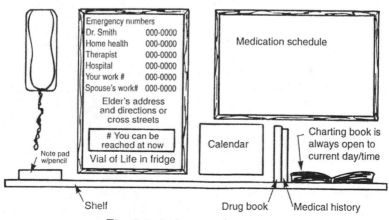

Fig. 9-3: Information center.

In some ways the information center is like an extension of the card with emergency numbers. A message board is used to contain all of the important phone numbers connected with the elder's care such as doctor(s) name and number, the names and numbers of any services you are using; your work number, your spouse's work number, etc. An open spot should be kept to write down the phone number of anywhere you will be temporarily (visiting, dinner, etc.).

A shelf or counter area should have a current copy of the elder's medical history and medication record as described in chapter 1. This is critical. Many times in an emergency the ambulance personnel need to know which drugs the elder is taking before beginning treatment, because the problem may be related to them. But—which ones? An accurate drug book will point out the likely candidates.

(Don't forget to keep a copy of this with you in the car. Not only do emergencies happen away from home, it's possible that in a panic you could leave vital information at home. A little extra time making entries in more than one book, or the small expense of photocopies, is a wise investment.)

If you have been keeping a daily chart (see chapter 10), keep this here, too. Always have the chart open to show the last entry. This way the most current information is quick to access in an emergency.

VIAL OF LIFE   Most emergency personnel are trained to look for a "vial of life" when responding to an emergency at an elder's home. A vial of life is any type of container labeled VIAL OF LIFE that holds a list of the medications the elder takes, known allergies, doctor's name, hospital's name, Medicare number, insurance number and the names and numbers of people to call in case of an emergency.

The vial of life container should be kept in the refrigerator's butter compartment, because this is where the emergency personnel expect it to be. Post a sign that says VIAL OF LIFE on the front door, the refrigerator door, and butter compartment door.

If you choose another spot, such as a cupboard, it's even more important that you clearly mark the location. Don't assume that you will be there when an emergency occurs.

Scheduling

During your family meeting, and later when you discussed living and care arrangements with your elder, you came to agreements on such things as chores, family time and private time for each person.

In our busy world, there are a lot of adjustments and outright changes in everyone's life from day to day. It's easy to become confused and to forget that soccer practice is now on Thursday night. When an elder lives with you, his or her entire routine needs to mesh with yours. The elder may not always remember your schedule when making plans. Conflicting schedules can cause more resentment and confusion than almost anything else.

To avoid this problem, write out several lists and post them in the kitchen. The first list should have chores: when they are to be done (daily, weekly) and by whom. A second list contains the routine family activities broken down by day.

The third list consists of seven pages, one for each day of the week. A new schedule is posted every Sunday for the coming week. Everyone's appointments and activities are listed according to the day and time. Transfer the medical appointments from the information center's calendar to the weekly list and balance the remaining time. Post all three lists separately with paper clip magnets to the refrigerator door.

It doesn't take long to write out the daily list on a weekly basis. You can make it a family ritual every Sunday morning over breakfast. The list promotes communication and helps to ensure that each of you is getting some of the things you need while living together. This is a friendly reminder of plans so that people are not infringing upon others' activities.

For example, Maurine is planning a pool and slumber party for her cheerleading group on Saturday starting at 3:00. It's

Grandma's turn to host a bridge game, and she scheduled it for Saturday completely forgetting about Maurine's party. If the schedule had been posted and checked, the problem wouldn't have arisen.

Remember that you're not running a dictatorship. When you're developing and writing the schedule, those involved deserve input.

Telephones

If your elder's vision or hearing is impaired, you may want to purchase a telephone designed to help. Here you have many choices. One features oversized buttons to make dialing easier. Another has a built-in amplifier. (This might go to a speaker or merely amplify the sound in the handset). Some have both.

Another common and handy feature is memory. This allows you to program in phone numbers so that the user only needs to push a single button. Someone in an emergency might have trouble dialing even a short number, such as 911. A longer number might be almost impossible. With a memory, only one button is needed to dial the number quickly and without having to look it up.

A light that flashes when there is an incoming call can be very handy for someone who is hard of hearing. It is also useful to alert you to a call when you have turned off the phone bell because you don't want a ringing phone to disturb someone's sleep.

Telephones are an important part of most safety services, which are particularly valuable when the elder will be left alone often. Some of the more complicated ones involve a complete household monitoring. If someone is breaking in, if there is a fire or if the subscriber is in some kind of trouble, the system connects through a phone line to professionals who monitor their subscribers around the clock. They can even listen and speak through the phone, if need be, and with the receiver still in it cradle. Other systems offer the subscriber the ability to access professional help by simply pushing a medical alert button, which is usually in the form of a necklace. When the button is pushed, the phone system automatically calls the dispatcher of a private emergency network. Often the phone or another device can then be activated to provide two-way communication. Your local hospital can supply the name of the firm in your area that supplies this kind of service.

CORDLESS PHONES   In an emergency, if you are the one calling 911 to help another, you will be asked a number of questions, such as "Is the person breathing?" Often the phone will be in one place, and the person requiring help will be in another room or even outside.

"Wait, I'll go see." You put the phone down, run to check, then come back and answer the dispatcher, who gives you a whole new set of questions or directions, which causes you to run back and forth some more, relaying information and trying to follow instructions. These are delays—dangerous ones.

This situation can be alleviated by the purchase of a cordless phone. A cordless phone can be taken to the site of the emergency, indoors or outside, up to fifteen hundred feet away from the base (although a hundred feet or so is more realistic). The elder can be taught to operate the phone and can acquire the habit of taking it along when going outside or even to a room where there is no phone. This builds a wonderful sense of security, especially if the elder is home alone.

An added advantage is that many cordless phones have two-way paging. Pressing a button on the handset causes a button on the base unit to beep, and vice versa. This feature can make it easier for the elder to communicate with the caregiver as well as with the "outside world."

Medical Equipment

As elder care progresses the use of special medical equipment usually comes into play to some degree. You might find your elder needing a wheelchair, walker, hospital bed or some other major (or minor) equipment. Always check with the doctor before purchasing or renting any equipment, because much of it is covered by insurance. When there is a choice, always have the most expensive pieces billed to insurance.

Earlier we discussed DRGs (diagnostically related groups) and how they relate to payment for an illness. DRGs also apply to durable medical equipment. Suppose your elder has a broken leg and must keep it elevated. You discuss the home-care situation with the doctor and decide that the elder needs a bedside commode and a wheelchair. It sounds reasonable, right? Well, an elder who has a wheelchair being paid for by Medicare is considered to be mobile and therefore to be able to get to the bathroom. It doesn't matter that the wheelchair won't fit through the bathroom door so the elder can use the toilet. It doesn't even matter that the elder can't get into or out of the wheelchair without help. Medicare still won't cover the commode.

Then you talk to the therapist, who says the elder will need a walker as well as the wheelchair—but Medicare will only pay for one of them.

Of the three items (bedside commode, walker and wheelchair) the wheelchair is the most expensive. Have the doctor write a prescription for the wheelchair. The type and size of the chair you receive will depend on the prescription. Be sure that it's the one needed. For example, the standard chair does not come with elevating leg rests, so if the elder needs to keep a leg elevated, make certain the rests are ordered on the prescription.

Some wheelchairs also have removable sides. This is an important feature if the elder will have to transfer from the bed to the wheelchair or from the wheelchair to another seat, perhaps into a car. Sliding across to make the transfer is much easier for the elder and the caregiver who may be assisting than standing up and turning around, as is often the case when the sides are not removable. Again, make sure this feature is written on the doctor's prescription if you need this type of accommodation.

The size of the wheelchair is important for the elder's comfort. If the elder is small in width and can sit comfortably in an eighteen-inch-wide seat, request a junior-size chair, sometimes called a small adult size. This chair is much more maneuverable than larger ones when it comes to getting into small bathrooms and through narrow halls or aisles in stores. However, a chair that is too narrow is going to be uncomfortable.

Wheelchairs also come in different weights. Some are very heavy and are difficult for elders with little strength to propel. The weight is important to the caregiver, too. You will undoubtedly need to transport the elder to doctor and therapy appointments. This means you will have to lift the wheelchair into the trunk or back seat of a car, the interior of a van or the bed of a pickup, or onto a carrier attached to the back of a car. You will want the lightest chair possible that is also strong enough to safely bear the elder's weight.

Long periods of relative immobility in a wheelchair are likely to cause decubitus ulcers (bedsores), and these can occur in as little as two hours. To help prevent this, specialty seats are available. The type and cost depend on the specific circumstances. If prescribed, these seats are usually covered by insurance. Talk to the doctor for a recommendation.

You will need to pay for equipment that is not covered by insurance (in our example, the walker and the commode). When you ask for rental fee quotes, check several firms, because prices can vary drastically from supplier to supplier.

If the elder will be using equipment for a long period of time, or the doctor expects that the equipment will be used again in the future, compare purchase price to rental price over the length of time the item will be required. Also bear in mind that equipment can be bought at garage sales and secondhand stores like Salvation Army for a fraction of its original cost. If the equipment is needed due to a specific disease, contact the foundation for that disease; many times the local chapter or related associations will lend the equipment free of charge. Also try the Red Cross for loans of equipment.

Medical supply houses will usually deliver equipment you rent or purchase from them. The person who delivers it should also show you how it works, how it is cleaned, and how it stores. For example, to the uninitiated a wheelchair looks fairly simple. It's a chair with wheels that folds for transport. Try folding it without knowing how, and you'll find out it's not as easy as it looks. The leg and foot rests might swing out of the way or might need to be completely detached depending on the brand and the model.

If the piece needs assembly or installation, such as a hospital bed, the delivery person should do this for you. Again, be certain that you understand its operation. When you are finished with the equipment, the person who picks it up should also disassemble it for you.

If a hospital bed has been ordered, make certain it is adjusted to the correct height for the caregiver. You should be able to place the palms of your hands on the surface of the mattress without bending over. Having the bed at this height will save strain on your back and make care much easier.

Bed size is also important any time you need to work with an elder who is confined for any length of time. This is especially true if the bed is not a hospital bed. A double or queen-size bed may be more spacious for the elder, but with these oversized beds there is more strain on the caregiver. They are difficult to work with when you need to change the bed with the person in it, or move the person. A twin-size bed will work just fine in most situations, and if a hospital bed is ever required, the twin-size linens will probably fit it.

For information on special mattresses, see "Bedsores" in chapter 10).

Miscellaneous Aids

For a list of mail order companies that provide catalogs, see "Aids" in the Resources section at the end of this book.

STACKABLE STORAGE BINS   When sickroom supplies multiply, it can be difficult to keep them organized. Many art-and-crafts stores, office supply stores and even some supermarkets sell stackable rectangular plastic storage bins that are open on one

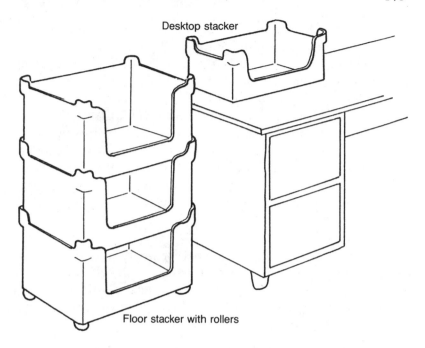

Desktop stacker

Floor stacker with rollers

**Fig. 9-4: Two types of stackable storage.
Others are also available.**

side. These are often used in the kitchen to hold such things as potatoes and onions, but they work well for keeping supplies in order. You can even find bin sets in which the bins are hinged on one side to swing out, and others with the bottom basket on wheels to make it mobile. Because the unit is compact, it is easy to cover with a pretty twin-size sheet when the elder has visitors.

WALKING TABLES   Tea carts are great for elders who have a difficult time carrying items and who also need the assistance provided by a walker. However, these carts are not meant for people who are unsteady on their feet. They won't stand up to much weight and are unstable if someone leans heavily against them.

Select a small cart with wheels and a handle for the elder to hold onto. Some carts also have a small shelf underneath. Both the shelf and the top tray of the cart should have a small lip around them to prevent objects from sliding off.

Inexpensive utility carts work well for this purpose, too.

Commode chairs can also double for this purpose, but only if the unit has locking wheels. If you own the chair, simply glue Velcro strips to the back side of the chair lid so that the Velcro shows when the lid is down, closing off the commode portion. Glue matching Velcro strips to the bottom of a TV tray. You may need to remove the fasteners that normally hold the tray to the legs.

CARRIERS   You can make a carrier for the front of a walker by attaching a plastic grocery bag over the middle with plastic bag closers. These often come with heavy-duty plastic trash can liners. The twist ties with wire in the middle won't work if the carrier is to hold much weight.

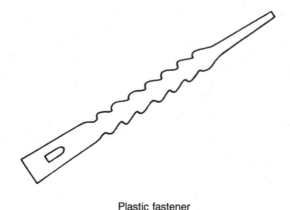

Plastic fastener

Fig. 9-5: This kind of bag closer works best.

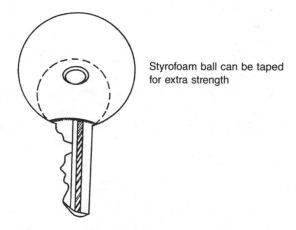

Styrofoam ball can be taped for extra strength

Fig. 9-6: One way to make a key enlarger.

KEY ENLARGERS   Cut or scrape a small opening in a small balsa wood ball or block. Styrofoam works well, too. The opening should fit the head of a key. Fill the hole with glue and insert the key. Let it dry. Paint the blocks or balls different colors: one color for the house, one for the car, etc. Balsa wood and Styrofoam are available at most art supply and hobby or craft shops.

HANDLE ENLARGERS   This is an easy item to make that is very helpful for elders with arthritis or stroke victims. Versions of it also work for eating utensils, pens, artist's brushes, hair combs, toothbrushes, tools for latching, and so on. The basic idea is to make the handle larger and longer so that it's easier to grip and easier to turn.

A bicycle handle grip that normally slides onto the handlebar is often all you need. A piece of stiff garden hose is sometimes a good choice. Plastic tubing comes in a variety of sizes for a good fit over an eating utensil or toothbrush.

Aluminum tubing can also be used. This is an excellent choice when the handle must be bent into a permanent shape to fit the contours of the elder's hand—for example, for a comb or brush. Cut the tubing to the correct length, shape it to fit the hand, install it on the item and wrap the tube with duct tape or fabric tape. This is to cover rough edges, to allow for a better grip and to eliminate getting gray aluminum oxide on the hand.

Styrofoam also comes in a variety of shapes and sizes and can be sanded to accommodate almost any needed configuration. The problem is that it's not very strong. You can give it some added strength by covering it tightly with tape or cloth.

Depending on what you're using as a handle extender, and the size of the item being inserted, you may need to make adjustments for a better fit. This can usually be accomplished with a combina-

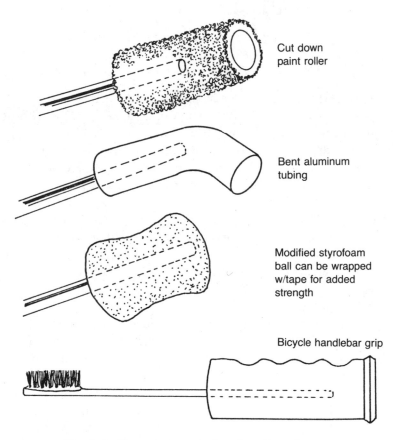

Cut down
paint roller

Bent aluminum
tubing

Modified styrofoam
ball can be wrapped
w/tape for added
strength

Bicycle handlebar grip

Fig. 9-7: Four ways to make a handle enlarger.

tion of tape, glue, a packing of modeling clay (one that remains pliable such as Plastalina), crimping and wrapping. You can even carve Styrofoam to make a filler. Keep in mind, however, that the greater the adjustments you make, the more permanent the device will be.

Faucet Adapters   Single-arm lever-type faucet handles are far easier to use than knobs that have to be twisted, even if those knobs have arms. If the faucets cannot be changed to lever type, you can make an adapter to make things easier.

If the faucet handle has four pronged arms, begin with a piece of wood 2″ square. Plywood ½″ thick will be sufficient, but almost any wood stock will do. Draw a 1⅜″ square centered in the middle of the wood. On the corners of this square, screw a 1″ screw though the wood. (It will be helpful to drill a pilot hole first.) These are the "fingers" that will grab the handle arms. A plastic "anchor" should be placed over the threads. This reduces the risks of damaging the faucet, or the elder, with the sharp exposed metal. Attach a handle 1″ wide by 6″ long to the wooden square and you have a lever.

Bath Aids   If hanging onto soap is a problem, get a bath mitt. It has a pocket the soap fits into, and the mitt fits over the hand.

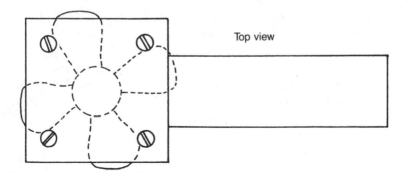

Top view

Fig. 9-8: Faucet adapter.

Fig. 9-9: Bath mitt.

If hard-to-reach areas of the body aren't being cleaned and a typical bath brush is too rough on the skin, try this: Buy a fly swatter and cover the swatting end with a washcloth or piece of toweling. Secure the cloth to the swatter with a rubber band. The thin side is great for getting between toes, while the flat side works well on backs.

UTENSILS AND GLASSWARE   Sometimes when movement is limited, self-feeding becomes difficult. One might be able to raise the hand to the mouth but be unable to flex the wrist. Another common problem is difficulty in maintaining a grip on an eating utensil.

Commercially manufactured utensils designed to help with these problems are available at many of the larger medical supply houses and in stores that specialize in products for the handicapped. Or you can purchase inexpensive lightweight cutlery and bend it into needed shapes.

If the elder has no grip at all, attach a handle to the cutlery as shown in Fig. 9-10. Glue wide Velcro straps to the handle. The straps need to be long enough to fit around the hand and overlap securely.

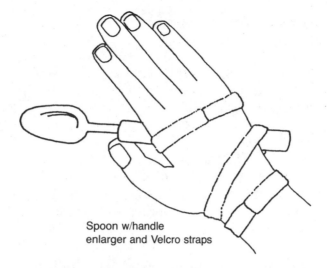

Spoon w/handle
enlarger and Velcro straps

Fig. 9-10: Adapting flatware using Velcro strips.

Another general consideration is the glassware used for eating and drinking. Even the most coordinated person can drop a glass. With an elder this can be an even bigger problem. Consider switching to unbreakable drinking glasses, cups, dishes and containers. You will still have to face spills, but at least you won't also be dealing with cuts from sharp pieces of broken glass.

Insulated mugs are available at most convenience stores. The smaller sizes (12–24 oz.) with sipping lids and oversized handles are great for elders. The lids help prevent spills and allow only a reduced amount of liquid to pass through the lid and into the mouth. If the elder is unable to lift much weight, simply fill the mug less full.

LANGUAGE CARDS   When a person is unable to speak, frustration levels for the elder, caregiver and family increase dramatically. Language cards tailored to your elder's needs can help diffuse the problem. Purchase pieces of poster board in three colors, perhaps yellow, white and pale blue. Cut the boards into strips two inches by six. Use one color for personal needs, one color for general needs, one color for conversational comments and questions.

For example: On each of the white strips print one personal need: TOILET, PAIN PILLS, WATER, COFFEE, or HUNGRY. Print general needs—TV, RADIO, GLASSES, FIX PILLOWS, SIT UP—on yellow strips. Use the blue strips for conversational needs: TIME? WHERE ARE YOU GOING? I WANT TO BE ALONE NOW. PLEASE STAY WITH ME. I LOVE YOU.

When the cards are finished, use a paper punch to make a hole in one end of each card. Put the cards on an oversized key ring or run twine through the cards. Use one ring for each color of card. This makes it easier for the elder to find the card grouping with the correct word in it.

PULL CHAIN AIDS   Pull chains can be difficult to grab when you don't have full use of your hand. Simply tie one end of a piece of bias tape (available at any fabric store and most supermarkets) to the pull chain. Thread the loose end of the tape through an oversized key ring or through a plastic sports ball that has holes in it (like Whiffle Ball) and tie the tape off.

Fig. 9-11: Using a key ring, or sports ball, as a pull chain aid.

Another solution is to tie a sturdy string to the pull chain and attach the other string somewhere else, such as to the wall. The result is a length of string in an appropriate spot. To activate the pull chain switch, simply catch the string anywhere along its length. This can be done even in the dark.

STANDARD WALL SWITCHES   This type of wall switch can be almost impossible to deal with if you have manual dexterity problems. Two solutions are possible. One is to change the switch to a dimmer switch with a large knob that requires only a push to turn on or off. The other is to glue a small piece of plastic tubing to the standard on/off switch to form an extension, making it easier for the elder to manipulate.

BED RAIL   If your elder needs the security of a bed rail to keep from falling out of bed, you can possibly use any of the several models available for young children. Most of these have arms that slide beneath the mattress. Others attach to the bed frame.

You can also make one very simply. Use three pieces of 1" × 1" wood or 1" doweling cut to the needed lengths. The two risers on the ends should be the same and reach about 12" above the mattress height when measured from the floor. (You may wish to use a third riser in the middle to provide additional strength.) The top crosspiece can be any length that serves the purpose. Usually 36" to 42" will be sufficient. Attach the pieces together securely with screws or brackets to form a squared-off U shape. Next attach two half-ring brackets to the side of the bed frame with screws. You may have to drill holes in the rails if they are metal and secure the screws with a nut on the reverse side. If side rails are wooden, attach with long wood screws. Space the brackets to the corresponding width of the rails. The opening in the brackets has to be large enough for the rail to drop through easily and small enough for the rail to be held upright without too much play between the wooden rail and the bracket. To install, simply drop the rail through the bracket.

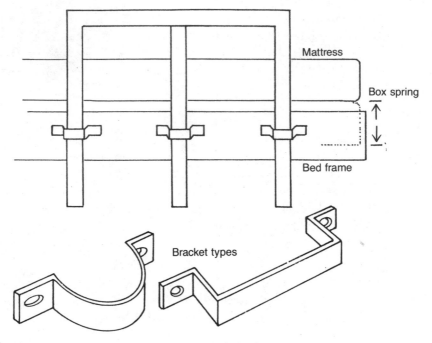

Fig. 9-12: Homemade bed rail.

FURNITURE RAISERS   Most furniture, including beds, is designed for the convenience and comfort of someone who is in
decent physical condition. For someone who has difficulty getting
in and out, or up and down, and also for the caregiver who may
have to bend over, the standard height is too low.

There are a variety of ways to raise furniture to a needed
height. However you do it, be sure that the risers are stable. It
makes no sense to devise a way to elevate a piece of furniture only
to be facing the constant risk that everything will topple.

You could build a complete platform, but this is time-consuming and expensive. It also doesn't solve the problem of furniture
that has wheels or that slides too easily. A common and easy
method is to use building blocks, which come in different
thicknesses. The legs of the furniture can go through the holes in

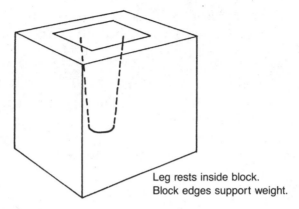

Leg rests inside block.
Block edges support weight.

Fig. 9-13: Using construction blocks to elevate furniture.

the block, with the base of the furniture then sitting on the block itself.

TIP-UP SEAT   This is a seat with springs beneath or inside. As the elder sits down on it, the springs within the seat compress. Then as the elder leans forward to rise, the springs respond to the decreased pressure and uncoil, helping the elder to get up. The independent type fits most normal-width chairs. Chairs designed specifically for this purpose are also available. Some of these use electric motors and even hydraulics.

LISTENING DEVICES   No one can spend twenty-four hours a day with an elder. Undoubtedly yours will need something when you are not in the room. There are better solutions than having the elder shout or bang for attention.

One option is to get a baby monitor. These are inexpensive and can even be found used in thrift or secondhand stores. The monitor plugs into a receptacle in the elder's room and transmits every sound in the room constantly. The receiver is usually powered by a 9-volt battery and is placed in the room where you are. Some models have a clip-on device so that you can clip the receiver onto a belt and carry it with you as you move from area to area. If the elder is unable to speak, provide a bell to ring. An old-fashioned metal (not glass) servant's bell works well. Test the distance the receiver can be from the monitor, as this varies from manufacturer to manufacturer.

Another solution is a more standard intercom. Many of these use the wiring of the home to carry the signals between the stations, making it possible to plug them in almost anywhere in the home. More expensive versions have a radio transmitter in the base that sends a signal to a portable remote receiver.

SIGNALING DEVICES   As an alternative, or a supplement, to an intercom-type system you might consider a simple signaling device. With this, the elder pushes a button that sounds a bell or buzzer, or causes a light of come on, in another room where the caregiver can hear or see it.

Many cordless phones have a feature that allows them to be used in this way, as discussed earlier in this chapter. You can buy signaling devices ready-made or, if you have a working knowledge of electricity, make your own. Instructions for making various types of signaling devices, from simple to complex, can be found in numerous books. Check your library or bookstore.

The bathroom is a particularly important place for a signaling device, especially if your elder is taking care of personal hygiene alone. He or she should have a way of letting you know if there's trouble—perhaps a fall or difficulty getting out of the tub.

CLOTHING   If buttoning and zipping zippers is a problem, consider removing the zipper or the buttons, sewing the holes closed and replacing these fasteners by sewing on Velcro (available at many fabric stores). To avoid changing the appearance of clothing that opens up the front, fasten the front, slit the garment up the back and use Velcro to create a new closure that will look like a back seam.

Some people who are forced to spend a lot of time in bed still loathe the idea of spending the time in nightgowns or pajamas. One solution is to use oversize cotton T-shirts. They are comfortable and allow the person to feel dressed. Because they are oversize they hang to midthigh, which allows the person to feel covered yet facilitates the use of a bedpan or bedside commode. Women especially seem to like having bits of decoration sewn to the collars (lace, ribbons, etc.) and for the shirts to be in bright colors. All-cotton T's can be decorated with fabric paints (a good hobby for the elder or a cherished wearable gift from grandkids) or purchased in pretty patterns. If getting the T's on and off over the head is a problem, slit them up the back and reclose with Velcro.

There are mail order firms and specialty shops that offer clothing designed for people with physical problems. Check the phone book. Also look in the resources section at the end of this book under "Clothing."

Keeping the Sickroom Clean

Keeping things clean seems to be a never-ending task. This is doubly true if the elder you are caring for is ill. Naturally a sanitary sickroom helps prevent contagion and reinfection. It also provides a more cheerful and restful atmosphere for the elder.

To keep things clean, most people use water and a disinfectant such as Lysol or Pine-Sol. Some elders object to the strong odors of these products, even if they have been using the products themselves for years. As we age and with certain conditions and medications, our sense of smell changes; things that we once thought were pleasant, like perfume, are now repugnant. If this is the case, move the person to another room while cleaning is being done. Take movable items to another room as well, so they don't absorb the disinfectant's smell.

Your elder may have less trouble with cleaning products made from natural ingredients, which have more pleasant odors. Simple Green, for instance, has a scent that some people actually like. You could consider cleaning thoroughly with a disinfectant and then lightly with another cleaner to remove the odor of disinfectant. Sometimes adding an air freshener to the room will help mask some of the odor. (And sometimes the air freshener will make it worse.)

Remove dust and dirt from wood furnishings with a product that will help trap dust, like Endust. A product such as Old English Lemon Oil furniture polish will provide a pleasant scent to the room and nourish the wood at the same time.

Many times you need to clean something in a hurry. Purchase a small dishpan or bucket, stock it with needed cleaning items and store it in the sickroom (perhaps under the bed) or in the bathroom that the elder uses. This way, when you need to clean, everything is ready and available. Here are some things you might include: paper towels, sponge or launderable rags, small scrub brush, spray bottle of multi-purpose cleaner, disinfectant, carpet cleaner.

To help keep the odors down, clean wastebaskets daily, remove and clean soiled linens and clothing promptly and discard all soiled dressings, adult diapers or pads immediately. Take all trash outside and place it in a sealed receptacle.

Change the water in humidifiers daily to inhibit the growth of molds and bacteria. The buildup, if allowed to happen, can cause not only unpleasant odors but also problems with allergies and even infections. Plants and cut flowers also need fresh water daily. If they are left in stagnant water, foul smells and bacteria will occur. Remove any dead or wilted flowers entirely.

If your elder is using a bedside commode, empty it promptly after use. Urine can have a strong smell, and it seems to permeate the plastic container that holds the fluid. Clean the container with any good soft-scrub cleanser to prevent scratching the container. When you reinstall the container, add two cups of water mixed with either half a cup of white vinegar or the juice of half a lemon or three sprays of Simple Green. Install an air freshener or use potpourri.

Odors may also come from the elder's body and may be especially strong in the case of particular diseases. Pay attention to the elder's hygiene. Make certain that appliances like catheters are kept clean. This is important not only to control odors but also to reduce the possibility of infection. A home health nurse or the hospital's nurse can explain and demonstrate the proper cleaning method.

Cleanliness is important to more than just the room. Washing your hands before and after working with the elder will also help keep the room clean and stop the spread of infection.

Stain Removal   Entire books have been written about stain removal. The following are hints on handling three kinds of stain that are fairly common in caregiving.

Urine. Remove boiling water from the stove. Add disinfectant according to directions and soak garment. When cool, wash as usual.

Feces. Soak garment in cold water. Rinse. Scrub stain with warm soapy water and a brush. Launder as usual.

Blood. If the garment is white, use a little ammonia or white vinegar in cold water to soak the fabric. All other colors use cold water only and a gentle soap like Ivory. If the stain has dried in, soak in warm, not hot, water. Gently scrub with toothbrush and Ivory. Hydrogen peroxide also works well but may discolor certain materials and is best used only on white.

Proctecting Furniture   An incontinence problem is not only embarrassing for the elder but can be frustrating and expensive for you when furniture becomes stained. You can eliminate most of this problem by having the elder sit on a specially made cushion. One advantage of this is that it doesn't call attention to the incontinence problem as a disposable pad would. It also provides extra cushioning on hard surfaces such as formal dining room chairs or park benches.

You can easily make your own. Purchase Velcro and some rubberized sheeting at a fabric store or in an infant's department. Make a pillow from any type of machine-washable fabric the elder likes. Some of the heavier cottons and cotton blends, quilted cottons and denim types are available in attractive patterns and colors. You can also use terrycloth towels or an old pillowcase. Cut the rubberized sheeting to fit one side of the pillow and attach it with the Velcro. Stuff the pillow to the desired firmness with cut-up panty hose and knee-high stockings or old socks. This stuffing material is easily plumped up for comfort, will absorb accidents and can stand up to the use of bleach products when washed.

When the pillow needs to be washed, simply toss it in the washer. To dry, remove the rubberized sheeting and pop the pillow into the dryer. The sheeting should be air dried. If this type of accident happens frequently, make several of the pillows.

Nicks, Dents and Crashes

Accidents will happen. This is especially true if you are caring for an elder who is now required to use unfamiliar medical equipment such as crutches or a wheelchair. Walls will be nicked, paint will be chipped, and furniture will be scratched. Most of the damage will be minor, and much of it can be prevented.

For example, wall edges and corners, primarily those leading into a much used hall, usually pick up the most damage from turns made too closely in a wheelchair. You can cover these edges by screwing or nailing on clear plastic moldings like those you see in many offices. If you have precious furniture in a highly traveled area, you might want to think about moving the pieces to another, less used room or placing them in storage for the time being.

The same is true for knickknacks, collectibles, figurines and other breakables many people keep around the house. At one point or another, the elder will knock over or fall against a table or run into it with a wheelchair or walker. There is every possibility that the elder will sustain cuts from broken china and glass.

As with fine furniture, put away other breakables, or place them on high shelves and then away from the edge. Both you and the elder will avoid the emotional trauma of breakage if the breakable item isn't there to break in the first place.

The Emotional Aspects of the Move

Helping the elder live life to the fullest is the primary job of a caregiver. The elder knows specifically what it takes to make him or her happy. Help your elder get it if it is at all within your power. Like all human beings, elders have a need for:

Respect No elder deserves to be treated in a demeaning manner.

Dignity Try to prevent situations where the elder may become embarrassed in front of others. If a situation does occur, handle it as discretely as possible.

Privacy Respect a closed door. Knock before entering. Allow them privacy to take care of bodily functions and grooming. If assistance must be given, use towels and sheets to provide for as much personal modesty as possible.

Safety Adapt the environment to provide as much physical safety and comfort as possible. Become trained in the elder's needs, like assistance in moving safely from a wheelchair to the bed. Provide visual cues for orientation if necessary.

Territoriality An elder should have his or her own place at the table, in the living room and a place to hold a private conversation or entertain a friend.

Control Elders should maintain as much control over their lives as they can. They should be encouraged to decorate their own rooms, see their friends, make their own decisions and set their own schedules whenever possible. They should exercise their right to choice on a daily basis. Even small choices like what to wear or what to eat encourage independence, bolster self-esteem and help elders feel in control.

Belonging Encourage, but don't require, the elder to participate in family planning and chores. Offer responsibilities consistent with capabilities. Encourage meaningful ways of interacting with others, such as a host or hostess, helper, tutor or friend.

Communication Let the elder know verbally and by touch that he or she is loved and valued. Encourage communication with other friends and family members, especially intergenerational contact (e.g., grandchildren).

Being needed To feel needed gives purpose, which in turn fosters a brighter outlook on life. Encourage your elder to pass on wisdom and skills. If your elder will be alone for large parts of the day, consider providing a pet of the elder's choice. Pet therapy is a wonderful way to stave off loneliness and depression, because the pet depends on the elder for care and in turn gives back affection.

Finishing business All people have a need to come to terms with death. Most have an urge to leave something behind to mark their passage on this earth. Encouraging and enabling an elder to leave behind memoirs or family histories not only leaves a legacy for future generations but helps the elder to come to terms with his or her life.

HELPING THE ELDER SETTLE IN   After a move, an elder must make an enormous psychological adjustment. Many times a move involves giving up physical reminders of a lifetime of experiences—a home, a car, furniture, mementos, a way of doing things, perhaps a hobby such as gardening. In the new environment someone else may be setting the schedule for meals and sleep.

Suddenly the elder is asked to accept and conform to different meals, different shopping, other forms of transportation and other living routines. All this comes after decades of making individual choices, of living alone or with a spouse. Is it any wonder the elder may feel uprooted and disoriented?

Some elders will feel overwhelmed and lonely. They may withdraw regardless of attempts to make them feel wanted or secure, be up all hours of the night, become demanding, even act in ways that others find embarrassing. If your elder has difficulty, try to remember that it will probably take at least ninety days for the elder to adjust to the new living arrangements. Intervention in this case is to help the person adapt.

Think back to the first time you moved to a new school or a different city. Remember when you and your spouse moved to a new neighborhood. How long did it take you to adjust and really feel comfortable in your new life?

Give everyone involved in the move time to adjust. Everyone is under stress trying to work the kinks out of a totally new situation. If you feel unable to cope, get professional help. Keep up the faith, too. Remind each other that though the adjustment is difficult, it can be survived, and in time the trauma of moving may lead to a pleasurable new life.

TEN

Day-to-Day Care

The vast majority of the physical care you will be called on to give your elder is easy to do once you know how. The medical professionals will teach you what you need to know if you ask. Rely on your home health professional for tips to make your job easier. *Ask questions!* If you don't ask, everyone will have the tendency to assume you already know.

When you receive instructions, *write them down.* Relying on your memory, especially for a task you seldom do, is bound to cause problems. The best idea is to purchase a small notebook or steno book and keep all your instructions together. Another option is to use a loose-leaf binder. The advantage is that pages can be added, taken out and reordered. However you do it, keep the book, labeled CARE on the outside, in your information center.

This chapter presents general tips that fit many circumstances, gathered from professionals in the field. It's critical that you keep in mind that a method suitable for one situation isn't necessarily suitable for another. That includes situations that *seem* to be similar. Disclaimers will appear throughout this chapter, again and again, to remind you that you should always check with the elder's primary-care physician or other health professional familiar with the case before you try any of these tips.

Never change a medication, its schedule or its dosage. *Never* administer a new medicine, even one that is sold without prescription, without talking to the primary-care physician first.

All drugs interact with each other and with the user's system. Normally there is no problem, but occasionally the interactions can be deadly.

Be aware that some of the procedures covered in this chapter bring a degree of danger. Moving the elder, for example, can cause injury to you, to the elder or even to both of you. Other procedures, if not followed correctly, can bring on other problems.

It's also important to remember at all times that the person you are caring for is a human being. Some of the procedures are highly embarrassing. As embarrassing as they are for you, they are worse for the person on the receiving end. Although there is no other choice, at least you can try to maintain the elder's sense of dignity.

Sickroom Supplies

The following is a basic list of supplies that are handy to have at your fingertips when caring for an elder. Adapt it and the suggestions that follow to fit your elder's particular needs.

paper, silk or other adhesive tape
alcohol
antibiotic cream
antiseptic wipes or baby wipes
disposable gloves
adhesive bandages
body lotion
cotton swabs
thermometer
facial tissues
gauze pads
reusable hot/cold packs
note pad and pencil
peroxide
petroleum jelly
scissors
tweezers

The adhesive tape should be one that will make a secure bond but still removes easily. Some adhesive tapes are difficult and/or painful to remove; some can actually damage the skin.

A digital thermometer is safer than the mercury-filled glass variety and is often easier and faster to use. Most are also extremely accurate. Even so, it's important to verify this accuracy against a thermometer known to be accurate.

If the elder is incontinent, add to the list of supplies a bedpan, urinal, disposable moisture resistant pads (like Chux), glycerin suppositories, Fleet enema (both oil and cleansing), citrate of magnesium and whatever else the doctor or health-care professional recommends.

Bed linens need to be laundered often, so stay away from those types such as satin that need special care or that stain easily. Instead select cotton or cotton-percale in soothing pastel colors and/or simple patterns. Buy the sheets with the highest thread count (180 +) that you can find. The higher the count, the softer the sheet and the easier it is on the elder's skin. Flannel sheets can make a nice change for the winter.

As mentioned in the previous chapter, use a mild laundry soap and be sure that the soap is completely rinsed out. Failure to do so can cause an increase in the number and severity of bedsores.

To protect a mattress use a plastic mattress cover (available from many department stores and major mail order catalogs) or lay an old shower curtain between the mattress and the bottom sheet. Tuck the shower curtain under the mattress.

Using plastic protectors on pillows usually cause the elder to sweat, which becomes uncomfortable and can lead to skin breakdown on the scalp. Instead use pillows with washable filling materials or air the pillows outside.

Backrests can be improvised from pillows and foam shapes. These can be covered in rubber sheeting to provide a moisture barrier before encasing them in an outside cover or pillowcase. Pillows in various shapes are available from medical supply houses, therapists and some chiropractic offices.

Charting Your Elder's Condition

Depending on the elder's condition, you may be asked to keep track of certain things on a daily basis. This procedure is called charting. Take this task seriously. You are the doctor's eyes and ears. Your information will help in the ongoing treatment of your elder's condition by enabling the physician to assess the program's overall effectiveness. It can help to spot problem areas, drug reactions and a host of other things. Your records can help define a new health problem when it's still in its early stages.

The doctor will tell you exactly what needs to be recorded. Not everything listed here will be required. The purpose of the following discussion is merely to give you an overall view and explain why such a record might be needed.

Basic charting should be simple for the caregiver to keep and easy for the home health professional or the doctor to read. If you have been asked to keep a chart, make certain the home health professional reviews it on every visit and that you take it with you when the elder sees the doctor in person. Always have the chart at hand when speaking with the doctor or the doctor's assistant by phone. Always record the information immediately, and always make sure a time is recorded with the information.

To keep track of the information, create a chart like the one in Figure 10-1. You might need to modify it to meet your own needs.

WHEN AND HOW MUCH   For a number of reasons, the doctor may need to know how often, and at what time of day, the elder is taking medication, eating and drinking or going to the bathroom.

Knowing what medication is requested or given at what times can help answer the question of how much pain the person is in. Sometimes new symptoms, such as nausea or drowsiness, will appear that may be caused by medication; knowing when what medications were given, and when what symptoms appeared, can be an important clue to discovering whether such a relationship exists.

Date	Food	Fluids	Medication Time Kind	Notes
To 11am Breakfast	soft-boiled egg toast w/jam _____ 4 crackers w/ peanut butter	coffee juice _____ shake _____ 1 coffee	2 pain 8:00 am 1 Keflex 1 softener	moderate soft formed
11am To 3 PM Lunch	1 c tomato soup 1/2 c fruit cocktail _____ 1/2 energy bar	iced tea	12:30 2 pain	
4 PM To 7 PM Dinner	2 oz sliced turkey 1/2 c mashed potato spinach 1/2 cooked carrot	coffee	4:30 1 pain	
7 PM To Bedtime	1/4 c bran cereal	2 oz milk	8:00 pm 2 pain 1 Keflex	Small formed

Notes: *Had good night - little pain. Ate very well.*

_____

_____

_____

_____

Fig. 10-1: Sample chart.

Listing the quantity of food and liquids consumed will translate into calories for the doctor. This information is important in relation to the person's gaining or losing weight. Is the elder consuming 3,000 calories a day and losing weight? Something is wrong! The types of food will also point out a vitamin deficiency. Remember that malnutrition is a problem for many elders. Malnutrition can be a problem for anyone who doesn't eat properly, not just those who are economically disadvantaged. The doctor may need to prescribe supplements.

Beyond recording what goes into a person, you may have to record what comes out and when. Be observant. If you are handling elimination with a bedside commode or bedpan, this is easy. You look and record your observation. Is the stool soft, hard, formed, loose, runny? Are there chunks of undigested food or pills? Is the odor "normal" for your elder? If the elder is handling his or her own elimination needs, ask if there was a bowel movement and what kind. Record this information.

Elders can become confused about days and sometimes preoc-cupied with their bowel movements. They may complain of constipation ("I haven't gone in a week") when the chart shows a bowel movement yesterday. If the elder complains of pain in the bowels, call the doctor; this could signal an obstruction or the beginnings of something else entirely.

Note the color or lack of it in the urine. A change in color or odor can indicate problems. Try to judge the amount, or put it into a see-through measuring cup that you keep solely for this purpose. (Remember, if you added water to the commode chair container, deduct the amount of fluid you added). If the elder is using a catheter, simply read the scale on the bag to find the amount. What goes in must come out. Taking in a gallon of fluid and returning a pint may be a symptom of fluid retention, kidney failure or another serious problem.

BLOOD PRESSURE AND RESPIRATION   A doctor will some-times require this information, especially when tracking cases of heart attack, hypertension and other cardiovascular diseases. This information will help the caregiver and the doctor track medication effectiveness and monitor both ongoing problems and newly developing ones. The nurse or home health practitioner will train you if this is something the elder's physician needs monitored outside of routine office visits.

TEMPERATURE   When diagnosing fever, an accurate temperature reading helps. Temperature, when combined with other symptoms, can help determine if a trip to the doctor's office or the hospital is necessary. Not everyone has the same temperature of 98.6 degrees Fahrenheit. Some people run slightly warmer or cooler than this naturally. Know what your elder's normal temperature is, and make certain the doctor and the home health professional are aware of it, too.

Thermometers are available in drugstores and medical supply houses. If you are not used to taking temperatures, reading a mercury thermometer can be difficult. Digital thermometers are inexpensive and generally very accurate. (Consider comparing the one you buy to a thermometer already known to be accurate.) Before each use, wipe off with alcohol to sterilize it and rinse it under running tap water to get rid of the alcohol taste. Follow directions for use, since they do vary. Typically you press a button to activate the thermometer, then place it under the tongue. When it is time to read the thermometer, it beeps. Remove it and read the digital display.

Other types of thermometers take the temperature from the ear. Still another is a strip you merely lay across the person's forehead. The latter is quick and easy but is generally the least accurate method.

GENERAL INFORMATION   General comments and observations can tell a health professional a lot about a person's attitude, which affects cooperation level, desire to get well and so forth. Noting how active they are, how much and how often they sleep are clues to insomnia and energy levels, all of which play a part in their overall well-being as well as their health.

Moving the Bedridden Elder

Moving a person, especially if the person can offer no assistance, can be tricky. If the elder has severe osteoporosis or cancer that has spread to the bones, moving the person can result in broken bones. When a bone breaks under these conditions it is not necessarily the result of your handling but rather a consequence of the illness. In other words, even gentle handling brings potential dangers.

The proper way to move someone should be demonstrated to you by a home health-care professional. The techniques you learn will be specific to the elder's infirmity. There is a difference between moving someone with a broken extremity and moving someone who has little or no use of his or her legs. The following are general rules, but before applying them, make sure you get professional hands-on instruction.

First, assess the situation. Think about (1) the size and weight of the person you are attempting to move, (2) the relationship to your own size, weight and strength, and (3) the general condition of the other person. Can the elder help at all, and if so how much? Also note the size and location of the bed and/or the medical equipment you are trying to get the elder into. Get all nonessential items (wastebaskets, telephone cords, etc.) out of the way.

When you are moving an elder, don't stop for any reason other than pain in the elder or in yourself. And once the move is complete, make sure that the new position is stable before you leave. Above all, *never* attempt to move the patient by yourself if you have back, leg or stability problems, if you have had recent surgery, if the elder is much larger or heavier than you or if the elder's condition demands two people for the move.

MOVING THE ELDER IN BED   If the elder is able to assist, ask him or her to help.

The bed should be flat (if it is a bed that can be moved into different positions) and clear of all pillows except one between the elder's head and the head of the bed or wall. Position yourself slightly lower than the elder's shoulder. Face the head of the bed on your elder's weaker side. Your feet should be about twelve inches apart with one foot ahead of the other. Bend your knees slightly. Place your arm that is nearer the bed under the elder's armpit (see Fig. 10.2). Have the elder bend the legs or leg, if possible. Ask the elder to raise the arms, or the stronger arm if only one moves easily, as far as possible and grip the bed rail (if a

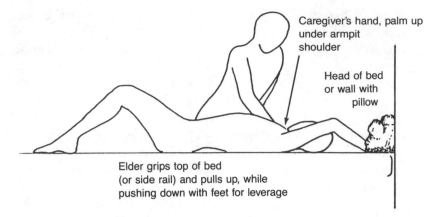

Fig. 10-2: Positioning yourself.

hospital bed) or the top of the mattress. Tell the elder you will count to three. When you reach three, the elder should push down with the heels and pull with the arm(s) while you lift upward and move the elder up in the bed.

If the elder is unable to help, follow the same initial steps of

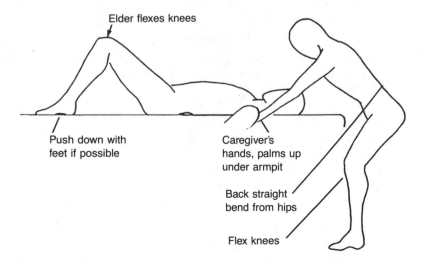

Fig. 10-3: Positioning yourself when the elder can't help.

getting the bed flat and removing the pillows. Stand at the head of the bed behind the elder. Lean over the bed and judge the distance you need to reach the elder's shoulders (see Fig. 10-3). You may need to stand on a concrete block or other riser if you have difficulty placing your arms under the elder's shoulders and locking them under the elder's armpits.

Ask the elder to bend the knees and push down with the feet (if possible) when you count to three. When you reach three, pull back. If the elder has the slightest discomfort, stop. Get help before trying again.

Always be attentive to the elder's discomfort, especially when the elder is frail, injured or postsurgical. Diseases, such as arthritis, can also cause the elder to experience pain when being moved. If a postsurgical elder experiences pain at or near the surgery site, have the elder press a pillow against the site. This procedure, called splinting, should alleviate some of the pain. If the elder has had surgery or has a broken bone, be sure not to put pressure on the sensitive area.

Sliding the Elder Toward You There are times when you need to move the elder sideways in bed, such as moving the elder toward you. This could be the first step in moving the elder from the bed to another location. Begin by turning your hands palms up and spaced close together, then sliding them under the elder's legs just below the knee (see Fig. 10-4). Pull the legs toward you. Repeat the procedure to move the hips (see Fig. 10-5).

Slide your arm that is closer to the head of the bed under the elder's neck and head so that the head rests on your forearm and is

Caregiver's hands, palms up.
Slide both legs together.

Fig. 10-4: Placing your hands under the legs.

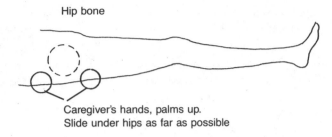

Hip bone

Caregiver's hands, palms up.
Slide under hips as far as possible

Fig. 10-5: Moving the hips.

steadied by your hand. Slide your other arm over the elder, grasp the shoulders and pull the elder gently toward you.

Moving the Elder to a Sitting Position As always, let the elder know what you're about to do and determine how much help the elder can provide. Place pillows or a backrest at the top of the bed close enough for you to grab once you have the elder in a sitting position.

If the elder can provide some help, stand next to the bed in a balanced position with your knees bent. Extend your forearm that

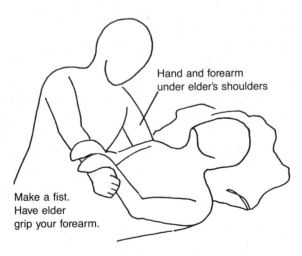

Hand and forearm
under elder's shoulders

Make a fist.
Have elder
grip your forearm.

Fig. 10-6: Getting positioned to help the elder to sit.

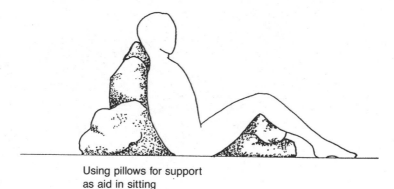

Using pillows for support
as aid in sitting

Fig. 10-7: Using pillows to prevent sliding.

is farther from the elder over the elder's waist. If you need to bend forward, make sure you keep your back straight and bend from the hips, *not* the waist. Have the elder grab your forearm. Slide your other arm under the elder's shoulders (see Fig. 10-6).

Tell the elder to use your arm to pull himself or herself up on the count of three. Stiffen your arm to give as much resistance as possible. As the elder attempts to sit, push the elder forward with the arm that is behind the shoulders. Place pillows or a backrest behind the elder.

If the elder is to remain in a sitting position, bend the elder's knees over one or two pillows so the elder does not slide down in the bed (see Fig. 10-7).

When the elder can't provide any assistance, place one foot on the floor, with the knee of your other leg on the bed. If possible, have the elder put his or her arms around your back and under your arms. Put your arms around the elder's back with your hands clasped on your own wrists. Your hands should be at the broadest part of the elder's back, over the shoulder blades (see Fig. 10-8).

You will be bending forward from the hips (with your back straight). Your weight should be evenly distributed, with the knee of the leg on the floor bent. When you raise up, you will straighten the knee of the leg on the floor, pushing with both thighs. Do not use your back muscles to lift the person. On the

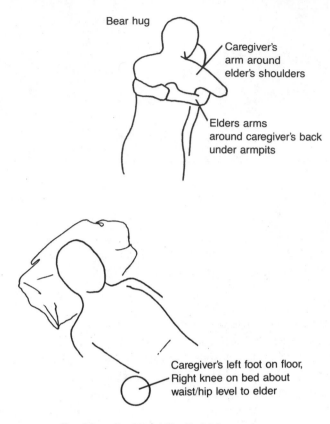

Fig. 10-8: Raising the elder who can't help.

count of three, pull the elder into a sitting position. Move the pillows or backrest into position.

Moving the Elder to a Chair There are special problems when the elder has to be moved from one location to another. A common situation is when the move is from the bed to a chair. First move the chair next to the bed and within easy reaching distance but out of the way. If it is a wheelchair with a removable side, detach the side nearer the bed. If the chair has detachable foot or leg rests, remove them on the side nearer the bed.

Following the instructions above, get the elder to sit up. Once this is accomplished, have the elder swing the legs over the edge of the bed. It's a good idea to put your arm around the elder's back. Place your other arm under the elder's knees and pivot the elder by pulling the knees toward you and the legs off the bed. Do not lift. The elder will now be sitting with the backs of the knees on the edge of the bed.

It's often a good idea to let the elder rest for two or three minutes while becoming stable. When you move a person who is weak or has been laying for a long time into a sitting position, the person tends to become lightheaded.

Bring the chair as close to the elder as possible and lock the wheels. Stand in front of the elder with your legs apart, comfortably straddling your elder's feet. Your legs should be slightly bent at the knee. Have the elder put his or her arms around your back if possible. Put your arms under the elder's armpits and around the back, then clasp your hand to your wrist (see Fig. 10-9).

Explain that on the count of three the patient should stand and the two of you will pivot toward the chair. Count to three. As the elder stands, lift with your thighs and pivot. When the elder is directly over the chair, lower the elder slowly (see Fig. 10-10).

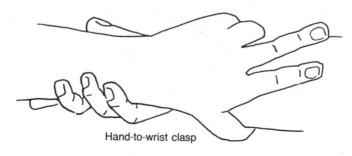

Hand-to-wrist clasp

Fig. 10-9: Hand-to-wrist clasp.

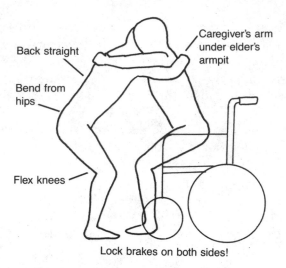

Back straight

Bend from hips

Flex knees

Caregiver's arm under elder's armpit

Lock brakes on both sides!

Fig. 10-10: Making the move to the chair.

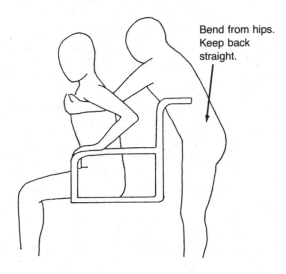

Bend from hips. Keep back straight.

Fig. 10-11: Assisting the elder to slide back in the chair.

Ask the elder to slide back into the chair until the elder's back rests against the back of the chair. If the elder cannot scoot or wiggle back into the chair, you will have to assist. To assist, stand directly behind the chair. Place your arms under the elder's armpits and around the chest. Lock your hands. Get a good balance with your knees bent. Count to three. On three, gently pull the elder back (see Fig. 10-11).

Moving the Elder From Wheelchair to Car This procedure is much the same as moving from a bed to a chair. However, there is more risk of strain on the caregiver's back, because most cars have lower seats than the standard chair height. This means the elder will have to be lowered into the car.

The best way to learn a wheelchair-car transfer is to have it demonstrated to you by a physical therapist. Never try to do this yourself unless you have considerable strength and balance and your elder is able to stand and help lower himself or herself. If this type of transfer needs to be done very often, ask the doctor to provide you with a prescription for a Hoyer Lift or to arrange medical transport.

Begin by detaching the wheelchair accessories. Move the wheelchair as close as possible to the car and parallel to the car door's opening. Lock the wheelchair wheels. Stand with your back almost touching the car door and your side near the car's opening. You should be directly in front of the elder, your feet about eighteen inches apart. Your right leg is about eight to twelve inches from the car's door sill. Bend your knees and keep your back straight.

Place your arms under the elder's armpits. Ask the elder to stand on the count of three. As the elder stands, you stand and pivot. Now stop. There should be less than six inches between you and the elder. Bring your left foot around so you are now facing the car's passenger opening squarely. The back of the elder's legs should be very close to the door sill of the car's opening.

Have your elder put his or her head on your shoulder or into your chest. The elder should have to lean toward you to do this. Your arms are around the elder's back. Bring one hand up to protect the elder's head. Clearing the car's roof without hitting the elder's head is the main goal. If you do collide with the roof, your hands, not the elder's head, will take the blow.

As you lower the elder, keep your back straight and your feet flat. If you must bend, bend from the hips. Ask the elder to sit. As the elder does this, he or she will naturally bend the knees and the elder's bottom will enter the car's opening and align over the seat. Continue lowering, and protecting the elder's head. As the elder gets closer to sitting, he or she will draw away from you. Let the elder's armpits naturally begin to slide down your arms, but no farther than your hands, which will brace against the elder's back. The closer the elder gets to sitting, the more of the elder's weight you'll be taking, so brace yourself well. You might find yourself sliding your feet forward as you lower the elder.

If necessary, help the elder pivot about a quarter turn in the seat. Have the elder lift the legs in. If you must help, lift both legs slowly into the interior. Assist the elder to sit straight and correct the elder's leg position. Fasten the safety belt.

If the car has a reclining or adjustable seat, pushing the seat back as far as possible and reclining the backrest can help. Lowering the seat as much as possible helps protect the elder's head from hitting the car's roof.

If the elder has a broken hip or knee, or a leg that must be kept straight, it's far better to arrange for medical transport or to transport the patient in a way that will keep the hip, knee or leg straight, such as on the floor of a van. The doctor will tell you how far any broken or damaged part can be bent or flexed. Make sure you do not exceed this limit when the person is transferred into or out of the car.

Moving the Elder From Car to Wheelchair Ask the elder to sit with the legs through the door opening. Assist the elder into this position if necessary. Pivot the elder about a quarter turn in the seat toward the outside. Lift both legs out simultaneously. Pivot the elder in the seat so the elder faces your squarely. Have the elder slide toward you to the seat edge (see Fig. 10-12).

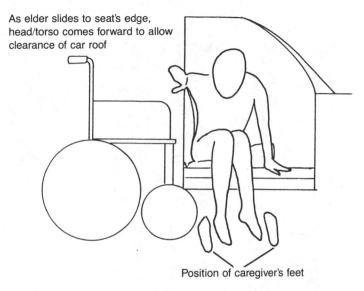

As elder slides to seat's edge, head/torso comes forward to allow clearance of car roof

Position of caregiver's feet

Fig. 10-12: Positioning the elder and the wheelchair.

With the accessories removed, move the wheelchair into position and lock the wheels. Position yourself directly in front of the elder with your feet flat, legs bent and back straight. If you must bend to reach the elder, bend from the hips. Slide your arms under the elder's armpits and use your hands to protect the elder's head. In this position, the elder's head will be outside the car and should be near your shoulder.

On the count of three, as the elder stands, you do as well, lifting with your legs. Keep your back straight. Pivot the elder to the wheelchair. Stop and check alignment of the elder's bottom in front of the chair. Gently lower the elder. Position the elder comfortably in the chair. Attach the chair's accessories.

CHANGING THE BED WITH THE ELDER IN IT This procedure is not as difficult as it sounds. If the elder can help with the turning procedure, great. If not, you can manage this on your own with a little practice. If the elder has a special medical condition

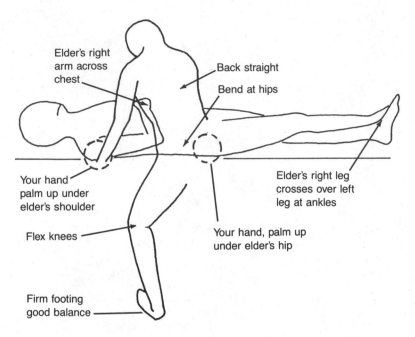

Elder's right
arm across
chest

Back straight

Bend at hips

Your hand
palm up under
elder's shoulder

Elder's right leg
crosses over left
leg at ankles

Flex knees

Your hand, palm up
under elder's hip

Firm footing
good balance

Fig. 10-13: Turning the elder onto his or her side.

such as being in traction or having compression fractures, get specific directions from the home health nurse.

First, gather all the bedding materials you will need. It's best if you explain what you'll be doing before you start so the elder knows what to expect.

The elder should be in the middle of the bed. Ask the elder to roll over onto his or her side, toward the edge of the bed. If the elder can't do this without help, while the elder is lying on his or her back, cross the right leg over the left leg (see Fig. 10-13). Place the right arm across the chest. Place your palms flat against the back of the elder's hips and shoulders. Make sure you are well balanced, with your back straight and your knees bent. If you must bend, make certain you bend from the hips. On the count of three roll the elder very gently toward the edge of the bed. If you use too much force you will roll the person either completely out of bed or into the bed's guard rail.

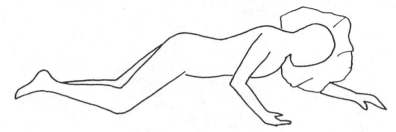

Fig. 10-14: Positioning the elder.

Positon the elder comfortably (see Fig. 10-14). Place a pillow under the head. Pull the left arm and shoulder into a comfortable position to relieve pressure on the arm, shoulder and chest.

Loosen one side of the soiled linen from the empty side of the bed. Fan-fold it and push it under the elder as far as possible (Fig. 10-15).

Put a clean sheet (and draw sheet if used) on the bed. Fan-fold these and push them under the sheets you are removing. If you are using a moisture pad or Chux, lay this on top of the clean linen in its proper position (see Fig. 10-16).

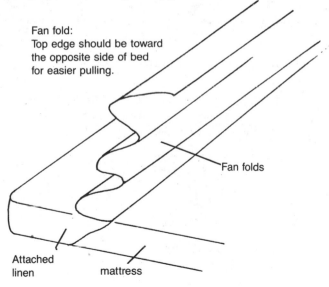

Fan fold:
Top edge should be toward
the opposite side of bed
for easier pulling.

Fan folds

Attached
linen   mattress

Fig. 10-15: Loosening and folding soiled linen.

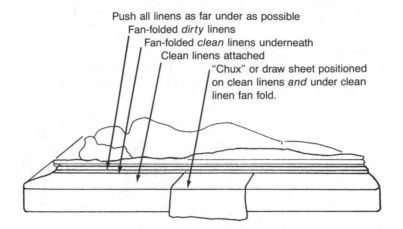

Push all linens as far under as possible
Fan-folded *dirty* linens
Fan-folded *clean* linens underneath
Clean linens attached
"Chux" or draw sheet positioned
on clean linens *and* under clean
linen fan fold.

Fig. 10-16: Putting on clean linens.

Position the elder for a full roll by crossing the left leg over the right leg and both arms across the chest (see Fig. 10-17). Raise the bed rail (if there is one) on the side of the bed you are rolling the elder to. Place a pillow between where the elder's head will be and the bed railing. Place the palms of your hands under the hip and shoulder that are on the bed. Using correct positioning for yourself, gently roll the person across the entire bed.

Pull out the dirty sheet (and draw sheet) by gripping the leading edge of the fan-fold. Remove from bed. Pull the clean sheet and draw sheet into proper position using the leading edge of the fan-fold. You can now position the elder comfortably and change the top sheet and blanket (see Fig. 10-18).

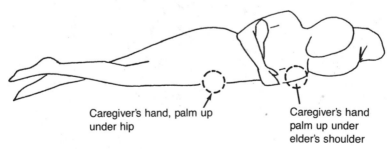

Caregiver's hand, palm up   Caregiver's hand
under hip   palm up under
                                 elder's shoulder

Fig. 10-17: Positioning the elder for a full roll.

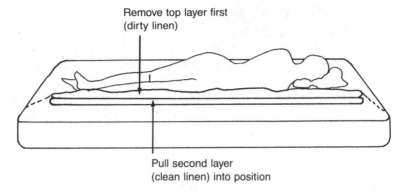

Remove top layer first
(dirty linen)

Pull second layer
(clean linen) into position

Fig. 10-18: Changing the linens.

General Hygienic Care

BATHING   Before the elder begins a bath or shower, it makes sense to prepare the bathroom first so that needed supplies are within easy reach. Supplies include a nonskid bath mat on the floor, two towels, washcloth, soap, shampoo and cream rinse, moisturizing body lotion, talcum powder or bath powder, deodorant and whatever else is normally used.

If there is room to move easily in the bathroom, supply clean clothes. If disrobing and dressing are difficult, have the elder disrobe and dress in the bedroom, wearing only a bathrobe and slippers between the two rooms.

Bathing is the perfect opportunity to observe your elder carefully. Look for bruises, skin breakdown, bedsores, rashes, bleeding and discharges. An elder who bathes himself or herself receives light exercise and increased circulation that helps prevent skin breakdown. If you do the bathing, you are providing stimulation and a soothing touch.

Check with the doctor about the frequency of bathing. Too often can cause the skin to dry out, leading to further complications. However, certain body parts should be washed daily to prevent pressure sores and infections. Underarms, elbows, heels of the feet, spine and buttocks, all bony protrusions, the genitals and the rectal area all require daily attention.

If the elder has limited mobility or is completely bedridden, it is a good idea to provide a small pan of warm water and a washcloth in the mornings so that the elder may begin the day with clean hands and face. An aloe cleaning wipe or a damp washcloth should be provided after every meal and use of bedpan or bedside commode so that the elder may clean the hands and the anal area.

Do NOT bathe an elder who is in severe pain and who says that the bathing process adds to his or her discomfort. Also be wary if the elder has mobility problems and the bathroom has not been equipped with safety devices such as hand rails, tub seats and so forth. If the elder is wearing a cast or has stitches, check with the doctor first.

The elder should always do as much of his or her own bathing as possible. The more an elder does, the more independent he or she feels and the easier it is on the elder (and on you). This is true whether the elder takes the bath or shower in a bathroom or bathes in the bed itself.

If the elder bathes alone, the bathroom door should be left open just a bit so that you can easily hear if the elder needs assistance. Never leave an elder alone who is depressed, unsteady on his or her feet, prone to fainting or dizziness, or confused. If you are staying with the elder during the bathing process, keep the door entirely closed, if possible, for the sake of privacy.

"Most accidents happen in the bathroom" is an often quoted truism. It's also backed by statistics. In the case of an elder, a bathroom can be a very dangerous place even though you've taken every precaution you can imagine. The more unsteady an elder is, the more likely an accident will happen. If an elder falls in the bathroom, do not attempt to move the elder yourself. Get help. If the elder falls in the bathtub or shower, drain the water, cover the elder with towels or robes and call for help.

Remember, too, that it is easy for an elder to become chilled. Make certain the room is warm enough and that the elder is covered as much as possible except when actually in the water. For an elder working with a bed bath, the same rules apply. Keep the person covered except for the area being cleaned. This not only prevents chills but helps keep the elder's dignity and modesty intact.

Bed Bath First gather the needed supplies, including a large towel, robe or sheet to cover the parts of the elder not being washed, a basin of warm water, three washcloths, mild soap, body lotion, deodorant, powder and two bath towels. You can substitute mild soap and lotion for a one-step cleaning with a product such as Septisoft, available at most drugstores and medical supply houses.

Protect the bedding with a large thick towel or plastic shower curtain placed under the elder.

Bathe in this order, cleaning then drying one part at a time: face (pay attention to the corners of the eyes) and ears, neck, arms and hands, chest (especially under the breasts), abdomen. Be certain any folds of skin are thoroughly cleansed.

Change the water and use a second washcloth to clean the back, underarms, navel, legs, feet and between the toes.

Change the water and use the third washcloth to clean genital and rectal areas. A woman should be cleansed front to back to avoid getting fecal matter near the vaginal area. Pay attention to the area alongside a man's scrotum. If it is within the elder's capabilities, ask the elder to bathe his or her own genitals and rectal area. If the elder is using a catheter, this should be cleaned according to the doctor's or nurse's directions.

Apply lotion to one body part at a time as before. Use deodorant if the elder can tolerate it. Use a light dusting powder under the breast area and in the folds of the skin.

Bathing an Elder Who Wears a Cast If the elder has a leg cast, a shower will be easiest, with the second choice being a thorough washing either in bed or sitting on the toilet in the bathroom. Do not allow the elder a tub bath, as it is all but impossible to get the elder in and out of the tub with a cast on, or to keep it out of the water while keeping the elder in a stable position.

Cast protection for the shower is easy. Select a towel large enough to wrap around the elder's leg at the top of the cast and have some overlap. The towel is secured with safety pins so that the majority of the towel is fastened around the elder's leg and a small part covers the top of the cast.

Next, take a plastic garbage bag (30-gallon size for above-knee casts, 13-gallon for casts ending midcalf) and place the elder's limb and cast into the bag. Secure it with an elastic loop or tie it with a necktie or scarf. Note that the bag is secured to the leg just *above* the towel.

When an elder is showering or even using a pan with water for bathing, some of the water will drip on the bag. Water can seep into the smallest opening, and the towel will help absorb any small leaks. Using this method, the cast will stay dry.

The same principle applies to an arm or hand that is in a cast. Suitable plastics can be from long bread bags or other small trash can liners, depending on the area that needs to be covered. Cast protectors are also available from most medical supply houses.

CAST CARE   Many times an itch will develop under a cast, and one's first thought is to shove something down the cast and scratch that itch. STOP! There is too much danger of "something" damaging an elder's delicate skin, which can lead to infection. Instead try tapping lightly on the cast over the itch with a blunt object such as an empty plastic bottle or rolled-up newspaper. Also, the tip of a bulb syringe can be placed next to the bottom or tip of a cast. Depressing the bulb causes air to flow up the cast and will hopefully relieve the itch. Keeping the elder cool also helps prevent the itches, so make certain the elder is not overdressed.

The edge of the cast can sometimes irritate the surrounding skin. Pad the area with a thin piece of towel or flannel. Allow the material to hang over the cast. If the problem is in only one or two small spots, you can use cotton strips from a roll of cotton or small pieces of sheepskin or moleskin. Just make certain nothing falls into the cast.

Do not use lotions or creams around or inside the cast. These can sometimes leave a sticky residue that irritates skin.

Never get a cast wet, as it will soften and will probably have to be redone. If the elder must be moved in rain or snow, use a cast protector or make your own protection as noted in the section on bathing.

If the elder is concerned about the cast's appearance, a little white shoe polish will clean it up. Do not saturate the cast, as it will soften. These days many casts are available in color; have the elder choose a favorite shade. Also don't forget the classic solution to wearing an ugly cast, namely to have friends and loved ones sign it or draw on it. A flower or other picture made by a loving grandchild not only brightens the cast, it can be a steady reminder to the elder that he or she is loved.

Cast Problems If the limb swells, elevate it. If swelling continues or does not diminish, call the doctor.

The elder should have feeling in fingers and toes even if there is a cast on an arm or leg. If there is pain, tingling or numbness, if the skin is bluish or if you cannot find a pulse in the foot or wrist, call the doctor immediately. The same is true if the elder cannot move the fingers or toes.

Toes and fingers need to retain good circulation. Squeeze them gently. They should turn white, then return to a healthy pink color. If this doesn't happen, call the doctor. Other indications that the doctor needs to be called are if there is any increase in pain, new pain developing in the cast area, or a discharge from under the cast. Also be aware of any unusual odors. This could be caused by something spilled into the cast, a skin breakdown or an infection.

If food or liquids get down inside the cast they will decay, causing an odor and possibly an infection as well. When the cast wearer is eating or drinking, it's a good idea to drape a small piece of plastic or a towel over the cast opening.

HAIR CARE   This is a fairly simple procedure if the elder is in the bath or shower and has a hand-held shower as recommended earlier. If the procedure must be done while the elder remains in bed, purchase an inflatable shampoo basin, available at many medical supply houses.

You will also need a plastic covering for the bed. (An old shower curtain or opened plastic trash can liner will do). Gather the needed supplies: three towels, shampoo, several containers of warm water (old clean plastic milk jugs work well), comb, blow dryer and bucket. If the elder's hair is long or has a tendency to snarl, you might want to add cream rinse to the list. There are a few brands on the market that do not require rinsing but remain in the hair as a conditioner or styling lotion. You can find them at a supermarket or beauty supply house.

If you have a hospital bed, adjust it to a comfortable working height for you. Cover the mattress with plastic. Put a towel over the plastic to absorb any spilled water, which would only run on plastic. Have the elder lie on his or her back, placing the head in the shampoo basin. The elder's head can be made lower than the shoulders by placing a flat pillow or additional folded towels beneath the shoulders. To help keep the elder dry and warm, place a towel over the shoulders.

Gently pour warmed water over the hair. Use small amounts of shampoo and work it into a rich lather with your fingertips. Do not use your fingernails on the scalp; use the pads of your fingers only. If your nails are long you may want to wear rubber gloves to prevent scratching or pulling hair. Rinse thoroughly.

Work as quickly and efficiently as possible so that the elder does not become overtired or chilled. If your basin becomes too full, empty it into the bucket.

Squeeze excess moisture from the hair, gently. Cover the hair with a towel and remove the basin. Gently comb or brush the hair, then blow it dry.

TOENAIL CARE   Adult toenails are often thick and difficult to trim. This is usually caused by fungal infections. Some of these infections respond well to over-the-counter antifungal medications, but most cases require a prescription medication to cure. Check with the doctor for the name of the preferred brand and to check drug interaction. To cut thickened toenails, provided they have not become deformed by infection, soak the feet in warm water. This will soften the nail so it can be cut. Always cut nails straight across, and never cut them below the quick. Problems such as ingrown toenails, major trimming on toenails and removal of calluses need the attention of a professional. Do not deal with these problems yourself.

Do NOT attempt to remove or tear off the dead skin that may have formed around calluses. Also do not use over-the-counter remedies for the removal of calluses. Arrange a medical appointment for their care.

SKIN CARE   Dry skin is uncomfortable, making the elder feel stiff. It can also lead to bedsores. Have the elder drink more water. Six to eight eight-ounces glasses of water per day is optimal.

Make certain the elder rinses well when bathing, because soap left on the skin is drying. The kind of soap also makes a difference. Switch to a mild soap like Ivory, or to a glycerin soap, which is available in many grocery stores and most bed-and-bath shops. Try to get an unscented soap or the type that is scented with oils rather than perfume that has an alcohol base. The glycerin soaps that have an odor are readily available in florals, which many women like. A man might prefer a musk or sandalwood scent. Products made for bathing babies are also good.

If you are giving a bed bath, consider adding an oil to the water such as Avon's Skin-So-Soft or Alpha Keri. Do not do this for an elder who is using a bathtub. Oils increase the likelihood of slipping, especially if the elder is unsteady on his or her feet to begin with.

Massage in a lotion. If massage is not permitted, you can probably still lightly stroke on small amounts. Good lotions are those that don't leave behind a sticky residue, which makes the person feel like he or she needs a bath all over again. Look for those products that are unscented, that are hypo-allergenic or dermatology tested and that have no alcohol.

Larger towns and cities may have a lotion shop or a lotion

counter in a bed-and-bath shop. These shops offer a variety of lotions made from jojoba, aloe and various vitamin combinations like A, D and E. Some of these not only help keep the skin soft but actually revitalize it. They can be scented with the person's favorite oil at your request or left unscented.

SPECIAL CLEANSING FOR A DIABETIC'S FOOT   Diabetes interferes with the blood circulation in a person's body. The circulation problem causes the elder's feet and legs to need special care. Openings in the skin, such as sores or cracking, may appear suddenly. These tend to be slow to heal with infection highly possible. To avoid problems (some of which can be life-threatening or may lead to amputation), follow daily care guidelines as given by your elder's doctor. They will probably include directions similar to the following.

Wash the feet daily in mild soap and slightly warmed water. Never use hot water or let the feet soak for extended periods or on a daily basis. A Dr. Scholl's Vibrating Foot Soaker helps improve circulation. Check with the doctor for instructions and for a prescription. Some insurances will pay for this if it is prescribed.

This is a good time to perform a daily foot check. Dry the feet, and pay close attention to the soles and the area between the toes. If you notice any redness, swelling, cracks or pus, call the doctor immediately.

The skin should be lubricated with body lotion daily. Do NOT apply lotion between the toes. Also keep in mind that it is important to keep the diabetic's feet dry. Apply talcum powder, especially if sweating is a problem.

If toenails must be trimmed, avoid nicking the skin. Do NOT trim nails shorter than the end of the toe. Trim the nails straight across. Due to the delicate nature of an elder's feet, especially if diabetic, the best approach is to get a recommendation to a podiatrist to have the nails inspected for fungal infection and have them trimmed.

Giving Medications

Occasionally an elder will refuse to take medication. In many ways, this is the elder's right. The elder may be sending an indirect message that he or she is annoyed, depressed, angry or frightened. It may also be a way of attempting to control a recovery situation where everything is being done for the elder, who is feeling powerless. It may be something else entirely. You'll never know unless you ask.

When the elder refuses you might ask, "Why don't you want the medicine?" You might have to probe further by asking, "Does the medicine taste bad?" or "Is it hard to swallow?" As you can see, there are legitimate reasons for not wanting to take medication.

If the elder says the medicine tastes bad, causes nausea or other side effects or is hard to swallow—if there is any type of logical objection—call the doctor. The physician may be able to offer a different type of medication, a different way of taking it (with food perhaps) or a different form of it (for example, liquid instead of tablets).

Sometimes the elder needs the medication despite side effects. Ask the doctor for another prescription that might counteract the side effects.

Some medications can be crushed and added to food. Others cannot. Always check with the doctor before giving medications in any form other than that in which they were manufactured. Timed-release medications can be dangerous when removed from the capsule and/or crushed into foods. Avoid problems; check with the doctor first.

To crush a pill, place it between two nesting teaspoons. Depress the top teaspoon with your thumb using a twisting or grinding motion. Commercial pill crushers are also available at most pharmacies.

If allowed, the ground pill powder can be mixed with juice or a small amount of applesauce or other soft semi-liquid food. Ice cream and puddings are good foods for this. Consider trying baby food like strained bananas or any other food taste the elder may like. Keep in mind that many adults will refuse to eat baby foods because they feel it is demeaning. You may be able to overcome this by making your own "baby foods" by putting acceptable foods through your blender.

When pills are pulverized they can impart a bitter taste. Mix them into one teaspoon of the food and give that first, then follow with water, juice or additional food that has no medication in it. You might also try adding the powdered pill to a small amount of jam, jelly or liquid ice cream topping.

Remember that certain foods can cause a reaction when coupled with medications. Always check with the doctor before mixing pills and foods. Be specific about the food you want to add the pill to, such as yogurt or raspberry jam.

If the medicine is already a liquid but the taste is horrible, suggest having the person suck on an ice cube before taking the medicine. The ice tends to numb the taste buds. Certain liquid medicines can also be mixed with other liquids such as flavored syrups or juices. A good way to administer these is from a medicine cup (available at most drugstores and medical supply houses). Simply measure in the required dose, add the chosen liquid flavor and stir. This is much easier than using a spoon because it allows a larger quantity and doesn't spill as readily.

Some medicines are available in suppository form. Follow directions for insertion. Remember to use disposable plastic gloves.

If you are to apply a powder to a wound, do NOT use your fingers. Instead sprinkle the powder on a gauze pad and gently press the pad to the wound. Apply an antiseptic cream while wearing a disposable plastic glove. Both of these measures help keep the wound site clean and reduce the risk of infection.

Giving medications to a confused or disoriented person can be scary for the caregiver. The most common caregiver fear is that the elder will choke or gag. In most cases the person's gag reflex comes into play and keeps such accidents from occurring. It is wise, however, to learn the Heimlich maneuver. The simple demonstration is given at many YMCAs, YWCAs, community colleges and fire departments.

For giving medications, follow these tips:

- Always administer the medications yourself. Never leave them with the elder.
- Make certain the elder is sitting upright.
- Always watch the elder take the medication, then either linger or check every few minutes to make certain the drug has worked and that no side effects have occurred.
- If giving more than one pill at a time, give them individually.

MISSED DOSES Occasionally an elder will miss a dose of medication or will vomit it back up. Do not readminister the medication or give medication off schedule. Call the doctor or home health nurse for directions. How you handle a missed dose varies with the medication. In some cases you will be told to give that dose right away. In others you should double up when the next dose is due. In still others you will be told to not worry about it.

Diet

When an elder has a bout with the flu, is released from the hospital or is about to undergo tests, and for any number of other reasons, the physician may request that the elder have only clear liquids or bland foods. The following lists are broken down into name and day. The name refers to the types of nourishment allowed. The day refers to the sequence a person is usually asked to adhere to if he or she has had or is preparing for a certain surgery, or has had recurring serious bouts with diarrhea.

Day 1: Clear Liquids A clear liquid is something you can see through. Examples include broth, tea, 7-Up, Gatorade, water, plain Jell-O and Popsicles. (The reason Jell-O and Popsicles are included even though you technically can't see through them is that they are mostly water and sugar, things that the body can easily assimilate). If your elder is diabetic or needs to take medication with food, ask the doctor how to adjust this diet.

Day 2: Full Liquids This day allows everything from Day 1 and adds liquids you can't see through. Colored pop like colas and root beers, coffee, soups made without milk, puddings (made with skim milk), sherbets and sorbets are included. The reason for the milk restriction is that milk and milk products are harder than other liquids to digest, especially for an adult. Generally milk products are not added until Day 5, if at all. Ensure can be given since it is made with soy instead of milk. If diarrhea occurs or returns, eliminate the milk-based pudding and return to Day 1 (*after* notifying the doctor).

Day 3: Bland Diet All foods from days 1 and 2 can be given. You may now add rice, noodles or pasta, mashed potatoes and gravy (preferably low in salt), breads (no butter), crackers, bananas and applesauce. *Some* other fresh fruits may also be suggested by the doctor or health care professional.

Day 4: Light Diet If your elder got through Day 3 with no problems, you can add turkey, chicken, eggs (soft-boiled, hard-boiled or poached), fish, and pureed cooked vegetables. Please note that raw vegetables and most fruits are still out. No fried foods.

Day 5: Regular Diet If there have been no problems the elder can now resume a regular diet or the permanent diet prescribed by the doctor.

APPETITE PROBLEMS   Some elders complain of nausea, which may be due to medications or specific medical treatments like chemotherapy. Check these possible solutions with your elder's physician:

- Anti-nausea medicines
- Eating crackers, lemons or pickles

- Small but frequent feedings
- Ice cubes made from non acidic fruit juices
- Avoiding liquids at meals (elder would drink one hour before meals)
- Drinking carbonated beverages like ginger ale and 7-Up
- Not allowing elder to lie flat immediately after eating (Sitting is better for the digestion. If the elder must lie down, elevate the head at least four inches higher than the feet.)
- Requesting a special dietary list and checking the suitability of baby foods

Difficulty in swallowing should be reported to the physician. It may mean a switch to soft foods. Consider easy-to-digest baby or toddler foods. If you do try these, serve them as you would adult food, on a plate or in a bowl. There is no need to advertise the fact that the elder is eating baby food by making him or her eat out of a jar.

Appetites can be affected by the appearance and texture of foods. One elder may prefer crunchy textures, and another may want bland or squishy foods. Ask what your elder likes and try to meet those needs.

Loneliness affects appetite, too. Have the elder join you for meals. If the elder is bedridden, join the elder. If an entire family is involved, make meals special. Give everyone a chance to dine alone with the elder once a week. The rest of the time, have two or three members or all of the family join the elder.

NUTRITION   Elders sometimes have digestive problems that need to be taken into consideration when preparing meals. As a rule, elders are less active than younger adults and consume smaller quantities of food. Many give up the practice of eating "three squares a day." Because they eat less and tend to munch on easy-to-eat foods, it is likely their nutrition is unbalanced, and they may also lose weight.

Check with the doctor about having the elder take a multi-vitamin or other supplement. Perhaps extra calcium is in order if the elder has osteoporosis or is female. The doctor may prescribe chelated calcium or Tums, depending on the other types of medication your elder is taking. Make sure you understand the doctor's orders as to the quantity the elder is supposed to take, and when.

A nutritional supplement drink like Ensure might also be recommended. Ensure is available in many drugstores and most supermarkets, especially those that have pharmacies or nutritional departments.

Any good book on nutrition will help you balance meals. Use this type of book in conjunction with the doctor's plan for eating. For example, if your elder is prone to anemia the doctor may suggest the elder eat foods rich in iron. A wheelchair-bound patient may need more vitamin C, while one who is prone to bacterial infections may need additional sources of vitamin A. The doctor can explain which vitamins an elder needs and which type of diet (such as high protein, low cholesterol, etc.) would be best. The nutrition book will tell you which foods meet those requirements. If the elder has a particular disease like cancer or heart disease, write to or call the foundation for that disease and ask for information and dietary guidelines. Check the library for books on the disease that also relate dietary information.

When an elder eats in small quantities or prefers to nibble throughout the day, you need to pack a lot of useful calories into a small amount of food. Sugar adds calories but not nutrition, so simply sweetening foods is not the best idea. Take the following suggestions to your primary-care physician or recommended nutritionist, who can double-check them against the elder's medications and needed calorie intake.

Special Drinks Ensure is a high-calorie, nutritionally complete, fortified soy-based drink. It is available in a variety of flavors, and it tastes best served well chilled.

You can also make your own fortified drink by mixing one or two envelopes of instant breakfast with eight ounces of milk or half-and-half. Read the box for nutritional balance.

To double the protein in each cup of milk without increasing the fat content, do this: Pour one quart of milk (homogenized, 2% or 1%) into a deep bowl. Add one cup of instant nonfat dry milk powder and beat slowly until milk is dissolved, about four minutes. Refrigerate several hours. Use as you would regular milk.

The Ultimate Milkshake

1 cup of milk, half-and-half, fortified milk or Ensure
1 large scoop ice cream, ice milk or frozen yogurt
1/2 teaspoon vanilla extract or other complementary flavor options: 1 banana; any type of berries (fresh or frozen); most canned fruits packed in their own juice; fresh fruits other than citrus and raw apples or melons; 1 tablespoon of a favorite topping like chocolate, butterscotch, pineapple, etc.

Mix milk, ice cream, extract and option choice in a blender at low speed until smooth and creamy. Makes two servings.

Fruit juices mixed with seltzer, 7-Up, ginger ale and the like are great over ice. Try cranberry juice and ginger ale; Mandarin orange seltzer with orange or pineapple juice; or grapefruit juice cocktail and 7-Up.

If the elder likes coffee (either regular or decaf), add a tablespoon of hot cocoa mix and some half-and-half or fortified milk to black coffee (use flavored coffee if desired). This is good hot or served over ice.

Your best option for any of the drinks above is to use them as a midmorning snack or serve about ninety minutes before bed.

Soups Soups are another way to increase fluid and nutrition intake. There are a number of good recipe books available that will give you basic soup ideas. You can make them different and give them a consistency that your elder may find more acceptable if you run the completed cooled soup through the blender. Try adding a little fortified milk to soups for a few additional calories.

Almost any soup can be "creamed" in this manner. Keep the soup thin enough to be drinkable from a mug.

Other Ways to Add Calories and Nutrition If your elder likes peanut butter, find interesting ways to serve it as snacks. It's a good source of protein and calories. Try it stuffed in a half of a celery stalk, on whole-wheat crackers, on chocolate-covered graham crackers, in fudge, on toast with jam, etc. Get creative with it. Some people like it with bananas and assorted fruits, while others prefer it with cheese.

Try an English, sourdough, French or deli roll, bagel or Boboli bread topped with pizza sauce and other favorite toppings. Use the same bread base and cover with tuna, diced meats, fresh diced tomato, a scrambled egg with Mexican seasoning or a little fresh dill. Melt a favorite cheese on top of any combination. Cut into nibble pieces.

If you can serve small meals more often, you have a better chance of getting the elder's calorie intake up. The elder may feel overwhelmed by a regular-size meal, so consider the off-hour routine: small breakfast at 7:30, snack at 10:00, lunch at 1:00, small snack at 3:00, and dinner at 6:00. If you keep the snacks small (say, two or three wheat crackers topped with peanut butter), you will have a good chance of getting all the food eaten.

Serve the elder's food on smaller than normal plates, such as salad or luncheon plates. Put soup in a coffee mug. The elder will not feel quite so intimidated by the quantity and will get a sense of satisfaction from having eaten it all.

Many medications need to be taken with food. Sometimes their time can be switched around so that the medications are taken at snack time. This can make the elder feel more like eating at the regular mealtime because he or she is not so filled with water and pills. Check with the primary-care physician to see if this will fit with your elder's treatment schedule.

If the elder's favorite snacks are still within his or her dietary limitations, leave them nearby for easy anytime munching. Try not to let the elder indulge in too many cakes, cookies and candies. The elder needs more nutrition than empty calories. If the elder insists on sweets, make them more nutritious: Add wheat germ or bran to cookies; use a standard oatmeal cookie base and toss in raisins, bananas, chopped dates, dried fruit, or applesauce; top frozen yogurt with fruit and fresh whipped cream; serve fresh carrot cake with cream cheese frosting; offer banana, apple or zucchini bread; try a fresh fruit pie. Many of these ideas can be adapted to low-sugar and low-fat diets. Check libraries, bookstores and health food stores for nutrition-conscious recipe books.

Alcoholic beverages such as brandy and wine stimulate some people's appetite. Check with the doctor to find out if a small amount of alcohol before meals is acceptable.

Add protein by cooking and dicing chicken, turkey or ham and adding it to gravies, sauces, pasta dishes, vegetable dishes, casseroles and salads.

Mix milk powder into hot cereals and use fortified milk on cold ones.

Add powdered milk, eggs (or powdered eggs or Eggbeaters), wheat germ, bran flakes or wheat bread to meat loaf.

Bread meats before cooking.

Crush cornflakes into a bowl with a scrambled egg. Add a can of tuna or salmon. Mix, then shape into patties and fry or bake. Serve hot as a main dish or cold (after cooking) with mayonnaise as a nibble food or the main filling in a sandwich.

Add mayonnaise to salads and sandwiches. Just one tablespoon has a hundred calories!

High calories can come from dried fruits and cheeses.

Add whipped cream as a topping to fresh fruit, ice cream sundaes, Jello-O or hot chocolate. You can make your own by adding vanilla extract and sugar to taste to a half pint of heavy whipping cream. Beat with mixer on low speed until cream thickens and forms peaks when beaters are lifted—about five minutes.

Offer high-energy bars as snack foods. These high-calorie bars are nutritionally balanced and available in many flavors. Find them at health food stores or in the nutrition section of your supermarket.

DO FOODS TASTE STRANGE?   The elder's sense of taste can be altered by a change in medication, by medical treatments or by illness. Once you have ruled out these causes with the help of a physician, ask the doctor to approve one or more of these ideas:

- Reduce strange tastes by having the elder drink more water over the course of the day.
- Clean dentures or teeth daily using some hydrogen peroxide on a swab. Rinse. Be certain the elder also cleans the tongue and gums. A visit to the dentist may be in order.
- Add beer, wine or mayonnaise to gravies and sauces to enhance flavors. Alcohol evaporates during cooking.
- Serve foods at room temperature or cold.
- If the complaint is bitterness or sour taste, increase sweet food consumption. Include things like candied yams, candied sweet potatoes, brown sugar and orange juice on carrots, sweet-and-sour sauces on chicken, pork or beef, Harvard beets and fresh sweet fruits.
- If the complaint is that the food is too bland, remember that taste sensations are sometimes diminished with age. Increase spices and flavorings. Add more garlic, rosemary, dill, sage and onion if the elder likes their flavors.

Dealing With Specific Complaints

PAIN   There are all sorts of pain, from sharp to dull, throbbing to aching. Pain comes from many sources, from a pulled muscle to disease. Regardless of the type and cause, pain is always a signal that something is wrong.

Pain is invisible, though its effects are not. It is impossible to know the exact intensity of someone else's pain. Each person's tolerance is different, and the sufferer can't pass the feeling itself to the listener, but can only describe the sensation in words..

Chronic pain is one of the most debilitating experiences. Any pain can be physically tiring, and chronic pain doesn't go away. Experiencing pain on a constant or semi-constant basis saps energy and enthusiasm for living.

Always check with the primary-care physician first before trying any treatment, including both medication (even aspirin) and physical methods (as discussed below). Be aware that some doctors feel that medication should always be kept to a minimum, while other believe that stopping the pain is of primary importance.

Many people in pain apologize for their condition. This can easily lead an elder to give up because of feeling so limited. Encourage the elder to take advantage of the moment. If the person feels good enough to do a cherished activity for five minutes, focus on the five minutes rather than the twenty-three hours and fifty-five minutes they were not able to perform the task.

The intensity of pain varies from hour to hour and day to day. Remind the elder that not being able to do something at this particular moment doesn't mean it cannot be accomplished later.

When the elder refuses invitations and entertainments because of pain, encourage both honest and positive thinking. "I can't handle doing that today, but I am sure I can tomorrow." Many times the anticipation of looking forward to something later will help make it easier to accept that it can't be done right at the moment.

When something like this is planned, encourage rest beforehand. Check with the doctor for any instructions or medication the person might need to help them handle the activity with more comfort.

Be aware that a person in pain has many emotional reactions to the condition and to the effects of the medication used to alleviate it. Anger, depression, fear and guilt are just some of the more common reactions. Imagine for a moment the frustration, and sometimes embarrassment, that accompanies having to continually explain why you can't do something. This situation causes many elders to withdraw from social interaction. If this is happening to your elder, contact the primary-care physician. You may be offered a referral for counseling, therapy or a combination of the two with the addition of a mild mood elevator and a different pain medication.

Treating Pain With Heat or Cold Applications of heat, moist heat, and cold to the affected area can help reduce pain. Heat and moist heat can be applied through a special heating pad available at most drugstores and medical supply houses. Cold applications can be provided with an ice pack or with ice cubes in a sealed plastic bag, wrapped in a towel.

Also available at most drugstores and medical supply houses is an inexpensive flexible plastic pack that is filled with gel and sold under a variety of names. Because it is flexible, it contours to the painful area for better heat or cold distribution and is more comfortable to lie on than ice cubes.

Stored in the freezer for cold application, the bag never becomes fully hard, just very cold. The same bag can be heated in the microwave on low or placed for a short time in boiling water that has been removed from the heat. Directions will come with the bag.

Whether using a homemade pack or a commercial one, *never* apply the pack directly to the skin, for either hot or cold application. Wrap it in a towel and apply.

The body will adjust itself to the heat or cold in about twenty minutes. Remove the pack or pad after this time. You can reapply the pad or pack in about twenty minutes. The standard rule is twenty minutes on, twenty minutes off. Be aware that some doctors are more conservative and with cold treatments recommend a maximum of six minutes.

Depending on the reason for the pain, a doctor may order alternate applications of heat and cold. In general, heat is to relax muscles, and cold is to reduce inflammation.

Exercise programs and range of motion regimens can also reduce pain and delay or prevent the condition's worsening. Check with the doctor or therapist.

Treating Pain With Medication Medication is effective for pain control. Again, you must check with the primary-care physician before giving any type of medication, even those sold over the counter without prescription.

If the pain is not handled by the dosage prescribed, DO NOT give more without talking to the doctor first. All pain medication works, but how effective it is depends on the patient's system. What works for one person will not necessarily be tolerated by another. Also keep in mind that different medications work faster—or slower—than others.

Matching the correct pain medication to the person, analyzing the drug's interaction with other medication the elder is currently taking and keeping the side effects (constipation, drowsiness, nausea, etc.) at a manageable level is often a trial-and-error proposition. It's important that you pay close attention.

An elder's body may build up a tolerance to pain medication, so the doctor may switch types to prevent having to give a higher and higher dosage of medication.

If the elder is terminal and severe pain is an issue, doctors should adjust the pain medication type and dosage to ensure the elder has a pain-free existence during the time remaining. If the primary-care physician is not willing to medicate for pain prevention in a terminal case, ask for a referral to hospice services. They will do everything necessary to assure your elder of pain relief.

If the pain is not handled effectively by medication, discuss with the doctor the possibility of pain blocks. The effectiveness of this procedure depends on where the pain is located, what is causing it and the skill of the anesthetist. The basic procedure takes about twenty minutes and involves injecting a type of anesthetic into particular nerve junctions to prevent the transmission of pain signals to the brain. One of the most common sites for injection is the spinal column. The duration of the pain block varies from patient to patient, lasting anywhere from a week to six months. The reason for pain will also affect its duration. Pain blocks are *not* a cure; they simply lessen or prevent pain from diseases and/or injuries.

Elder Participation in Pain Control The elder can do a number of things to actively participate in managing pain.

Have the elder describe as clearly as possible the types of pain he or she is experiencing. Write this information down and note the time along with the frequency of recurrence. Again, it's important to note any side effects the elder relates regarding pain medication. All this information, when given to the primary care physician, can be used in further diagnosis of the cause (it could be a worsening of the present condition or the beginnings of a new problem) or indicate a dosage or prescription change.

Encourage the elder to concentrate on something other than the pain. Many people find that their pain seems to lessen if they become engrossed in a book, game or movie. What's happening is that the person is being distracted rather than concentrating on the pain.

Your elder may benefit from such methods of pain control as biofeedback or self-hypnosis. Their effectiveness depends on a number of factors, including the elder's being willing and able to learn and use the techniques. Ask your primary physician about a referral to a pain control center. Remember to check insurance coverage and treatment costs.

Encourage activities that do not stress the painful area. (This excludes doctor-suggested therapies used to increase mobility and lessen pain over the long term). A person with painful hands may not be able to do fine crafts work but may enjoy walking. Someone with a spinal problem may not be able to walk for long periods but can enjoy games, puzzles, crafts, and so on.

Ask the elder to be specific when saying he or she cannot do something because of pain. If you can identify *how* the pain interferes with the activity, you may be able to adapt the activity to work around the elder's problem.

One man loved to travel around his state visiting friends. A spinal injury made sitting in a car long enough to travel a hundred miles agony. In addition, the stiffness that came on from sitting made it difficult to walk, and the pain put a further damper on his visits. Rather than end his passion for traveling, he and his wife sought a solution. Since she drove on the trips, the doctor prescribed a painkiller and muscle relaxant. He advised a rest stop every thirty minutes when the husband would get out of the car, do some mild stretching exercises and walk a bit. His wife also made additional pillows to use as cushions and to allow for comfortable repositioning in the reclinable seat. The man was still limited in what could be done, but with those few easy steps he wasn't completely denied. Encourage the use of aids to get around disabilities. See chapter 9, especially "Miscellaneous Aids," for specific suggestions.

Chronic Joint Pain Chronic pain is a pain that doesn't go away. A common cause in the elderly is arthritis or another joint stiffening problem. Some diseases can also cause chronic pain. The person may be able to find relief for symptoms without taking more pain medication. As always, talk to the primary-care physician before trying the ideas presented below. Some may be useful in managing other kinds of chronic pain as well.

The elder may benefit from losing excess weight (slowly). Excess weight puts more strain on stiff joints.

Exercise, in particular a water exercise class, may be useful. Pain is reduced in the water, and the body is more buoyant, so the elder has more range of motion with less pain. Yoga stretching exercises may increase flexibility. Yoga and water exercise classes are available at many YMCAs, YWCAs, colleges and health clubs.

Applications of heat and cold as described above may help.

Try heat and eucalyptus ointment. Eucalypta-Mint is a thick oil-based product, suitable for both rheumatoid and osteoarthritis. Apply the product to the affected joint and wrap in plastic wrap. Moist heat can be applied by an additional wrap of a warm wet towel. For hands or feet, apply the ointment and soak in warm water. Eucalypta-Mint is available from Therapeutic Supply and Services Company, 1924 Cliff Valley Way, Atlanta, GA 30329.

Many people feel stiff in the mornings. Your elder may benefit from giving muscle ointment before going to bed at night and from exercising hands, arms, feet and legs before getting up in the morning. A warm shower helps loosen arthritic joints.

Help your elder reduce stress. Learning to relax helps mental attitude. A person who is tense mentally also tends to tense up physically. Soothing music, as well as meditation and other techniques learned in classes and through books and tapes, can reduce stress. Even on a good day, things should be done in moderation. A person who overdoes it will likely pay for it the next day in stiff muscles and sore joints. On the other hand, a bad day shouldn't be used as an excuse to do absolutely nothing. If muscles and joints aren't used at all, eventually mobility will decrease until the condition is permanent.

Some people have reported pain relief in specially designed flotation tanks, also known as sensory deprivation tanks. The principle is based on stress reduction. It appears that as the body, mind and muscles relax, endorphins, the body's natural painkillers, are released. There are two hundred centers around the country that have floatation tanks. For more information contact the Floatation Tank Association, P.O. Box 1396, Grass Valley, CA 95945, or check with a local clinic that offers pain control and stress reduction therapies.

CONSTIPATION   Constipation can be the result of pain medication, disease, not enough fluid intake, poor diet, changes in diet or lack of exercise. Like any other medical problem, this one needs a physician's attention. The doctor should find out what is causing the problem and try to correct that situation. For example, if it's determined that constipation is probably being caused by a certain medication, the doctor may give the elder a different one.

Depending on the cause in your elder's case, and on dietary or other restrictions that have to be taken into account, the doctor may recommend "natural" treatments for constipation. These usually involve changing the diet to include more roughage (often with bran, fresh fruits—especially grapes, raisins, prunes and prune juice—and multi-grain breads) and increasing exercise.

Sometimes a liquid fiber supplement is recommended. However, these can cause bloating and gas in some people. You might want to try a product called Life Cleanse II +. It is made from natural substances and works gently and reliably without unmanageable side effects. The product mixes with juice or other liquids and is available with or without added sugar. To get the product or receive more information, contact Lifestyle International, Inc., 1017 15th Street Northwest, Ardmore, OK 73401.

If the problem continues, the next step in the normal course of action is to add stool softeners to the medication routine. This is followed by laxatives if the stool softeners do not work. When laxatives fail, the next step is either suppositories or an enema.

Please note that elders who have a history of bowel problems such as colitis, colon polyps, cancer of the colon, anal fissures or severe hemorrhoids, need specialized care for constipation. Do not use any laxatives, stool softeners, suppositories or enemas without specific directions from the physician.

When selecting an over-the-counter laxative, rely on the doctor, pharmacist or home health practitioner for advice. Normally professionals will select the mildest form that will do the job. This makes it easier on the person's system. Stubborn cases may require a bottle of citrate of magnesia taken orally. This product may work very fast (within twenty minutes) or more slowly. The person using this or any other laxative should stay near bathroom facilities.

If the elder cannot handle the insertion of a suppository alone you will have to help. The easiest way is to have the elder lie on his or her left side with right knee drawn up toward chest. Put on a pair of disposable plastic gloves. Use one hand to firmly part the buttocks and fully expose the anal opening. Gently insert the suppository into the opening. Push gently on the suppository with one finger until the suppository is as far as it will go past the anal sphincter. If you meet with resistance or the elder complains of pain, STOP. There may be a blockage that must be softened before it will remove itself naturally.

The suppository can take ten to twenty minutes to dissolve and do its job. The elder may sit during this time if it is more comfortable. When the urge to defecate comes on, caution the elder not to strain, which can cause internal tears and bleeding if the fecal matter is extremely hard.

An enema is often (but not always) actually two enemas. When using the Fleet brand, the first enema is an oil, which will probably be fully absorbed by the stool. This softens the stool, making it much easier for the elder to pass the fecal material. The second is a cleaning enema, which removes excess oil and encourages the fecal matter to pass. Fleet is a reliable brand, and their products work in conjunction with each other. They are available at drugstores and supermarkets. Follow package directions, and avoid mixing brands.

To give an enema, have the elder lie on his or her side with the top leg drawn up to the chest as far as is possible comfortably. Lubricate the enema's applicator tip and shaft with a small amount of petroleum jelly or mineral oil to ease insertion. Wear disposable plastic gloves. Spread the buttocks with one hand. Insert the applicator nozzle slowly and gently to a depth of about four inches.

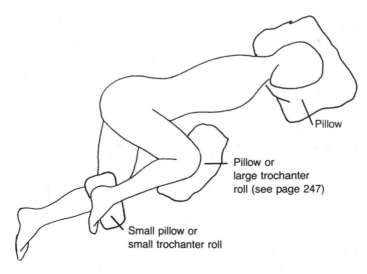

Pillow

Pillow or
large trochanter
roll (see page 247)

Small pillow or
small trochanter roll

Fig. 10-19: Positioning the elder for an enema.

If you meet with an obstruction or the elder becomes uncomfortable, STOP.

Gently empty the applicator bottle of fluid with a steady, even squeeze. Remove. Have the elder continue to remain on his or her side. This should not be a problem for the oil enema. When the second enema is administered, the fluids can become harder to hold. Having the elder remain in this position as long as possible will help the fluids to flow into the intestines and be more effective.

Ask the elder to retain the fluids for the length of time directed on the package. This is usually about twenty minutes. Many elders have a difficult time with this, so ask them to do the best they can. Remember that the urge to defecate may come suddenly. The ambulatory elder may want to sit on the toilet and hold the fluids using the sphincter muscle.

Receiving an enema is one of the most embarrassing procedures an elder can go through. You need to talk to your elder about it and reassure him or her that the procedure is "no big deal." If giving an enema is a problem, discuss the situation with the primary-care physician or home health worker. A professional may have to do the procedure.

As you are actually doing the procedure, talking about what you are doing sometimes help the elder prepare mentally each step of the way. Talking about other subjects during the waiting times will help ease embarrassment. The more calmly and casually you treat the procedure, the easier the elder will accept it.

Elders, being people, usually have a great deal of personal modesty. It is very difficult being unclothed in front of someone, especially one's child. Needing help with something as personal as bathroom functions is traumatizing. Reassure the elder as much as possible. Use a sheet to cover all but the area you must be working on. Allow the elder dignity, especially in this most undignified position. Make certain you and the elder have privacy, with no interruptions, when you are dealing with this delicate situation.

If your elder has a problem with bowel control, or moves slowly so that using a commode chair or getting to the bathroom in time could be a problem, take some precautions. The fear or reality of an accident can be even harder on the elder than the enema procedure itself.

First, remember that under these conditions, fecal material is expelled with force. To make cleanup easier and to prevent staining on furniture, mattress or carpeting, slit two thirty-gallon plastic trash bags so that they open flat like a sheet. Place one end under the elder's hips and upper thighs so that a barrier is created between the elder and the bed linens and mattress. Allow the rest of the plastic bag to drape down over the side of the bed.

Part of what will be expelled is liquid and needs to be absorbed. Some type of absorbent material that you will discard or wash needs to be between the elder and the plastic. A clean old blanket or sheet, or even newspaper, works well.

The carpet needs protection, too. Lay down the second plastic sheet and cover it with newspaper. If you are using a bedside commode, be certain the area between the bed and the commode is covered with plastic and newspaper as well.

For people who are bedridden or who have a difficult time reaching the commode under urgent conditions, have a bedpan handy.

After the procedure the person will need to bathe, shower or have a sponge bath. Pay special attention to areas where the skin folds can trap fecal materials, If a sponge bath will be the cleanup procedure, try using a wipe like the type used when changing a baby's diaper. These are available in most drugstores and many larger supermarkets. Several brands are made with aloe that is very soothing to the skin. Whatever type you select, try to get one without alcohol or with the lowest alcohol content you can find. While alcohol is a disinfectant, it also dries the skin, which in turn can cause skin breakdown leading to bedsores.

DIARRHEA   Almost the opposite problem is diarrhea. This is not only embarrassing, it can become dangerous. If the condition persists more than two days, depending on the severity and the person's overall health, the person runs a risk of dehydration or other problems. Call the primary-care physician for directions.

An occasional one- or two-day bout with diarrhea is usually due to a viral infection, and the best solution is to let it run its course. It is a signal that the body is trying to rid itself of an infection. If you or your elder feels that the diarrhea is not caused by an infection but is related to something else entirely, *call the doctor immediately!*

In certain situations diarrhea is not caused by a virus but is a reaction to specific foods or medications. As adults age, many develop an intolerance for lactose, which is found in milk products. If you suspect a lactose intolerance, have the elder abstain from milk products for a week. If the diarrhea has abated, begin reintroducing milk products in measured amounts and record how the system reacts. Some people have problems with the amount of products while others have problems with the type. For example, they cannot drink milk but can tolerate small amounts of cheese. If it does turn out to be a lactose intolerance problem, you might want to try lactaid products and nondairy substitutes. They are available in most supermarkets in the dairy department. An additive (made from lactase) that helps the body digest milk products is available at most health food stores. You simply open the premeasured capsule and dissolve it in the milk. For more information on lactose intolerance call toll-free 1-800-LACTAID.

Antacids with magnesium can also cause diarrhea in some people. If you suspect this might be the culprit, check with the doctor about switching to an antacid that contains only aluminum hydroxide. This type is less likely to cause the problem but is also reported to be less effective. The physician will tell you how much antacid should be taken, and when.

Ask the doctor to check your elder's medications. Certain antibiotics, lactulose, colchicine, quinidine and many other drugs can also contribute to diarrhea.

At-home treatment for diarrhea includes giving lots of fluids, especially cool water. A clear diet is recommended for the first day, full liquids for the second day, and a bland diet for the third. (see "Diet" in this chapter).

Diarrhea can be caused by large amounts of poorly absorbed carbohydrates. Foods that can contribute to this problem include pasta, bread and other wheat products, processed bran, corn, potatoes, oats, apples, prunes, pears and peaches. Soda pop, which is frequently used to settle the upset stomach that sometimes accompanies diarrhea, can also cause gas, which irritates an already overstressed bowel.

If the diarrhea must be stopped so that you can make an appointment that can't be rearranged, ask the doctor if you can use an Imodium product. These are available over the counter in both liquid and capsule form. Imodium works by causing the bowel to contract, which helps delay passage of the feces.

Hydrophilic products such as Kaopectate and Pepto-Bismol may be useful for mild cases. Aluminum hydroxide antacids also have hydrophilic properties that may help.

Soft processed cheese foods like Velveeta, sharp cheeses like sharp cheddar and Swiss, bananas, barley and carob powder have been used to reduce diarrhea's symptoms by binding the bowel. They do nothing to eliminate the cause.

BEDSORES   Bedsores are also known as pressure sores and decubitus ulcers. These skin ulcers can appear in as little as two hours. They are caused by unrelieved weight (pressure) on body parts and/or poor circulation. If the sores are not treated immediately, they become quite painful and can become infected. Severe cases can require hospitalization and can occasionally cause death. In all instances, it takes much longer to clear a decubitus ulcer than it takes to get one.

In the first stage, a shiny red spot appears on the skin, Many times this spot will lack sensation. In the second stage, the skin opens. It may or may not ooze or "weep" (pass clear fluid). In the third stage, the skin cracks open, oozing blood and/or fluids. Dead black tissue may appear at the edges of the wound. There is usually a foul odor. The dressing usually needs to be changed at least once a day. In other words, the situation is already becoming serious. By the fourth stage the ulcer has deepened to the bone. Complete rebuilding of the tissue is required. Surgery is sometimes necessary.

A pressure sore can appear anywhere, but certain bony places on the body are more likely to develop the sores first: shoulder blade, buttocks, coccyx (tail bone), elbow, back of the head, ear, hip, knee, ankle and heel. Pressure to these areas from sitting, lying, medical devices, even bedclothes, can cut off blood circulation, and the skin begins to die because it is not being nourished.

People who are more prone than others to develop sores include:

- Those who are bedridden or wheelchair-bound for long periods
- Those with circulation problems
- Those with sensation losses
- Those without proper hygiene or who are incontinent
- Those who are diabetic
- Those who are immobilized due to wearing medical appliances or bandages or being in traction devices.

Before anything else, remove pressure from the affected area. Call the doctor or the home health nurse. Because of the potential seriousness of this condition, it needs prompt medical attention and directions for home treatment.

There are also some home remedies that you can use (but *always* check with your doctor before trying them). One is to apply the gel that comes out of the leaf of an aloe vera plant to the cleaned area, then cover with gauze. Another is to apply a small amount of honey or granulated white sugar to the area.

Prevention Do not allow a bedridden elder to stay in the same position for more than two hours without moving. Help the elder into a new position if necessary. Once the elder is turned into the desired position, you must make him or her comfortable in a way that relieves pressure and allows for good blood circulation. If the elder is lying flat on his or her back, place a pillow under the head

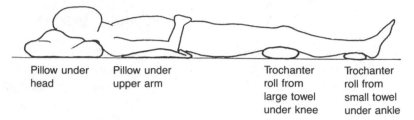

Pillow under head   Pillow under upper arm   Trochanter roll from large towel under knee   Trochanter roll from small towel under ankle

Fig. 10-20: Elder lying on back.

and one under each arm to a comfortable height. Roll two towels. Place one behind the knees and one under the ankles (Fig. 10-20).

If the elder is lying on his or her side, position the shoulder that is in contact with the bed into a comfortable position with the arm extended or bent at the elbow. Place a pillow under the head and another between the knees. Place a rolled towel or rolled soft cloth between the ankles. Prop pillows behind the back to prevent the elder from involuntarily rolling over onto it (see Fig. 10-21).

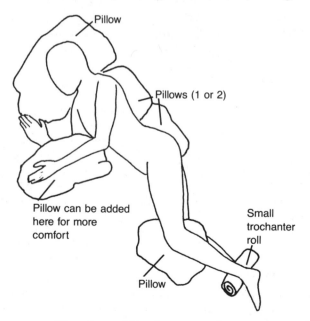

Fig. 10-21: Elder lying on side.

FOLD TOWEL IN THIRDS

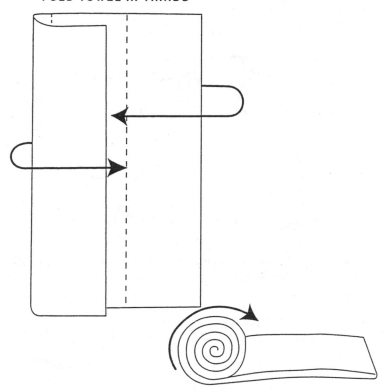

Fig. 10-22: Trochanter roll.

If you are short on pillows, you can make a trochanter roll. Use any size towel. Fold in thirds the long way and roll. The roll can be used in place of a pillow or behind a soft pillow to add stability.

Wheelchair patients need to shift their weight from side to side about every fifteen minutes. Sitting on a specialty pillow (not donut device) that takes the weight off of the tail bone also helps. These pillows are available from a medical supply house.

Check daily hygiene. Bathing helps to stimulate blood flow and helps prevent tissue breakdown. This is especially important in hot weather when bacteria and salts can easily become trapped in folds of skin, which speeds tissue breakdown and infection.

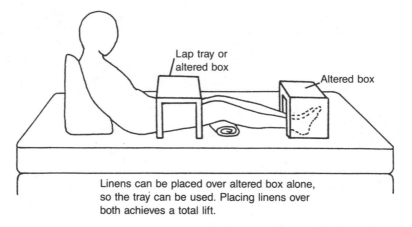

Lap tray or altered box

Altered box

Linens can be placed over altered box alone, so the tray can be used. Placing linens over both achieves a total lift.

Fig. 10-23: Making trays to "tent" the linens.

Incontinent people need to have the urine or feces removed from the area immediately after each episode. Make certain the catheter is clean also.

Keep a close watch on the bedclothes. Food crumbs and wrinkles can cause skin irritation, which in turn can lead to bedsores.

Avoid washing sheets, blankets and anything connected with the bed in harsh detergents that could leave a residue on the fabrics. If you must sanitize them, rewash them in a mild detergent (either a natural product or one made for baby clothes) followed by fabric softener. Use unscented products if your elder is bothered by the smell. Also consider double rinsing before the final spin cycle.

Sheepskin heel and elbow pads, egg crate foam mattresses, air and water mattresses and other products help relieve pressure. Check with the doctor because these items may be paid for by Medicare or other insurance.

To relieve pressure from bed linens, elevate them by draping them over a footed tray placed over the elder's lap. This makes a "tent" of sorts (see Fig. 10-23). You can cut a cardboard box into this tray configuration: Simply remove the flaps from the open end of the box and cut U-shaped holes in two opposite sides large enough to fit over the elder's lap and allow for movement.

INSOMNIA   The need for sleep differs between elders and also depends on the elder's condition. Sleep patterns can be easily disrupted by a variety of things including change in environment and/or routine, medication, pain or anxiety. If the complaint of insomnia persists for more than two days, contact the primary-care physician. In the meantime try the following:

Avoid serving caffeine (found in coffee, tea, certain soft drinks, cocoa and chocolate).

Avoid heavy evening meals. Instead serve the heavier meal around noon and a lighter meal for dinner. Serve a light snack like Jell-O, yogurt or ice cream an hour or so before bedtime.

Discourage stimulating activities before bedtime. This includes watching exciting TV programs, listening to fast-paced music, exercising vigorously and reading exciting books.

Prevent afternoon naps entirely or limit them to thirty minutes. (Note—consult with the physician before doing this. That nap could be so needed and important that insomnia is of no concern in comparison).

Simple stretching exercises coupled with deep breathing can help release tension. Check with the doctor regarding the proper exercises for your elder's condition.

Touch is very relaxing. Gently rubbing lotion into hands and feet can help the person fall asleep. Remember, however, that your goal in this case is to relax, not to stimulate. Use gentle pressure and long strokes only.

Music can be very restful and reassuring. Consider a CD or cassette player instead of a radio. Even those stations that play steady music for long periods have commercial and other interruptions. The music selected generally should be instrumental and of a peaceful nature. A music store can guide your selection. Consider music with nature sounds or "meditation" music, but be aware of the elder's tastes. What is soothing to you isn't necessarily soothing to someone else.

The Elder's Need for Privacy

Even a young child begins to develop a need for privacy. Parents sometimes intrude upon this for good reason; at other times they find it amusing. After the child reaches a certain age, the right to privacy is almost a given. It continues through adulthood. Then suddenly, for many, it disappears again.

"Mom, I *have* to help you take a bath! Now bend over."

The physical reality of aging might mean that Mom bathing alone results in an incomplete cleaning or is even dangerous. If so, there is no other viable choice: The person's privacy must be "invaded" to some degree. The situation is complicated if you are of one gender and the elder needing this care is of the other. To be blunt: It can take some doing to get yourself to scrub the elder's genitals, so much that you might forget that the elder hates it even more than you do.

Respect your elder's dignity, and don't put him or her into situations where it is compromised. For example, would you like to use the bedpan in a room full of people? Would you consider getting up if you knew that your clothing left half your anatomy hanging in the breeze? When you must help your elder with private functions, make sure that you two are alone and the door is closed.

When you assist with hygiene, let the elder do as much as possible. Offer a sheet or towel to cover areas that are not being cleaned at the moment. Let the elder direct the course of action. If necessary, remind the elder that not bathing is *not* an option.

Some elders are highly embarrassed at having a grown child help with bathing or enemas. There are two possible solutions here. First is to talk to the elder and explain that it in no way embarrasses, if this is indeed true (and perhaps even if it isn't). Discover what specifically embarrasses the elder about the needed procedures. It may be something that you can overcome. For instance, a father might be embarrassed by having a daughter bathe him, just as a mother might cringe at the thought of having her son do the same; having a spouse (someone of the same sex as the parent) help with the function instead may solve the problem. The second solution is to have the primary-care physician or home health nurse arrange for an aide to help with this chore.

Like anyone else, at times your elder will want you to join in a conversation and at other times will want conversations with others to be private, even if they tell you all about it later. A telephone in the elder's room will allow him or her to talk privately with friends and relatives. Something as simple as the caregiver's closing the door, or even leaving the room, when a visitor comes adds to the sense of privacy.

Balancing your protection of the elder's privacy, of course, must be your careful judgment of the elder's condition, and your even more careful handling of the situation. An elder whose mind is completely intact deserves all the privacy he or she deserved before caregiving was needed. One who is becoming prone to difficulties, mental and physical, deserves a degree (as little as possible) of monitoring. It's sad to say that some relatives could try to coax the elder into making a new will, or otherwise take advantage. Far more common are the well-meaning visitors who simply don't recognize that the 2:00 P.M. nap really is important.

The Elder's Need for Touching

Everyone needs to be touched. A warm, gentle, loving touch conveys caring and empathy. It also feels good. Holding a hand, a gentle hug, simply stoking a face can communicate support and love more clearly than words. Research has indicated that people who are rarely touched frequently have higher levels of anxiety than people who are often touched.

As elders age, they face an increasing number of problems. As their self-esteem lowers, they need even more reassurance. Touch is one way to provide this. Even elders who have been physically undemonstrative in the past may welcome a hug now, especially if they are somewhat isolated due to communication difficulties, physical disfigurement or emotional problems such as anxiety, depression or fear. Those elders who are confused or uncommunicative can sometimes be reached best through touch.

If you are wondering if your elder will accept your touch, try this approach. Sit close, facing the elder. Maintain eye contact if possible. Smile. Think warm, loving thoughts about the elder. Those thoughts will show in your face, and even an uncommunicative elder will be able to read them. Slowly reach out and gently stroke or hold the elder's hand. If the elder does not pull back and is physically able to, he or she has accepted your touch.

Massage is an extension of touch. The simple act of gently massaging lotion into the skin feels wonderful to the recipient. It also stimulates blood flow, nourishes dry skin, provides passive exercise to muscles and helps to prevent bedsores. And it is a nonthreatening form of touch when used properly and appropriately. If you are contemplating this form of beneficial touch for your elder, you can learn the techniques from many fine books available through your bookstore and library. Keep these points in mind.

1. Always check with the elder's primary-care doctor first. There are certain physical conditions that preclude the use of massage except by therapists or other professionals.

2. Never massage a person who is in pain.

3. Never massage a person who recently had surgery, infections or hemorrhages. Never massage a person who suffers from clotting disorders or has hypertension.

4. Never massage an elder who feels uncomfortable about it.

ELEVEN

Emergency Warning Signs

Most people who become at-home caregivers have little or no medical background. Elder-care situations can change drastically and without warning. Whenever there are changes in an elder's condition that concern or alarm you, *call the doctor immediately!* If the situation appears to be life-threatening, *call 911 immediately!*

Don't hesitate. If you feel reluctant, keep in mind that the doctor is your employee. You are paying, often substantially, for that expertise. Your tax dollars go to pay for emergency services. These people are there for a reason, which is to help. Although it's not appropriate to make such a call when there is no emergency, it's just as inappropriate *not* to call when you suspect that the situation warrants it.

The purpose of this chapter isn't to make you a medical expert, nor even to offer medical advice. Instead it's meant to give you a very basic understanding of how to spot the signs of potential problems. We advise that you invest in a book that covers medical emergencies in more detail. Also, strongly consider taking classes in first aid and emergency medical care such as CPR.

What's Normal?

Each elder is an individual, and each elder's reactions to illness, disease, medication and treatments are individual. Elders do not necessarily exhibit the signs "normally" seen with a diagnosed illness. When you are a caregiver, you will have countless hours to observe your elder, their reactions to medications or disease and the subtle signals that mean "something" is wrong. If you have a hunch something is not right, call the doctor. If you think it's life-threatening, get the person to an emergency treatment facility.

Trudy had a recent history of deep vein thrombosis (DVT) or blood clots. After having been released from the hospital where she had undergone treatment, Trudy was doing well and her doctors were pleased with her progress. Though she was weak from so much enforced rest, she was able to walk on her own and did most things for herself.

"Mom and I were watching an old movie on television," said Marie, her daughter. "I looked over at her and she appeared 'off.' I don't really know how else to describe it. I asked her how she felt and she said fine. I assumed I was overreacting. I'd also been told that when you give care for a long time and have had a lot of emergencies, you sometimes anticipate problems needlessly.

"By the time the movie was over, Mom still didn't look any better, though she was cheerful and ate a decent lunch. She didn't have a fever and said she wasn't experiencing any pain in her leg. When I touched her right leg where she had the DVT, it wasn't hot when compared to the left leg. All seemed to be just fine.

"Later that afternoon I took her temperature again, and she told me to quit fussing, but I just couldn't shake the feeling that something was wrong. I discussed it with my husband. He said if I felt that strongly about it, we'd take her to the emergency room.

"Fortunately they weren't swamped, but even so I had a hard time convincing the ER doctor to check for DVT. She pointed out that Mom wasn't showing typical symptoms. I knew that, but told her that Mom didn't always show symptoms. I reminded her that Mom had been in the hospital just three weeks ago with DVT in her right leg. I kept insisting that she check. She finally agreed.

"About ninety minutes later Mom was readmitted to the hospital. One of the scans showed four clots, this time in her left leg. The ER doctor wanted to know how I knew there was something wrong. That's when I found out that 'She didn't look right' is not an acceptable medical diagnosis. But it should be!"

It's easy to overreact in caregiving situations. You are under a lot of stress, especially when there have been many medical problems to handle.

Sometimes the elder may deny that anything is wrong. There are a number of reasons for this. The elder may fear another trip to the hospital. The elder may feel unable to cope with or even survive another ordeal. The elder may not want to face the seriousness of his or her condition. The elder may sincerely be tired of the life he or she is living and may not want any further treatments, feeling they will only prolong suffering. And sometimes the elder is actually not aware of what his or her body is saying. This is fairly common when the elder has been through a prolonged illness; the elder tries to ignore the body and the illness as much as possible. It's a type of denial and even withdrawal.

Whenever you are faced with a questionable situation, gather as many facts as you can to support your idea that *something* is wrong. Learn to look for signs of change. Ask the home health professional to teach you the warning signs for your elder's condition and those related to it. When possible, read books on the appropriate subject. It's not a bad idea to invest in a book that lists medications and their possible side effects. At least ask the doctor or pharmacist.

Keep in mind that each person is different. A medication that "follows the book" in 250 million patients *could* cause serious side effects in others. This is why it is so important for you to become aware. As the caregiver you are an important part of the overall medical team. Remember, whenever you notice significant changes that you have not been warned to expect, *call for help!*

When assessing a medical situation, know what is normal for your elder. The first thing you should know is your elder's temperature. While 98.6 is what everyone *thinks* of as normal, a "normal" temperature is the one a person actually has when he or she is not ill. This temperature can be anything between 95.2 and 99.5. Body temperature also tends to change during the day and can vary substantially due to causes other than disease.

You could take a person's temperature, get a reading of 99.6, and think that the person is running a degree above normal, when actually everything is just fine. At the same time, if the individual has a "normal" temperature of 96, the reading indicates a fairly serious condition. One of the reasons a doctor writes temperature on a patient's chart is to get a record of *that* person's "normal."

How and where you take a temperature also matters. A rectal reading is one degree higher than an oral reading. The reading you would get in an armpit would be one degree lower.

If you have been asked to keep track of blood pressure or respiration, you should also be aware of what is normal for your elder. The same direction applies if you have been asked to keep track of any other kind of measurement, such as urine output or the circumference of an ankle in the case of swelling.

Warning Signs

Once again it is important that you realize that there are no hard and fast rules. It's also important that you not try to diagnose alone. Chest pains might mean indigestion. Assume that, however, and you could be facing a heart attack. A chest pain linked with a pain in the arm is an accepted symptom of a heart attack. This could be the real thing, or it could be something entirely innocent and safe.

Even those who have spent years in school and then a lifetime in practice don't know all the answers. In fact, one of the signs of a good doctor is when that person readily admits to not being quite sure.

FEVER

100° F.—Mild fever.
102° F.—High fever in an elder. *Call physician immediately!*

Fevers often indicate that the body is fighting some kind of infection but can be brought on by a variety of other things. They may be, but aren't necessarily, a sign that something serious is wrong. The rule of thumb is to become concerned when the fever comes on suddenly, if it occurs for no apparent reason, if it reaches

103 or higher, if it is accompanied by shakes and chills or if it lasts a very long time.

Fevers can be lowered at home, but in the case of elder care normally should be only with a doctor's direction. For example, generally do not give aspirin to lower fever unless you have permission from the doctor to do so. Certainly don't plunge the elder into a cold bath or shower. Especially, call the doctor immediately if you suspect that the fever might be from a drug interaction. This is normally indicated if the fever has arisen soon after a new treatment or medication has been given or if the fever is happening in conjunction with other medical abnormalities.

BLOOD PRESSURE   Blood pressure is used as a general and rough indicator of the cardiovascular system and can also help to spot other problems. Depending on the circumstances, you may wish to purchase your own testing unit. Be aware, however, that the "consumer" grade may not be accurate or may not give consistent results. If you get one, it is a good idea to bring it along on a visit to the doctor so that you can compare its readings with those of the doctor's professional equipment.

Blood pressure is a concern if there is (1) a large drop or rise in pressure readings from what is usual for your elder, (2) a major difference between the pressure taken when the elder is sitting up and when lying down or (3) a large rise or fall in pressure readings after giving new treatments or medications.

BODY MOVEMENTS   Changes in the way the body moves can be brought on by a number of things. Your concern usually will involve sudden changes. Once again, knowing what is "normal" will help. This includes what is "normally" expected to happen from treatments.

Gait Watch for uncharacteristic movements such as limping, unsteadiness or balance problems. The person might lean forward or to one side while walking. It is also fairly common for an elder to lean to one side when standing yet to believe that he or she is standing straight. Another problem might be that the arms and legs are out of sync when moving. More serious is paralysis.

Possible causes are malnutrition, stroke, side effects from medication or a new medical problem that may or may not be related to existing ones.

Extremities Watch for involuntary tremors or shakiness in the arms or legs, and particularly in the hands. Toe tapping, finger drumming or any other repetitive movement that indicates that the person has a difficult time being still can also be a sign of trouble.

Contracture has occurred when an arm or leg is unable to stretch to its full extent. Ultimately, this contraction of the muscle shortens the arm or leg and the limb is drawn close to the body. This a major cause of immobility.

Possible causes are medication interaction, stroke, anxiety or a new medical problem.

Facial Changes Facial changes include excessive blinking, out-of-synch blinking (one eye blinks and the other doesn't), no blinking, fixed stare, drooping of one or both eyelids, drooping of one or both sides of the mouth, twitching similar to nervous tic, inability to furrow forehead normally as when frowning, puffing up the cheeks, a sucking motion with the mouth and chewing sounds that weren't made before.

Possible causes are stroke, nerve disorder, medication interaction, mental disorder or a new medical problem.

BREATHING   Become aware of your elder's breathing patterns. Normally a person breathes between twelve and twenty-four times per minute. The quality of breathing, whether it is gentle and noiseless, varies from person to person. Know what is normal for your elder.

Hyperventilation Hyperventilating is indicated by shallow, rapid breathing that can be accompanied by dizziness, faintness, tightness in the chest, anxiety or panic. It usually occurs in elders with a prior history of hyperventilation but can first occur later in life. Most often it is brought on by emotional stress or anxiety. The episode generally responds to emotionally based reassurances, particularly those that help calm the person. Treat as directed by the doctor. If it continues, call for medical help. Hyperventilation can be a symptom of more serious problems.

Shortness of Breath Shallow rapid breathing that looks like hyperventilation but does not respond to reassurances could be a sign of an emergency situation. Take the vital signs if possible and call the doctor or emergency number. This is particularly important if the person has never hyperventilated before or if it continues for more than a few minutes. Keep in mind that it doesn't take long to suffocate, and less for lack of oxygen to cause permanent brain damage.

Among the possible causes are respiratory infection or disorder, emotional disturbance, medication interaction, heart attack or failure, COPD (chronic obstructive pulmonary disease), exacerbation and obesity.

Coughing Coughing can be dangerous for some postsurgery patients, mostly because of the muscular spasm that is part of coughing. It may be a sign of something serious when it is persistent and/or exhausts the person.

Always call the physician if the cough is accompanied by fever or pain, and certainly if there is blood in the discharge or if there is a bloody, yellow or greenish sputum.

Possible causes are respiratory infection or disease, COPD or a new medical problem.

Wheezing Certain medical conditions have wheezing as part of their pathology. If wheezing is unusual for your elder, has worsened or is accompanied by fever, by bloody, greenish or yellow sputum, by difficulty in breathing or by chest tightness, call the physician or emergency number.

DISCHARGES   The flowing of liquid-like substances from the body's surfaces or orifices is called discharge. These may be natural and normal or could be the sign of a medical problem. Abnormal discharges fall into three main categories: bloody, watery (thin and usually semi-transparent) and creamy or thick. There are also a combination of types such as bloody-creamy or bloody-watery. When describing discharge to a doctor, emergency operator or health-care professional, be certain to describe the type, its odor, if any, and where it is coming from.

All abnormal discharges are potentially serious and could need immediate attention. Be aware, however, that some medications have unusual side effects. One might cause excessive sweating, sometimes with an unusual odor. Another could cause the urine to become orange or reddish, leading you to think that there is blood in the discharge.

Bleeding Bleeding is abnormal when it doesn't stop, is occurring for no apparent reason or is happening inside the body.

Of particular concern are patients who are taking blood-thinning medication, such as for clotting disorders, or who are undergoing chemotherapy. A simple cut or bruise can become serious. Often the bleeding is internal and can't be seen at all. Have the doctor or home health practitioner explain the symptoms of internal bleeding to you as it applies in your elder's case.

Any sign of abnormal bleeding requires immediate attention. Call the doctor or your emergency number.

DRY MOUTH   Dry mouth is rarely serious unless it occurs with other symptoms. Call the physician or emergency number immediately if dry mouth is accompanied by shortness of breath, blurred vision, dilated pupils, nausea or vomiting or pale, cold, moist or clammy skin.

EYE AND VISION CHANGES   Sudden vision or eye changes can indicate serious medical problems. If the elder's eyes exhibit a marked change such as a change in the color of the whites, bulging, a sunken or drooping lid, twitching, discharge, a blood spot on the eye, pain or burning, cloudy cornea, remaining excessively bloodshot for more than twenty-four hours, abnormal eye movements (for example, the eyes do not look together at the same time) or discoloration around the eye, call the physician immediately.

SKIN CHANGES   If the elder's skin or the whites of the eyes take on a yellowish cast, it could be a potentially serious symptom of a disorder such as jaundice. This affects the liver, gall bladder or pancreas or comes as a side effect of blood disorders. Unless you've been told to expect it as something normal in your elder, because of disease or medication, call the physician.

The onset of a jaundice condition with other symptoms like vomiting, fever or abdominal pain is almost certainly a medical emergency. Call the physician or emergency number.

SPEECH CHANGES   Changes in your elder's ability to speak can be serious. If you notice slurred words, difficulty putting syllables together, stuttering or a new speech impairment such as difficulty finding and using the correct word, call the physician immediately. Chances of recovery are improved with early treatment.

Possible causes are medication interaction, stroke, high fever or a new medical condition.

DEHYDRATION   Severe dehydration can kill. Elders at risk are those who do not drink enough fluids and those who sweat frequently or severely. Unfortunately, it's not uncommon for elders to reduce fluid intake, and sometimes they do not even exhibit any signs of thirst.

To test for dehydration take the skin on the elder's forearm or forehead between your thumb and index finger and squeeze gently. The skin should return very quickly to its normal position. (Try it on yourself to get an idea of how fast it happens.) If the skin remains in the pinched position or takes an abnormally long time to return to normal after you have released pressure, the elder is very possibly dehydrated.

This situation isn't necessarily an emergency unless it has gone on for some time. Even so, call the physician immediately and follow the instructions. It's possible that all you need do is increase the amount of fluids. It's also possible that the problem is much more serious.

The opposite extreme is taking too many fluids, especially plain water. This can also cause problems such as low sodium.

Signs of a Heart Attack

NOTE: Not all signs need to be present.

- Shortness of breath
- Intense chest pain often described as heavy pressure
- Pain radiating into left arm, shoulder, back or neck, teeth and jaw
- Prolonged pain in upper abdomen
- Fainting episode
- Nausea and/or vomiting
- Intense sweating

A heart attack isn't necessarily fatal. It's possible that a person in excellent health can have a heart attack and not even know it has happened because the symptoms are so slight. That doesn't mean it isn't serious, even in such a minor case. Scar tissue will form, which increases the chances of another heart attack, and its severity. A serious complication following a heart attack can be irregular heartbeat.

As a person ages, the critical nature of a heart attack—and its likelihood—increase. The body can function without food for weeks, without water for days, without air for minutes. But if the heart stops, blood stops. Almost immediately the brain begins to die. Without quick intervention, even if the victim is brought back to life, brain damage can be severe.

This is not a time to be cautious or hesitant. Emergency medical personal realize this even more than you do. They would much rather be called, make the rush to the home and find out it was a false alarm than have someone wait until the victim is already unconscious.

Should You Call an Ambulance?

As stated in the opening, this chapter isn't intended to turn you into a medical expert. There are plenty of books and courses available for this, and you are again advised to at very least take a course in CPR.

In the list below, not all signs need to be present for the situation to be an emergency. As with a heart attack, in many cases just a single symptom is enough to call 911.

- Breathing difficulties
- Shock
- Heart attack symptoms
- Unconsciousness
- Diabetic shock or coma
- Poisoning
- Severe allergic reaction
- Stroke
- Spinal cord injury
- Internal bleeding
- Broken bones
- Major burns
- Dehydration
- Choking
- Any other symptom the elder's physician has warned of as being dangerous to the elder's condition

With the advent of 911 it's rare for a person to call an ambulance directly. The only exception would be if your area doesn't have 911 service, or if that service is temporarily inactive.

It's still wise to understand what an ambulance service is, and especially to understand what is available. Depending on the size of your town, there are usually three types of ambulances available.

A hospital ambulance is dispatched from the hospital, picks up the patient and returns to the hospital. This type of ambulance is usually fully equipped to deal with emergencies. Normally the cost is rolled into the overall care bill if the elder is admitted. If the elder is not admitted to that hospital, you may be asked to pay immediately for services, or the hospital may accept insurances.

Some larger cities have citywide ambulance services that will transport the patient to the hospital of the patient's choice. Usually full emergency services are available. Some expect immediate payment, others will bill insurances, and a few cities offer the services as part of the property tax payment. Check how this service is paid for in your area.

Many larger towns have private ambulance services. The patient is transported to the care facility of choice. The service may or may not offer emergency services and equipment. It may expect immediate payment or may bill insurances.

The amount of training of the personnel handling the service varies. Usually the minimum level is that of an EMT, or emergency medical technician. These people have had the training needed to handle most medical emergencies. With more training and experience the person can be licensed as a paramedic. Although a paramedic is not a doctor, there are some physicians who in an emergency would rather trust their lives to these people than to other physicians. They are specialists in handling such cases.

The question of when to call for an ambulance, directly or through 911, is almost identical to the question of when to call 911. Call for an ambulance if the elder:

• Is unconscious
• May have had a heart attack

- Has breathing difficulties
- Has back or neck injuries
- Is bleeding severely

In some areas ambulance service is slow or of poor quality. If this is true in your area, the primary-care doctor can recommend the most reliable form of transport.

Do not attempt to transport the elder yourself if you are too panicked to drive safely.

If you live in a rural area, a typical ambulance service may be slow, or not available at all. However, there should be a helicopter ambulance available. This service may be called AirEvac, Air Rescue, Flight for Life, or something similar. Emergency air transport services like these also operate in urban areas. Check with police or your doctor in advance of an emergency to get instructions on how to use the service.

TWELVE

Communication

Complete communication is the giving and *receiving* of information. There is a give and a take, a speak and a listen.

Incomplete communication is the root cause of most relationship problems. Self-help books, therapies and courses have addressed the topic of communication skills, yet "We just don't understand each other" is one of the biggest complaints in any relationship today. Children say it about parents, wives about husbands, bosses about employees, brothers about sisters, elders about adult children and vice versa in every case. We all like to think we are good communicators and fair-minded, so how does this happen?

There are a number of reasons. At center is that we are all just human beings and imperfect. We learn things, and we also make mistakes. We have needs and react in certain ways when those needs aren't met. We develop ideas, notions, prejudices, philosophies—in short we develop a personality. This affects how we communicate and also how we interpret the communication of others.

At its best, communication is imperfect. Words convey meaning, but many times the exact meaning isn't there, and other times words are simply not enough to get the idea across. As an old adage suggests, try to describe the color blue to someone who is sightless.

Another ancient story, also using people who are blind, tells of a group of men who find an elephant for the first time and are trying to describe the animal without being able to see it. Each has his own interpretation of what the animal is. One feels the leg and says it's like a tree. The others each describe it in a totally different way, depending on their perceptions and interpretations. All of them are correct in some ways—yet all of them have missed the reality of the elephant in its totality.

Consequently, truly complete communication is nearly impossible. Interpretation is needed, but that means that mistakes can be made. What you *think* the other person is trying to tell you may be correct, may be a close approximation or may be totally incorrect.

Imagine an extreme case. It has been decided that your mother-in-law will be coming to live with you. Perhaps you haven't gotten along all the time in the past, but you want to make amends and you definitely want her to know that she is welcome in your home.

You spend a great deal of time and money to get her room ready. The walls are decorated in her favorite colors. You move some of her furniture and mementos in. You buy a brand-new color TV complete with remote. In one corner you have built a special table and light as a craft center, aware that this will be more comfortable than using the kitchen table, and certainly safer since the children won't accidentally break or damage those crafts. You even have a telephone with a private number installed so she can call her friends and other relatives in privacy. You do everything you can to make her room comfortable and like her own home.

Her reaction to it isn't quite what you expect. What *you* see is an effort to welcome her and to make her feel at home. What *she* sees is that you're trying to isolate her from the family and that she isn't welcome. You got her a TV, and her response is "Am I not welcome to watch TV with the family?" This is stressed more strongly by giving her a place to do her crafting. She has her own phone, which she interprets as you being worried that she might tie up your own phone with trivial, unimportant calls or might run up your own phone bill.

To you, the room has been made self-sufficient for her comfort and to allow her privacy, dignity and independence (and a quiet place away from the noisy grandchildren). Your effort to make the room comfortable is seen by her as proof that you don't want her elsewhere in the house. Worse, you've changed the lock on the door so that you can get in if there is an emergency—a clear sign on your part that you intend to violate her privacy!

Communication has broken down because of misinterpretations. And justified or not, it's something you have to deal with.

Nonverbal Communication

It is said that at least 80 percent of all interpersonal communication is nonverbal. It happens with facial expressions, placement of the arms and legs and the general body posture.

Since birth we have been telling the world of our wants and needs. A baby cries. The world, usually the parents, responds. Mom checks the diaper. It's dry and the baby is still crying. She attempts to feed the baby. It doesn't want food and still cries. She picks the baby up, holds it and walks the floor while rubbing its back. The baby stops crying.

The child communicated a need without saying a word. The same child might tell you that a particular kind of food is unwelcome by grimacing or spitting it out. As the child grows older it might express the same need to be held not with crying but by holding out its arms. Or it might show anger or fear by tucking the body into a ball in the corner of the crib.

The process continues throughout life and becomes increasingly complex. Often the signals are obvious. Sometimes they're not.

Imagine that you've just told your teenage son that he can't attend an unsupervised party. He actually agrees with you that in this case there just might be trouble. Still, he doesn't *say* "Okay, I'll stay home," he snaps it. He does so with his arms held tightly against his chest. He tells you that he'll spend the evening studying for tomorrow's history test and slams the door to his room.

The words indicated agreement. Even if he'd managed to say them without letting anger get into his voice, the nonverbal aspects clearly show anger.

At the same time it's important to remember that nonverbal signals are often prone to misinterpretation. In an episode of an old TV series the grandparents temporarily move into the home of their daughter. The grandparents have just taken a class in nonverbal communication and proceed to "dump" this on the daughter and grandchildren. One morning the grandmother announces that the eldest granddaughter is angry. Her reasoning is that the girl was holding her arms across her chest when the grandmother wanted to use the bathroom first. The mother explains that it wasn't anger, it was that the girl's robe had no belt to tie it shut.

It's important to pay close attention to nonverbal signals. This can become critical if the elder is suffering from a disease that makes verbal communication less certain or impossible. At the same time, nonverbal signals are easy to misinterpret. This is where your personal knowledge of the individual comes into play. The trick is knowing when to accept those signals, and when to realize that they may not be what they seem and then to ask.

Rule 1: Never Assume

Never assume you know what another person wants, thinks or feels. Ask. Never assume another person knows what you want, think or feel. Tell the person.

The rule sounds easy, but it isn't. In order to tell someone what you think, want or feel, you must feel safe in doing so. In this case "safe" means that you are able to state the truth without being punished or ridiculed. "Safe" means there will be no retaliation as a consequence of speaking. "Safe" means you are accepted, warts and all.

To give the truth you have to feel safe. The same is true when you expect to *get* the truth from someone. Imagine that you ask someone "What can I do to make this better?" The person answers, but you don't like the answer, and then you let the person know that you don't. The next time you want honesty from this person, it may not come.

Sometimes it is very difficult to talk straight. Often, for good reasons, we have developed social inhibitors that cause less than honest communication. Every time we try to open up, these social inhibitors ("I may hurt his feelings if I say that") are combined with fears ("If I hurt his feelings, he may not love me anymore"). This produces a mental gag.

When we try to talk straight, sometimes we back off or try to soften what we say, especially when we see that straight talk isn't accepted. Many times this polite softening of backing off allows the space needed to clarify the situation. Other times it simply leaves the other person more confused than ever. It can also leave the other person feeling attacked, defensive, angry and hurt.

Ideally, everyone will be up front and honest with everyone else, while remaining kind—and everyone will be understanding. If that ideal seems to be taking place, be very careful.

Be honest and encourage honesty. Keep in mind, however, that there is a careful balance between "honesty" and "cruelty." Honesty is not a license to say mean, cruel, vindictive things under the guise of truth. There are times when sensitivity is more important than honesty.

Rule 2: Be Clear

"I hate it when you slam the door!"

Most people would agree this is a simple and truthful statement. To a degree it is. It's also something that can be misinterpreted. Look at the wording. "I hate it when *you* slam the door!" The implication is personal, or could be taken as such. The real situation might simply be that the spring that closes the door is too strong for the elder to control, in which case your statement is a reminder of the elder's increasing physical problems.

It started when the elder slammed the door, which brought to your immediate attention that you hate slamming doors. But you didn't say that. Instead you said, "I hate it when you slam the door!" Saying it this way makes it personal. It singles the other person out as being wrong. Furthermore, it could subtly imply that when anyone else slams a door it's okay. No, that's not at all what you meant—it's how it was interpreted.

If you say in a calm voice, "Loud noises, like slamming doors, startle me," you have made the same statement, but you have not accused anyone nor made anyone wrong.

Recognize that communication is imperfect. You can misinterpret and can be misinterpreted. Don't assume that you know what the person is trying to get across, especially when it seems to be negative. Work hard on being clear so that you aren't misinterpreted. Make sure that you are both talking about the same thing and in the same way.

Rule 3: Listen

It takes practice to listen. It also takes an open mind. Most people would rather talk than listen, as though their ideas or opinions are more important than anyone else's. These are the same people who wonder what went wrong when a relationship of any kind falls apart.

Listening is twofold. It means to hear what is being said *and* to understand. Once again, be careful in how you interpret.

Learn to listen to what is said, don't guess at what is meant. Your spouse says, "Having your mother living here really upsets me." If you respond with "Why do you hate my mother?" all you have done is put the person on the defensive. You have made it unsafe for the person to express feelings and needs. Worse, you have interpreted what was said and have not waited to understand.

Try a different approach. "What is it specifically that upsets you?" Now instead of putting the person on the defensive you have simply asked for more information in an effort to get to the root of the problem and hopefully to discover a solution.

At this point you need to do a few more things. You need to show that you are indeed listening and interested in what the person has to say. Assume a comfortable, casual posture. Folded arms, clenched fists, frowns, hands on hips and similar signals telegraph that you are not ready to listen and that it's possible you are ready to get in a few zingers of your own in defense of your mother.

When you truly listen, you might find that what your spouse is really trying to communicate is "I haven't seen you alone for more than ten minutes in the last three weeks." It's fairly obvious that your mother is not directly to blame, lousy scheduling is.

From your point of view, you're harried, never doing fewer than three things at once. Now here's this fully grown, perfectly capable person trying to pull you in yet one more direction. You'd both agreed this situation probably wouldn't be easy, and you'd both promised to be understanding. Laying guilt over time is definitely not being understanding. *He (She)* should be more understanding. *He (She)* should be trying to help you. *He (She)* should...

Stop! You're not listening, you are interpreting again and being defensive. Are you so certain that a guilt trip is being laid? Is it possible that the person has discovered that a particular need is stronger than estimated when this arrangement was agreed to? Could the person be afraid that he or she is no longer important to you? There are lots of possibilities, but you won't find out unless you ask.

"You know, you're right. We haven't spent much time together, and I miss you. Can we talk about what we can do about the situation?" This response shows that you listened. It shows understanding of and agreement with the other person's feelings ("You know, you're right"). It acknowledges the problem ("We haven't spent much time together") and communicates an emotional tie to the other person ("I miss you"). This approach unites the two of you in a common cause and even begins to cure the actual problem.

Rule 4: Paraphrase

Because understanding another person can be difficult, don't take chances with it. You can ask a question to help clarify. The other person may not have expressed himself or herself exactly the way he or she wanted to, and this gives the person another chance.

"You seem to be devoting so much time to your mother and her problems."

Your response might be "You're saying that we need more time together, is that right?"

"Not exactly. The amount of time isn't really so important. We knew this would be difficult and we probably would have to make do with whatever time we could get. What I object to is feeling so shut out that I can't reach you."

Paraphrasing has opened a deeper problem than was first observed and allowed the person to express the feeling behind the situation.

Rule 5: Address the Feeling

People work from emotion. Most people can understand anything intellectually, but it doesn't change how they feel. When push comes to shove, it is emotion that drives a person to behave in a particular manner. If you can find a way to satisfy the emotional need in a positive manner, most problems will be solved.

"What I object to is feeling so shut out that I can't reach you."

"What makes you feel shut out?"

"We never talk the way we used to. When I come home, you ask me how my day was, but I don't think you really want to know. When I ask you how your mother is doing, all I get is a short answer and you're gone again. I don't know what you're feeling or what's really happening with your mother."

Before you answer, take a moment to think about it. Don't simply dismiss the matter. Feelings are not governed by logic, and though they may be difficult to quantify and measure, they are real nonetheless. Something is obviously happening that brings this feeling to the forefront of the person's emotions. You may be contributing to the feeling by your actions, or maybe not. However, you will not improve the situation until you really look at it.

If you say to the person, "There is no reason for you to feel that way" or "You shouldn't feel that way," in essence what you're saying is "You're *wrong* to feel that way."

Statements that begin, "You ought," "You should," "You have to" or "You must" are commands that set up opposition. They are ways of correcting behavior (which means that you think the person is wrong, otherwise the behavior wouldn't need correcting) and of setting up control. Telling someone that he or she must or should behave in a specific manner or feel a particular way sets up resistance. You have told the person he or she doesn't have a right to feel what the person feels, or that your feelings (or someones else's) are more important. You have reinforced the negative while telling the person that it is not safe to express himself or herself. Instead of opening communication, you've closed it.

Before you speak or react to a situation, consider the next rule.

Rule 6: Show Empathy

To understand another person's feeling, put yourself in the person's place. This is empathy (not sympathy). Try to look at yourself, your actions and the situation through the other's eyes. If you can do this without holding onto "But *I'm* right!" (which automatically makes the other wrong), you have a better chance to come to an understanding that satisfies both your needs.

We all have expectations. When someone doesn't live up to ours, we feel anger and frustration. The only way to lessen the feeling is to build tolerance. Empathy does this automatically. If you have looked at the situation and can find no way to see the other person's point of view, let the person show you. Understanding and empathy must be communicated; they can never be taken for granted. None of us are mind readers.

"You have a right to feel the way you do. I have some difficulty seeing your point of view, but if you'll explain it to me, I will try to understand."

Rule 7: Respond

An old, and very sad, story tells of a man sitting in a bar (or somewhere else, depending on the version), frustrated after a fight with his wife. He has no idea what is wrong. He came home to find her crying, then screaming at him. When he asked what was wrong her reply was "If you don't know I'm certainly not going to tell you!" Then she slammed the bedroom door and locked it.

Whether your view of the problem is positive or negative, the person you are communicating with is owed a response. The person took a big risk in letting you know how he or she feels. The person put his or her emotional well-being on the line, and for most people this requires more courage than facing an IRS audit. Always let the other person know your position, your feelings and suggestions for a solution. Express yourself in a kind and gentle manner. Anger only makes a bad situation worse.

"You're right. I haven't been listening very well when you tell me about your day, and I dread it when you ask about mine. You agreed to try this new living situation, but only on the condition that it didn't ruin our lives. I was afraid if I told you everything that goes on, you'd insist it isn't working and force a change. I thought I was disrupting your life less by not talking about the problems."

Rule 8: Reach an Agreement

The goal of communication is mutual understanding. In personal relationships we have to push understanding until a mutually workable agreement is reached when there is a problem that must be solved. A well-adjusted couple can agree to disagree on whether or not a mayor is doing a good job running the town, and their relationship is unlikely to be harmed by their differing opinions. When the issue is important, where their lives together are affected by a decision, as it is in elder care, a consensus must be reached.

Reaching an agreement will be difficult if the couple view themselves as adversaries. "I'm right, you're wrong" has no place in a discussion. When the other person has objections, don't ignore them. Instead, ask for cooperation in considering all solutions, yours and the other's. You are then working for a solution that fits everyone's needs.

Changing your stance on an issue does not mean you have lost some type of battle. It means that you are mature enough to see that there are two people in a relationship and that you each have different needs. These needs must be met if you are to have a healthy happy life together. Both parties have to give so that both parties will gain. It is never a fifty-fifty proposition 100 percent of the time. Sometimes one will do most of the giving on an issue. On another issue the other will do more giving. If you're keeping score, you need a therapist.

Finding Maturity

The rules work if they're consistently applied. Naturally they work better if both people are using the same techniques. If even one of you begins applying them, the other will tend to learn them as well because you are teaching by example. If the others involved in your relationships like the clear message you're sending, and most will, they'll learn to use the rules, too.

Learning to communicate using these eight rules may be easier between you, your spouse and children than between you and your parent(s), but it is always dependent on personality and maturity level. We will deal with the special problems of communication between parent and adult child later in this chapter and again in chapter 13.

Even a young child can be taught to identify his or her feelings and to express them acceptably. The problem begins when children are taught not to acknowledge and express certain feelings. No one has to come out and say "It's not okay for you to show anger." The child could learn to suppress anger by the way a parent responds to it. If that response is sufficiently traumatic, either physically or psychologically, the child knows it is not safe to express anger and develops a social inhibitor.

This inhibitor will continue until it is consciously replaced. Many people never replace or modify the inhibitor, which is why there are communication problems when the person tries to express anger as an adult. It's also why so many children and adults express things like anger and frustration inappropriately. In many cases, it's all they know.

Inhibitors learned in childhood affect every area of the emotions. Abandonment, fear, love, joy, anger and sadness are only a few of the more readily identifiable ones. The inhibitors are incorporated into the personality, making one person controlling and another timid or nonexpressive. When you deal with communication you are also dealing with personalities. These personalities began their development in childhood.

No one got out of childhood unscathed. Even if the parents were absolutely, totally and completely perfect (impossible—they're just humans, too) society will have taken its toll. And this continues into adulthood. To gain the most success from these communication techniques, a person has to be willing to face himself or herself and injustices maturely. Sometimes this requires the help of a professional. Other times a person is capable of reflection and building a new, mature attitude about the incident(s) alone or with the help of a spouse or good friend.

Maturity is not something that automatically comes with age. This is why a relationship with your parent can be extremely tangled. Maturity is a state in which pettiness and past injustices must be left behind in favor of forgiveness and new beginnings.

People, including elders, do not mature at the same rate. Indeed, some elders never mature to the point that they can allow their fully grown child adult status. Some adult children refuse to see their parents as individuals; as a result the elder remains locked in a mental box labeled "parent" long after the parental mode should have ended.

To stay balanced in all your relationships, including caregiving, you need to go that extra mile in the area of maturity, if only for your own peace of mind. It's difficult to accept responsibility when the other person seems only to want to blame unjustly; to let go of the past when the other one only wants to hold on tight; to relate as equals, one to another, while the other insists on role relationships like parent-child; to have self-esteem and trust while another demands constant reassurances and plays manipulative games. Maturity is knowing you can only control yourself and your own responses.

Maturity also means taking risks with yourself. It is a risk to talk straight about your own feeling and needs, especially if you haven't done it before. You may be afraid that you will be rejected, that the other person will think you are being a child or, worse yet, laugh at you. But without this risk to your ego, you build an invisible wall that closes everyone out—a wall behind which your needs go unmet.

Your Children

Children also have needs that go unmet. Caregiving situations can drastically affect your children. The younger ones especially may not know how to communicate these effects. They may not feel comfortable talking about what's going on, or they may not be able to identify the source of their discomfort. Children, like adults, may express their unhappiness in ways that do not obviously relate to the cause of the problem, but the changes in their behavior indicate something is wrong. Watch for these warning signs:

- Disturbed eating or sleeping patterns
- Withdrawal from family life or favored activities
- Changes in temperament (a boisterous child becoming much quieter or an easy-going child becoming more argumentative)
- Reversion to outgrown behavior patterns such as bedwetting
- Clinginess where independence was sought before
- Inappropriate behavior
- Sulkiness or moodiness
- Problems at school or with friends
- Fights, either verbal or physical

It's your job to keep a close eye on the children. What you do, and don't do, can affect them for the rest of their lives. Often all that's needed is ten minutes to cuddle while reading a story, or five minutes to share a cup of hot chocolate. Perhaps they can help prepare lunch.

It's important to remember, however, that children are young, not stupid. Honesty is more important than ever. Don't be falsely condescending. Even young children will pick up on this. They might accept it, if that's all they can get, but they won't like it any more than you do.

Just what you do and how will depend on the age of the child. Whatever the age, keep in mind that children, teens, adults and elders are all human beings, not different species.

Communication Breakdown

"We grew apart" has to be one of the saddest excuses for a failed relationship. It means that two people stopped communicating, stopped risking their egos from fear the other would reject their new thoughts, dreams, needs and wants. They stopped trusting that the other person would want to grow with them. As life deals you a new set of circumstances, different needs come to the fore and old issues need to be resolved again.

The old issue of lack of communication came up again for Marian and Steve. Steve is a quiet, thoughtful man from an undemonstrative family. Marian is a highly verbal individual who is prone to discussing issues and feelings to discern the reasons behind them. During their courtship and the first few years of marriage Steve's quietness occasionally bothered Marian, who needed to exchange ideas and points of view on a variety of subjects. Steve admired Marian's ability to express what was on her mind and learned to open up more as their relationship grew. Through twenty-six years of marriage they had developed a comfortable way of being together. Steve became a good listener, adept at discerning what Marian wanted from her frequent verbal dissertations. Marian was delighted with the way Steve always seemed to know what she wanted, never realizing she was actually telling him.

Steve always liked Marian's parents, especially her mother, Phylis. He had gotten along well with her father, David, despite his sometimes biting wit.

Tragedy struck. A car accident took Phylis's life and left David partially disabled and emotionally devastated. As time passed, Marian assumed more and more care for her father, who insisted on remaining in the house where he and Phylis had lived, though he was too frail to cope with managing alone. A series of housekeepers were driven off by David's bitter and complaining attitude. Marian grew quiet. Insomnia drove her from the bedroom night after night, and Steve's attempts at comforting her failed.

"I came home from work one day to find her curled up in our bed, crying. David had been railing at her again. I didn't know what to say anymore. I didn't know how to comfort her. I wanted to hug her, but she's rejected me so often that I didn't want to risk that again. So I just walked out of the room and let her cry. I feel awful about that, but I didn't know what else to do. She won't tell me what she wants. If I knew I'd do it."

Steve and Marian researched every possibility for David's care, from a nursing home to bringing him to their own home. David refused to be moved. When Steve suggested it, the result was a big fight, first between David and Steve, then between Steve and Marian.

The two who had enjoyed such open communication suddenly weren't speaking. Marian complained Steve just couldn't understand that she loved her father. "Somehow he has changed," she complained. She had the same complaint about her father. "Everyone blames me for everything."

When a serious problem develops in a relationship, it's never solely one person's fault. In this case it would be easy to blame David. It was his stubbornness and caustic personality that caused many of the problems. Or you could blame it on Marian, who became so frustrated that she stopped talking to Steve, and then blamed him for being the one who changed. You could also blame it on Steve for not being more patient, more understanding.

Sometimes it takes the help of a therapist to break the deadlock and get communication started again. If this is where your relationship is at the moment, seek guidance. If your spouse won't go with you, go by yourself. The counselor can help you utilize the best coping methods for your situation.

One-Sided Communication

Sometimes even your best efforts fail. At the beginning of this chapter was the simple truth that communication is a two-way proposition. It requires speaking *and* listening, with both of these used in an honest effort to communicate fully and completely. If you aren't willing to do both, communication will break down. The same is true if the other person refuses.

If this happens, first carefully and honestly examine the situation to see if any of the fault is yours. Could it be that you *think* you're asking for honest input while being guilty of turning that input into a fight?

Second, remember that people often learn by example. Demonstrating your willingness to listen openly and honestly can eventually lead to others around you behaving the same way. This usually means that you have to take the first step and first risk. It also requires that you accept the possibility that it will never work. The other person's social inhibitors may be so ingrained (including some you planted?) that he or she is unwilling to change just because you have.

If you and your spouse have gotten into the habit of hiding your true feelings, and you read this chapter and decide you need to open communication... well, old habits are hard to break.

It's also possible that the other person has built up mental walls over the years that have nothing to do with you and/or that you won't be able to do anything about. At such a time the most you can do is accept it and keep on trying.

Manipulation

After her father, Robert, suffered a massive stroke he came to live with Sondra and her family. Their relationship had always been turbulent. Great affection punctuated with manipulation caused Sondra to leave home at eighteen. Sondra's dream was to earn a degree in business administration. Robert's idea was that she should become a teacher, as her mother had been. In his mind, this was how Sondra should prepare herself for motherhood.

He ridiculed her decision, then refused to help her financially, stopped talking to her for a while and continued to make it clear in the following years that he didn't approve. The situation improved a little after she married Jeffrey and had children, but he still withheld his approval. Sondra also complained that he still treated her as a nine-year-old. In fact, he'd given more respect to Sondra's children than he did to her.

After he moved in, his efforts to manipulate her increased. He used all the same "techniques" and now added guilt to it. She tried to reopen communication with him, tried to share the positive things in her life, but it seemed that the harder she tried, the worse things became. It reached a point that Sondra hated even bringing him lunch.

There are all sorts of ways to manipulate people. Robert tried several. He withheld the reward of helping financially ("Carrot and Stick") when she wouldn't give up her dreams. Later he refused to speak to her, then treated her badly ("Withholding Approval") and then used guilt.

He could have used competition ("Your sister always..."), comparison ("My friend Helen has a son who calls her every day"). The "Prove It" method demands that you perform a certain task ("If you loved me, you'd...").

Manipulation is almost invariably destructive to relationships and to all the people involved, including the person doing the manipulating. The only way to stop being manipulated is to take responsibility for your own choices. In other words, when someone says, "If you loved me you'd visit me more often," ignore the manipulation. Look at the request.

If you *want* to visit more often, you can deny the manipulation by ignoring it, since it doesn't apply to your choice. "I'm here now. I do want to visit with you more often. Let's make plans for it, okay?"

If you can't or don't want to agree, take responsibility for your decision and stand up to the manipulator. "I visit as often as I am able. Please accept that I do love you." If you want to state a reason, do so.

If you would be comfortable with a compromise, offer one. "Because I do love you, I visit as often as I can. One thing we can do is talk more often. Why don't we pick a special time every Sunday evening and talk by phone for half an hour?"

In any case, arguing will only cause more problems. Sometimes the only technique you can use is stonewalling. This is where you simply state your position and don't deviate from it. "I simply can't do what you want. Please accept my decision and believe that I do love you." Then change the subject. If the person continues to press the argument, you have two options. You can either listen in silence or give the person a choice. "I have given you my decision."

If you select the choice method, you must back up your word. "I visit as often as I can because I do love you. But your pressing for more frequent visits is ruining the time we do have together. I would rather cut this visit short and leave now than fight with you. Do you want to change the subject or do you want me to leave?"

Competition or comparison is another form of manipulation. This is easy to spot because you are always lacking in the comparison (to whomever—a sibling, friend, or actor/actress on TV). The comparison can be implied, as in "Your brother always brings my favorite chocolates when he visits," or stated, as in "Your sister always asks about my roses and you never do." Either way, it is an attempt to get you to go one better in some area.

The easiest way to overcome this kind of manipulation is to respond calmly and compliment the comparison. "I'm glad my sister shares that with you. It's a special bond between you, like when you and I..." Adding a reminder of something special that you share with the person underscores your relationship in a positive light and changes the subject.

Withholding affection or approval is one of the hardest forms of manipulation to deal with because it is never-ending. You no sooner accomplish one task than another is set. The best thing you can do for yourself is to accept the fact that no matter what you do or how perfect you become, this manipulator will never give you what you seek. Learn to approve of yourself. Learn to accept yourself and what you do. Learn to love who you are, warts and all, because in the final analysis you are responsible for yourself and your actions. You can't change other people's opinions of you, they have to change it for themselves.

Sarah's Story—A Harsh Reality

Sarah was a warm, loving human being with a generous spirit who was loved and admired by her many friends and family. A former university professor, she gained much joy from tutoring children in their studies. To all outward appearances, Sarah was leading a rich, full life. No one realized Sarah's life was turning into a nightmare.

It began with little things. She forgot a name, then it would suddenly be there. Birthdays would slip by unnoticed, something that never happened in the past. Sometimes she had trouble thinking of the precise word she wanted to use in conversation.

Sarah put the problems down to getting older. She compensated by making notes to herself. It worked very well for a while. She no longer forgot what she wanted to say to a friend when she called on the phone.

As the years passed, Sarah began to get worried. Sometimes she would leave her house to have lunch with a friend or to shop, and things she knew seemed strange. She remembered going to the store to purchase a scarf and becoming frightened by the salesclerk. Sarah knew the woman was speaking to her in English, but she couldn't make any sense of it. Even with friends she would lose the point of entire conversations, but because she was socially adept she didn't think most people noticed.

The episodes were sporadic, and Sarah didn't want to talk about these problems to anyone. She feared that they might put her away or treat her like a child when she knew very well she wasn't. So Sarah managed on her own and compensated the best she could.

Her son, Scott, remarked to his wife, "Mother seems to be

slipping a little." Still, it didn't appear to be too serious. Sarah had given up tutoring and much of her social life, claiming she wanted more time for other projects, but was vague as to what those projects were.

Sarah was rapidly becoming terrified. She would wake in the night and for a short while not know where she was. She knew something was dreadfully wrong. She felt her mind slipping away. There were whole chunks of time when she couldn't remember what she'd done. She would reassure herself by going over all the people and things she *did* remember, in hopes that she would keep the memory.

Then Sarah got sick. She was so very tired and frightened. Perhaps a day in bed would put things right. Scott became alarmed when Sarah didn't answer her phone and rushed to her home. He found Sarah with a high fever and mumbling things that didn't make sense. She didn't seem injured, so Scott bundled her into the car for a trip to the emergency room.

Scott was facing a crisis. Sarah faced something quite different. One moment she was home and safe. The next moment was almost like being on an alien world. What was this strange room? Who were all these people? Why were they doing such rude things to her? The things they said and asked her to do made no sense. Of course she could breathe into that stupid bottle, but why should she want to? Didn't they know it hurt to do that? They should know, she had told them. At least she thought she did. Where was her robe? Where was the bathroom? Who put rails on her bed so she couldn't get out?

The doctors told Scott and his wife that Sarah had pneumonia and that it was complicated by chronic obstructive pulmonary disease (COPD), which seemed pretty far advanced. The halluci-nations were either the result of the fever or from the lack of oxygen to the brain cells. They would do further tests as Sarah recovered. However, they should make plans for Sarah's future now because she would need care when she was released from the hospital.

Slowly Sarah got better. The pneumonia cleared up, and most

of the dizziness passed. But the confusion, disorientation and forgetfulness remained and sometimes seemed to be worse. She couldn't understand what had happened to all her things, or why Scott and Connie didn't get her out of this place and take her home where she was safe.

Scott and Connie had spent most days and some of the nights with her, but Sarah simply didn't remember. They were hurt and felt guilty when Sarah accused them of abandoning her. She sounded so confident and sure of herself, just like she always had. Maybe Sarah was right?

People came and went. They all looked the same to Sarah in their white coats. Some were nice, some were brusque, and they all talked. Everyone seemed to want something from her, and usually Sarah tried to oblige. She remembered her social skills. Smile, nod, look people in the eye. They seemed pleased with this, but she didn't really understand what they wanted from her.

Fortunately no one ever asked her to explain or repeat what was said to her. Sometimes she remembered the responses she was supposed to make, and then everybody seemed happy. Why should I care who the president is? Sarah wondered. Personally, I always preferred Mr. Roosevelt.

Scott and Connie were coming today to take her home—home to her favorite chair and the violets blooming on the kitchen window sill. Home where all her things were, where she knew how to function and, most of all, where she was safe.

Scott and Connie were beaming and hugging her. That felt nice. But why had they brought her to their home instead of her own? They said they had told her but she didn't remember. Why were some of her things in this room? Where on earth did they put the rest of her possessions? They said they told her but maybe they lied? Could her things have been stolen while she was held prisoner by those horrid people in the white coats?

Suddenly she was angry. Sarah didn't care what Scott and Connie said. This wasn't her home. She had a right to be in her own home. Her independence was lost, her belongings were gone. Her life was gone. Sarah felt her world crumbling and was overwhelmed by fears she couldn't name.

Sadness engulfed her. She watched life move around her, but often she couldn't make any sense of it. Sometimes old friends came to visit her and talked of things she vaguely remembered. Sarah tried to hang on to these visits like the gold they were, but as often as not they slipped away. Everything seemed so mixed up. It was getting harder to tell today's reality from yesterday's memory.

Sometimes she remembered a person or a place, and it was like a ray of sunshine piercing a fog. A fog that was filled with stirring shapes of unknown dread. When a memory came it was wonderful and she had hope again. The music Connie sometimes played for her sparked flashes of youth. The pictures of her handsome husband in his army uniform holding baby Scott were an oasis of joy in an otherwise confusing world.

Sarah didn't understand why Connie was so mean to her. Of course she knew what a button was and what a zipper was, it was just that her hands didn't seem to know what do with them.

Then came the day when Connie insisted on helping Sarah with her bath. The room was so scary. Sarah didn't trust the water because it always played tricks. It was too hot or too cold, or it wouldn't come when you wanted it to. Sometimes it came too much and it wouldn't stop no matter what you did. The water could kill her just like it did the little girl who lived down the street from her when she was six. Didn't Connie know these things? Sarah tried to tell her, but she didn't seem to understand. Maybe it would be okay with Connie there, or maybe Connie was trying to kill her in that scary little room.

Sarah sometimes felt overwhelmed by terrors she couldn't name. Years before she had developed the habit of going for a walk when she was scared or worried. That's what she did now. She wandered the street feeling that if she could just find her way back home everything would be all right again. But the streets kept changing, and her frustration increased, and she couldn't remember how to get back to where she was supposed to be.

She felt so much anger but couldn't figure out why. She knew her things were gone—her mother's precious clock, her father's flag—all gone. They must have been stolen, or maybe her mother took them away. She accused Connie and Scott of theft but just as quickly forgot that she had.

If only William would come home from work, everything would be fine. He wasn't a perfect husband, but he always took care of things. But William had betrayed her, too. He'd left her. No, he died. She remembered the funeral and the loss.

If only he'd come home! Why was he so late?

Sometimes Connie took her to a strange place with lots of laughter and friendly people. Sarah relaxed and chatted with the people, but she never remembered what the conversations were about. It was nice, though—lots of bright colors, and the people there always seemed glad to see her. The only bad thing was the way they kept moving the rooms around.

Then the day came when Connie and Scott took her to another place that had another room. It was okay. It had some of her things there. But how did they get there? Where did Connie go? Her panic seemed to last forever, but it eventually passed. "Oh dear God, don't let me forget Connie and Scott, too."

Connie and Scott came back sometimes. But not very often, it seemed to Sarah. Mostly it was strangers. But why did they cry? Two of the strangers were a nice young man and a pretty woman. They gave her lots of hugs, and that was nice.

Special Communication Problems

Sarah was suffering from Alzheimer's. This disease, and others that affect the elderly, can make communication difficult or even impossible. The world narrows and becomes a scary place for those with any type of memory loss. In Sarah's case, the loss was extensive. Her paranoia was the result of the disease and a subsequently damaged brain trying to process information, to find a reassuring reason for inexplicable events. It is the paranoia that the caregiver and the family find so difficult to handle, especially when efforts to communicate are useless. The person looks and sounds the same as always. It is hard to believe someone you knew as truthful and well-balanced would suddenly make up wild tales.

Some of what the person says is only mildly off the wall and contains enough truth or logic for you to believe in its possibility, especially if you've been holding a normal conversation with the person and one of these strange statements lands in the middle of it: You're talking to Mom about your childhood days. She seems to remember your eighth birthday party perfectly. Then suddenly she begins to tell you something terrible about your brother. Could it be true?

Even when the short-term memory starts to fade, which is fairly common, there is fear—fear on the part of the person experiencing it and fear in the family. "I don't know how to cope" and "Will this happen to me?" are only two of the most common worries and fears.

People suffering from dementias of various sorts are not always "out of it." Depending on the person and the cause of the mental state, the elder can have periods or flickers of reality all day long or a brief time of normalcy when he or she is cognizant of the world and the situation before lapsing back into what a layperson might term unreality. Moving back and forth between reality and memory is random and as such cannot be predicted. It is a mistake to assume a person in this condition is totally unaware of what is happening or does not need stimulation and human contact. In fact, it has been observed that if people in this condition are ignored or talked about as if they were not present, their behavior worsens and they are more prone to withdrawal.

Sometimes a victim of dementia-type illness or severe stroke who has damaged speech centers will withdraw and/or become depressed. Again, this does not necessarily mean the person is totally incapable of understanding.

Regardless of your elder's condition, treat the person with respect, compassion, kindness and love. Most of all love, for the world is very bleak without the connection a loving touch can bring. The following are ways of communicating with elders who have impaired mental faculties. They apply to nursing home visits as well as caregiving at home. Adapt them to your elder's capabilities.

Visit regularly. Some elders keep close track of the time and day. They do look forward to it when you say you will visit on a particular day at a particular time.

Be conscious of your elder's needs. Sometimes an hour will be great; at others ten minutes is enough. Frequent visits are usually better than long ones.

When you visit, make certain you want to. Your body language will communicate more than words. Even an uncommunicative elder can read your attitude. Let yours show love and caring.

When you communicate to the elder, try to seat yourself at eye level. Take the elder's hand. Smile. Speak slowly and clearly. There is no reason to overemphasize this, and certainly no reason to shout. (This doesn't help even if the elder is hard of hearing, because it blurs the vowel sounds. Shouting or loud noises of any kind tend to upset those with mental impairments.)

Use a normal tone and volume when speaking. Don't talk to the elder as you would to a child. Respect the elder and leave his or her dignity intact. Nearly all elders will respond according to the way they are spoken to and treated.

Provide reality for the elder. If the elder says it's Sunday and it's not, don't agree. It simply confuses the elder further, especially if he or she hears someone else remark that it's Tuesday. If the elder asks the same question three times, answer it three times. Don't brush it aside.

Provide reassurance. If the elder answers a question correctly, respond, "That's right." Nod or smile your agreement, too.

Acceptance helps a person's self-esteem. It encourages the person to stay as grounded as possible instead of giving up and withdrawing.

Never respond to verbal or behavioral peculiarities with anger. Your elder may sometimes "act up" due to frustration and anger, especially when trying to unsuccessfully communicate. Stay calm. Show the elder you understand some of the frustration by holding his or her hand and soothing the person. Tell the elder you understand, but in a noncondescending way.

When an elder has a hard time communicating, rely on

watching body movements. You can tell the difference between anger and fear by looking into the elder's eyes. Watch the elder's body language. If the elder is nervous or anxious, chances are the hands will tremble or clutch repeatedly at clothing or blankets. Often simply being reassuring will help. The human touch—just holding a person, rubbing a back or holding a hand—can work like magic to calm and reassure.

Always identify yourself and who is with you. Remind the elder of the day and time. It does help center the elder in the present. If your elder asks a question, answer it honestly. This is part of reality therapy.

Take advantage of the past. Go through snapshots relating to the elder's past. Work on making an album of these photos with captions. This is a form of reality therapy that can turn into a cherished family keepsake.

Get the elder to relate old family stories and record them on cassette. These can become a wonderful part of an oral history and a vital legacy to grandchildren.

Take the elder for a walk through the house or facility, or outside if possible. An afternoon at a park or the zoo is wonderful.

Everyone loves opening gifts. Consider wrapping needed items in gaily colored paper with big bows. Gifts don't have to be strictly for birthdays and holidays. Presents can brighten anyone's day. You might consider a magazine from forty or fifty years ago, a blooming plant, pajamas, a dressing gown, new clothing, a warm cardigan for the winter months, sheepskin-lined slippers, cologne, lotion, mobiles, pictures, cards and posters. Gifts made by young children often have a wonderful effect.

Sometimes there will be silence. Your elder may be having a bad day, may not be feeling well, is depressed or simply doesn't feel like talking. This is when tactile stimulation is very important: Hold the hand, brush the hair, rub the back or stroke the arm. The elder may remember more of twenty years ago than yesterday, but he or she is also in tune with now. Your elder can feel your love and compassion more than you might realize.

If the elder is fortunate enough to have friends who are

concerned and want to visit, keep them up to date on the elder's condition. Especially if they have not visited in a while, make certain you are candid about what they can and can't expect. This will prevent or at least minimize misunderstandings. Discuss the guidelines in this section that apply to the elder's situation to make their visit more meaningful for themselves and the elder.

Illnesses of any type do not always conform to the categories and descriptions you read about. This is true of mental impairment as well. Because the person may *seem* so familiar, may *seem* otherwise healthy, it can seem as though they are doing or saying these strange things on purpose.

Your feelings may be deeply hurt when the elder accuses you of abandonment or thievery or says, "I know you hate me." You wonder how the elder could not know you. Surely if the elder had ever loved you, if you had ever been important in his or life, the person couldn't forget you or confuse you with someone else.

The simple fact is, they have no choice. But *you* do! You love the elder. You can have patience. In your own mind, you can separate the elder from the disease. Learn more about the illness. A good book to gain a broad understanding of these problems and their solutions is *The 36-Hour Day* by Nancy L. Mace and Peter V. Rabins.

Join a support group for your elder's illness. You and your family need the support of other people who are going through what you are experiencing. They will offer networking information and nonjudgmental attitudes. This is not something to be ashamed of. It happens to people from all walks of life, all ethnic backgrounds, all socioeconomic backgrounds, all educational backgrounds. There are no boundaries with this illness. Support groups provide acceptance of you and the problems you face. They can help you find the most joy possible in this situation. And joy is what you need to share with your elder.

THIRTEEN

When You're Having a Bad Day

Your daughter Coral is worried that no one will come to her birthday party. Her friends know that Grams is dying and say they are afraid of ghosts. Jimmy has had a fight with his best friend. Your husband comes home saying the car has to go into the shop.

In the normal course of things you could handle all this quite well. You could have comforted Coral, invented something really special for her party and probably patched up Jimmy's quarrel. Auto repairs are just a part of owning a car.

But "normal" was a long time ago. (Or maybe that was last month and it just *seems* like a long time ago?) Mom refused to take her medicine, barely touched lunch, rang her buzzer more than a dozen times, then chided you for responding too slowly. With a growing sense of guilt, you find yourself relieved that the birthday party might be canceled, and you snap at Jimmy to take care of his own damned problems. Although you don't say it (because it sounds too silly, even after a day like today) inside you wonder why your husband would pick this time to break the car.

Your elder is needing more and more care. Help from family and friends *seems* to be dwindling while the demands they seem to be making on you are increasing. So are the fights. You've reached the point of exhaustion and need rest, but sleep doesn't come often, or easy. When you look in the mirror, a stranger with a grim set to her mouth and shadows under dull eyes looks back.

It's a bad day. Worse, it's just another bad day, same as yesterday and the day before. Things just aren't going as you'd expected. Of course you knew that it wouldn't be easy. You expected to work a little harder, maybe give up a few things now and then. You even expected that your mother would gradually decline and that eventually you'd be making funeral arrangements. You *thought* you were prepared for all the realities.

What you didn't expect was a growing sense of futility and frustration, and anger, and guilt, and then the whole cycle of emotions all over again.

Yes, it has been a bad day. There have been others, and the newest reality is that there are more coming, with no way out. How do you deal with all these things? How do you cope with a situation when there appears to be no end in sight?

Take a Time-Out

The first and most critical step is to sit down, lie in the tub, go out in the yard...do whatever feels the most comfortable, and come to grips with the true reality of what is happening. You're not a superwoman (or superman). You're a loving, caring human being with many strengths and distinct limitations. You need a time-out. Take it!

Imagine that you have a particular long-term task to get done. To accomplish it you ignore the fact that you need rest. First you get tired. Then you become exhausted. The work drags more and more from you, with less and less getting done. Mistakes are made, increasing in number and severity as you keep pushing yourself beyond the limits. Eventually you will collapse. Refuse to sleep and it's not a matter of *if* this will happen but *when*.

If that's not convincing enough, think of yourself driving on a highway. The person coming toward you has gone beyond the limits but due to a false sense of duty has refused to rest. What would be your suggestion to such a person for the safety of everyone?

Take some time. Rest. Recover.

To continue pushing is dangerous, not just for yourself but for everyone around you. In the story above, two children were hurt needlessly, and an otherwise strong marriage was threatened. Things are falling apart. The caregiver has gone too far, to the point that the very reason for giving care has disappeared.

If you got involved in caregiving because you thought it would be fun, you've been badly misled. If you find yourself giving up your whole life to it and dragging everyone around down into the same hole... it's time to step back. In fact, it's well *past* time. It should never reach the point of desperation.

When you feel the beginnings, find a way to get some time to yourself. It doesn't have to be long but *does* need to be inviolate.

Accept Yourself

A second and very important step is to accept yourself. No one is perfect. All of us have flaws, weaknesses and limitations. All of us also have strengths and many good qualities. Mixed in are a variety of emotions. Often these can be controlled, at least to a degree, but there is a major difference between controlling an emotion and not having it in the first place.

"I never get angry" is an unrealistic statement. And there's nothing wrong with feeling angry. It's a part of being human. The same is true for feeling frustrated, jealous, sad or any other negative emotions.

The problem comes when a person swallows all these emotions, keeps them repressed deep inside and, worse, feels guilty about having them in the first place. It's not Mom's fault that she's growing older. It's not even her fault that she snaps at you now and then. So, how dare you get angry with her!

The answer is simple. You're human. Accept it. Once you've done that you can begin to accept the flaws in other people more easily.

When you are a caregiver it's easy to fall into the trap of thinking that your feelings don't count. It's a short step from there to feeling guilty about each and every negative emotion. Accept yourself and the fact that you have needs the same as everyone else. Accept that others have feelings, too. Accept that you'll feel all those emotions (and that others will), including guilt.

Write It Down

Take a few minutes to write down the feelings you've experienced in the last forty-eight hours. Name every one of them, the "good" and the "bad." Now make complete sentences about each feeling. I am furious at _____ because _____. I am sad because _____. I felt good because _____.

This is a time to explore. It's important that you be brutally honest—and you can be, because when you're finished writing all this you're going to destroy it. No one else will see it. Also, as you write remember that feelings are simply feelings. They aren't logical. You can't reason them away, but you *can* learn to deal with them. To do that, first you have to find out what those feelings are and how they are affecting you. You have to externalize those emotions, and writing them down on paper can help do that.

Another purpose in writing this down and exploring what is going on inside is to discover what is causing the emotion(s). Notice how the above sentences are phrased. Writing them isn't just to say that you feel anger or sadness; it includes the reasons why, the causes and whatever else seems needed.

This isn't a casting of blame. Instead it's exploration. Recognize that you are feeling that emotion, then find the cause. You need to be aware of your feelings *and* their source. Look for ways to treat, or at least deal with, that source. Then learn how to release and/or express the emotion.

The trick of expressing and releasing emotion is to do it in a constructive, or at least nonharmful, manner. Releasing anger doesn't mean screaming at the children or slapping your spouse. But then, controlling anger doesn't mean repressing it. If you deny your feelings, and are repressing everything, you will undoubtedly end up needing care yourself.

Quality Time

All of us need time to ourselves now and then. Especially on those "bad days," this is important. It's also important to remember that you're not in this alone. Others are involved. Beyond this, you have a life of your own and relationships that will continue after caregiving has come to an end.

One of the great problems of caregiving is the feeling of being alone. This may seem to be in conflict with the idea that you need to find time to *be* alone, but it's not. You can stand in a room full of strangers and still feel alone. Or you can spend every minute around others you know and love well, and truly *be* alone. The difference is the quality of the time. Ten minutes laughing over a card game with your spouse or child is far more therapeutic than an hour of arguing.

More than this, just as you need time to rest and recover, you need time with others. Sometimes the best "time alone" is time spent with other members of the family. This gives you, and them, a sense of unity and a sense of normalcy.

It's easy to fall into the trap of seeing things from only your own point of view, especially when you're approaching burnout. Withdrawal will only make this worse. It will also make worse your family's own sense that *you* have abandoned *them*.

Just as you need reassurance, so do they. In giving it, you get it back. Then all of you become a family again, perhaps even stronger and closer than before (instead of being driven apart). This isn't easy. It requires thinking, then action and sometimes sacrifice. The rewards, however, are well worth it.

Coping With Your Negative Emotions

Dealing with the positive emotions of love, happiness, elation and so on is easy. Even when they become overwhelming, almost any way you handle them will be fine. You won't find many books or articles out there hoping to teach you how to cope with the problems of positive emotions. In caregiving, feeling love and affection or having it shown to you isn't the problem. Such times are the boosts that can keep you going. These are the good days. The bad days can bring on a flood of negative emotions.

ANGER   This is one of the most prevalent of the emotions. You feel anger at the illness that caused this situation, anger at your family for not being more supportive and anger at yourself for not handling the situation as well as you wanted to. Anger comes from frustration, from loneliness, from burning your finger on a hot pan.

Accept that anger is a natural part of the situation and a natural part of any human being. Accept it and then deal with it. If this means slamming your hands against pillows, fine. Or consider burning off that energy in planting a garden. It's generally best to find some constructive way of getting your anger out, because in doing so you will have replaced a negative emotion with something positive.

You might have thoughts of lashing out at the situation, your family, even the elder. If that urge comes, don't feel guilty. The *desire* to strike out is normal—but recognize it and stop before it becomes a reality! Recognize the urge for what it is: a warning that the emotion is getting out of control. You may need to seek help. Talk with a trained professional such as a counselor, social worker or minister. Consider joining a support group for caregivers. Being able to discuss your feelings will help you get some perspective on the problem and plan a course of action.

JEALOUSY   Many times the underlying cause of anger is jealousy. When an elder is ill, people call to ask the caregiver about the elder's condition. Some give advice, some regale you with tales of their own elder's condition, and some callers just want to tell you how great *their* life is going (or so it may seem). Doesn't anyone care what *you* are going through?

Your family was great in the beginning, but now that everything is settling into a routine they seem to be getting on with their own lives and leaving you to cope with the mess. How can everyone so blithely disregard what you're going through? Most of your life has been pulled out from under you, and what is left is dictated by someone else's needs. You are jealous of everyone else's freedom and of the attention that the elder is getting. You even find yourself a little jealous of Coral's birthday. It would be so nice to have one of your own and, more, to be a child again where your greatest worry is how many friends will show up for games and cake.

It sounds ugly. It is also understandable. You know how hard you work each day, how much you do to make the entire situation function. It's rough at times. Real or imagined, it can seem that everyone around you is living "the good life" while you struggle along on two hours of sleep.

It may help to talk openly, honestly and calmly with the others involved. Ask them for help, which in essence is also asking for attention to your own situation.

This is the perfect time to *take* some time. One of the main causes of jealousy is having no time for yourself and nothing that brings you joy. Use some of the suggestions at the end of this section to combat this problem and get back in control of your life. Indulge yourself.

A common reaction, unfortunately, is guilt. As you sit on the back patio sipping some herbal tea and enjoying the sound of the birds singing in the tree, for that brief moment you are putting yourself first. How dare you! There is so much to do. Mom needs you. Everyone needs you. And indulging yourself in this way must be wrong. So of course you feel guilty, right?

Wrong! It's true that others need you. It's even true that it's wrong to *always* put yourself first while ignoring the needs of others. It's *because* these things are true that you deserve that indulgence. Why? Because you are a person, too. You have needs the same as everyone else.

DEPRESSION   Your lifestyle changes radically when you are a full-time primary caregiver. You have given up many things to do this. Over the long haul, caregiving with its labor-intensive chores is draining. The one factor that is never far from your mind is that no matter what you do, the elder will die.

As with the other emotions, a terrific "medicine" for depression is a healthy dose of selfishness now and then. You need to take special care of yourself. You need to replenish the joy in your life or at least to grab onto a bit or normalcy. Call a friend, go for a walk, have your hair done, take a relaxing bath, brush the dog, spend an hour working on a favorite hobby, read a book, watch a movie, listen to music, write a letter. These are just a few ideas that can give you a needed mental break from caregiving.

Taking time for yourself is necessary. Imagine what would happen if you denied yourself time to sleep. Before long you'll be tired. Later you'll reach the point of exhaustion. Let it go on too long and you'll collapse. Exactly the same can happen if you deny yourself the time to relax now and then.

If depression lingers your effectiveness as a caregiver will diminish, your relationship with the elder will deteriorate, and your life will become increasingly difficult. Use the services of a professional counselor, cleric or social worker.

FEAR   A main fear a caregiver may encounter is the fear of inheriting the disease that the elder suffers from. This fear is not necessarily unfounded, as many illnesses appear to be linked by heredity. If you are concerned, talk to the primary-care physician about the possibility. Join a support group for your elder's illness. Many of the others in the group will have gone through the same fears you have and will be able to provide insights into the problem. Contact a foundation for the elder's disease. It can supply information about the disease and help keep you abreast of the most recent research, studies and treatments.

A second fear is abandonment. This fear can become especially strong if the elder has a terminal prognosis. It is not easy to face the loss of a parent, regardless of your age. The elder has always been there, a guiding force even if the two of you have not been physically close. The bond we form with our parents is special, and when they die a hole is torn in the fabric of our lives. We feel alone, abandoned in a way that cannot by filled by the reassurances of friends, family or even a spouse.

The fear does diminish as we learn that we can survive and know joy again. We can stand on our own. Believe in yourself and your capabilities. Think about the positive things you have going in your life. Talk with your minister, counselor or social worker. There are support groups for families of the terminally ill. The members are experiencing the same feelings you have. You are not alone. Reach out for the help you need.

FRUSTRATION   The variety of situations that can frustrate a caregiver is almost endless. Beyond everyday problems of family life and career concerns, a caregiver is faced with dealing with doctors and other medical personnel, insurance companies, paperwork, appointments and the general physical care of the elder. Things get worse if the elder refuses to receive care from anyone other than the primary caregiver or to follow the prescribed treatment plan, or if the caregiver manages to arrange for services from the community or hires help and the situation doesn't work out.

It often helps to find and join a support group for caregivers. The group is one place you can safely vent your anger and frustration without being judged. The networking ability of these people is astounding. They can help you find services and offer suggestions and techniques to help solve some of the problems you are facing.

Focusing on the Positive

The feelings described above can take over your life if you let them. Fear and frustration fuel jealousy and anger, which can start a bout of depression, and then the whole cycle starts all over again. To prevent that from happening, think your way to new feelings. It *is* possible. The basic technique for doing so is to accept the reality, accept that the negative aspects exist, then do your best to replace the negatives with positives.

Think of all the good things you do during the course of the day. Be proud of your accomplishments and love yourself. Look at the gift of time you have with the elder. If it wasn't for your care, how many moments of joy would have been missed? How many opportunities to create a special memory would have vanished if not for you? Has the elder expressed thanks, or told you how much you mean to him or her? Cherish these moments. Focus your thoughts on them. These joys are what caregiving is about.

When you begin to feel frustrated, angry or depressed, say to yourself, "I *am* in control of my life. I have the power to choose my feelings. I choose to feel good about myself. I choose to feel happy to give care to my elder."

Turn your thoughts to the special, wonderful moments you've shared with your elder. This is not done in an effort to deny feelings of anger or any other emotion. These positive statements are used to reinforce the good things that are also happening in your life. They help keep you balanced and remind you that nothing is ever totally devoid of good. When you are calmer and in a more reasonable frame of mind, you can choose to deal with the problem that caused your anger or frustration. You will have a better chance to find a solution when you are feeling in control.

One easy way to cope involves just three steps. You can use your journal to do this.

1. Ask yourself how or what your are feeling—mad, sad, frustrated, etc.
2. Who or what is truly responsible for this feeling?
3. What are you telling yourself? "Listen" to what you are thinking, and write down those thoughts.

From here, decide what you can do about the situation now, and also what you can do the next time it comes up. In this way, you're trying to form a plan of action, or to recognize that the situation is one that has to be tolerated. If it's the first, you can do something to change the situation. If it's the second, you will know that there's nothing to be done, which by itself helps you to accept the situation as it is.

Avoiding Manipulation

Manipulation may come suddenly but is more likely to build over time. The elder needs your help. You've always gotten along well, so it wasn't a difficult decision to bring the elder into your home and agree to accept a caregiving situation. At first all goes smoothly. Bit by bit you feel control of your life slipping away and the demands made on you increasing. It could be a progression of little things, like having to stop what you're doing to hand the person a newspaper or magazine he or she could have easily gotten. It could be something more obvious, like the person using manipulative techniques such as "If you really loved me you would...".

You can tolerate this for a while, but sooner or later you'll begin to feel like a slave. But even this might be dismissed for a while longer. After all, when you accepted caregiving you agreed to be a servant. Still, this can build to the point of absurdity.

In Laura's case, the situation had deteriorated to the point that she would sometimes weep for no obvious reason. Excusing, dismissing and explaining away the cause had become so automatic that even the effort to recognize what was really happening brought on guilt.

She couldn't remember her old life anymore and didn't know how to get a new one. She began to consider leaving with the kids and "going home" to her parents' house in Wyoming. Then the image of her husband's careworn face imposed itself. How could she leave Jim? She loved him. This wasn't his fault.

As a mother-in-law, Marlene had always been terrific. That's why Laura supported Jim's decision to have Marlene move in when Jim's father died. It was a good decision at first. Things went well the first eighteen months, though Marlene depended on Jim a great deal and valued his opinion in making decisions.

Then Marlene fell and broke her hip. She recovered physically but feared that it would happen again. She became very dependent on Laura and turned to Jim more and more often to make even the smallest decisions. Marlene simply abdicated responsibility for her life.

Though she loved Marlene, Laura couldn't cope with her frequent demands for attention, especially when they were based on Marlene's refusal to do things she was perfectly capable of doing for herself. Making it worse, Marlene's physical condition was deteriorating through inactivity.

The doctor lectured Marlene about not moving around and exercising as she was instructed. So did the physical therapist and the home health nurse. Marlene got angry at Laura for "tattling." Laura was lectured by the doctor, the physical therapist and the home health nurse because Marlene was overly dependent on her.

Laura tried to follow their advice. When Marlene wanted a cup of coffee that afternoon, Laura reminded her that the doctor said she was supposed to get that for herself. Marlene became infuriated.

Laura maintained her position. Marlene spent the afternoon without coffee. When Jim got home from work, Marlene burst into tears as she told him how mean and cruel Laura was. Then she begged him to help her into her bedroom where she would be safe. That night Jim and Laura had the biggest fight of their fourteen-year marriage. As if this wasn't enough, the social worker heard about the incident and accused Laura of possible elder abuse.

Marlene didn't improve because she refused to do her therapy. The therapist warned that the problems would only increase, and they did. Marlene began to manipulate Laura more and more, knowing at least subconsciously that Laura couldn't fight back. The big fight with Jim proved that. She got her coffee the next day, and Laura brought the vegetable soup back to the kitchen and replaced it with the clam chowder Marlene was "in the mood for."

Laura couldn't discuss the situation with Jim because she didn't feel safe. He understood how hard it was for Laura to cope and that she was slowly being destroyed by caregiving responsibilities. Still, Marlene was his mother, and she was in pain.

Laura's "bad day" had begun, and she didn't seem to have a way out.

A caregiver's job is hard enough even when the elder is cooperative. It becomes almost impossible when the elder refuses. In Laura's case, Marlene gave up and from there learned to get her way through manipulation. Others helped her to do this, even though they meant well.

Laura could have tried to make a verbal contract with Marlene. "We miss having you at dinner with us. It would sure be nice if you would join us at least for this one meal. Would you do this for us tonight to see how it works out?" If Marlene balked, Laura's response could have been to remind Marlene of the many other dinners they'd all enjoyed together.

It starts with an agreement to one dinner. That takes the pressure off in one regard (Marlene wouldn't be agreeing to come to dinner *every* night, just this one time). At the same time it applies another kind of pressure since the first pressure has been taken off. Marlene would likely feel foolish to refuse such a simple and temporary request, and thus would be more likely to try it "just this once." And once the first dinner has been successful, the way is open to the future.

Another possibility is to get therapy for the elder. Someone who deals with this kind of behavior on a professional level may be able to teach the elder new coping skills.

Handling doctors is easier. The only trick is to make sure you keep them informed. Tell them that the elder is refusing to cooperate. If they offer advice, try it—and let them know if it worked or not. This kind of situation is nothing new for someone who has worked in the field.

Even the social worker can become an ally. Explain what is happening, and have it verified by the doctor or home health-care nurse. Don't be ashamed to ask for advice on how to handle the situation. In a case similar to Laura's, once the social worker understood the situation, she went to the elder for a talk.

"Doctor Smith tells me that you have been refusing to cooperate with him and your treatment program. That's your right, of course, but you must know that you can't expect your son and daughter-in-law to wait on you constantly. If you think you really need this kind of care, perhaps we should consider placement in a professional facility where you can get the care you need."

The shock value took effect almost immediately. Confronted with the choice of cooperating or being moved to a facility, this particular elder made it a point to be at dinner that night.

Accept, however, that there are times when nothing works. The only other alternative is to accept the situation as best you can. In such a case, consider getting therapy for yourself, so you can deal with the frustration you're bound to feel.

Make a Personal Declaration

Many caregivers get so caught up in their elder and the elder's problems that they forget the life they had before caregiving. Sometimes, especially when caregiving goes on for years, it becomes hard for the person to even think of himself or herself as separate from the caregiving task. This is dangerous to the caregiver because it throws coping skills out of balance. Think about the following statements. Make them part of your caregiving plan for you.

- Taking care of myself is necessary if I am to give care to others.
- I know my own limits and strengths. I seek help when I need it, regardless of what anyone including my elder might say.
- I have the right to feel what I feel and to express those feelings in a calm manner.
- I maintain the right to my own life outside of caregiving. Not only does this nourish my caregiving abilities, but it will help sustain me when my caregiving responsibilities have ended.
- I take pride in my accomplishments and in the courage it takes to perform these tasks.

- I realize I cannot control the happiness or well-being of another person. I cannot fulfill all his or her needs. No one person can.
- I have the right of choice, to decide what I will or will not do. This includes the right not to be manipulated by anger, fear or guilt by my elder.

Add your own rights to this list. Being yourself, and maintaining that, is one of the most difficult—and one of the most important—battles.

Learn to Relax

This has been mentioned several times in this chapter. Part of taking care of yourself is discovering ways to relax away from family and caregiving responsibilities. The problem from ignoring this comes with time, or more accurately, the lack of it. Schedule one hour every day as your time. It may have to be the hour after dinner and before the elder needs help getting to bed. It may be during the day when the elder naps. You may find you have to get up earlier or go to bed later to manage the hour, but do it. You'll find this one Golden Hour can save your sanity.

If you wish or need to, break the hour into two thirty-minute periods twice a day. There are only two rules: First, no one is allowed to interrupt this time period unless it is a life-threatening emergency. Second, you must do something that is self-indulgent!

Here are some suggestions to keep positive focus in your life:

- Begin a journal in a blank book. Use it to express your feelings, hopes and dreams for the future. No one sees it but you, so use the journal as a path to your secret self.
- Put on a favorite piece of instrumental music or purchase a tape or CD of music with nature sounds. Recordings with ocean, rain or meadow themes are very relaxing. Turn down the lights or light a candle. Stretch out in a comfortable position. Let the music guide peaceful mental walks. Let your imagination take flight with positive, joyful images and

fantasies. Pretend you are a leaf, floating on a stream. Perhaps you are a sea gull soaring over the ocean at sunset. Did you discover a castle in a secret wood?

- Meditate or pray.
- Think back to when you were a child. What interested you? Get books on the subject from the library or bookstore and study the subject.
- Start a new hobby—puzzles, drawing, music, crossword puzzles, crafts, anything that engages your full attention.
- Exercise. Go for a walk, learn yoga or tai-chi or do gardening. You can even exercise in a bathtub! Fill the tub with warm water and add bath salts or oils if you like. Soak for at least five minutes. Sit up straight with your legs out in front of you. Raise your elbows to shoulder height and press the palms of your hands firmly together for a count of five. Relax for a count of ten, breathing slowly. Repeat five times. Hold on to the sides of the tub for balance and sit with your legs straight out in front of you. Raise one leg about six inches and point the toe as far as possible, keeping the leg straight. Hold for a count of five. Lower the leg and relax for a count of ten. Repeat using the other leg. Alternate right and left legs three times.
- Curl up with your favorite beverage, perhaps an herbal tea, and indulge in a good book.
- Indulge in any activity you can do by yourself that calms your spirit. The importance of being alone is to help you maintain a balance of self. This time is in addition to the time you spend with your family and friends. Remember that when you hire someone to care for an elder, that helper's working time is usually eight hours, not the twenty-four you've been spending at the task.
- Find a volunteer to spend several hours with your elder. Try churches, the Older Woman's League, Red Cross, the caregiver's support group network. As an alternative, hire someone.

- Take a vacation. Part of the solution to the problem of feeling overwhelmed is time away from caregiving. One or two days away can made an enormous difference in your feelings and enhance your ability to cope with a difficult situation. If you have hospice services, talk with your case worker. Hospice can provide someone to help with care for a few hours or even a few days.

- Call for respite services. Some city and state governments make recommendations or supervise services. Otherwise call your physician or home health nurse for a referral. Check with hospitals and skilled care facilities in your area. Respite care is being offered more frequently due to increased need. Some other volunteer groups are also providing services.

Recognizing Burnout

People are different; they have different needs and capabilities. One person can draw a picture; another can type a hundred words a minute. Neither ability makes one person better than the other. The world doesn't end and the person is no less than before if he or she decides not to draw or type. Those statements seem so obvious you might wonder why anyone would bother to write them down. As obvious as it is, caregivers tend to miss the point when it is applied to them

Caregivers have limits like anyone else. As hard as they try, they are not superpeople, able to endlessly give of themselves. Simply put, caregivers are human beings, and like people in any situation or profession they can suffer burnout. Are you experiencing any of the following symptoms?

- Disrupted sleep patterns, including insomnia or habitually oversleeping; never feeling rested, even when you have managed an uninterrupted nine hours; sleep being troubled by disturbing dreams or nightmares

- Altered eating patterns, including not being able to eat or overeating; weight gain or loss in excess of five pounds

- Increased alcohol or sugar consumption
- Increased smoking or a strong desire to start again after having given it up
- Frequent headaches or sudden onset of back pain; increased reliance on over-the-counter pain remedies or prescribed drugs
- High levels of fear or anxiety
- Don't think you can handle one more problem or crisis
- Overreacting to commonplace problems like dropping a glass or misplacing something
- Overreacting with anger toward spouse, children or the elder in situations that a month ago you would have considered a minor annoyance
- Feeling yourself emotionally withdrawing
- Feeling trapped
- Laughter and joy having all but disappeared from your life
- Life looking gray most of the time
- Resenting the elder and/or the situation
- Mistreating the elder
- Frequent thoughts of simply disappearing or running away
- Wondering which will end first, the situation or your sanity
- Frequently feeling totally alone though your friends and family are physically there
- WIshing simply to have the whole thing over with
- Playing the "if only" game: "If only _____ would happen" or "If only _____ hadn't happened"
- Thoughts of suicide

A caregiver will have some of these thoughts or feelings some of the time. It is burnout when even a few of these symptoms are daily companions. It is a crisis when you begin to strike back by mistreating the elder (or others in the family), neglecting your own health or having thoughts of suicide. Seek professional help immediately!

Talking with your spouse is always the best first step. Sometimes there are stumbling blocks, such as when you feel guilty because the elder is the spouse's parent and not yours, or when you've tried talking and can't come to a resolution. In that case the first step to getting your life back on track is to honestly discuss your feelings and situation with the home health nurse, hospice worker, primary-care physician or other professional. They can help you evaluate your needs and help you find answers.

Consider Outside Placement

It may be that the professionals with whom you discuss your situation will suggest an alternative placement for your elder, at least on a temporary basis. This is when most caregivers experience a major guilt attack. Feelings of failure abound and are compounded if the caregiver has promised never to send the elder away. Before you fall into the morass of guilt, think back to why you undertook caregiving in the first place.

You love your elder. Caregiving has pushed you mentally, emotionally and physically to the brink of exhaustion. It is time for the ultimate expression of love. Put your elder's needs before your guilt and provide the care the elder needs by placement or accepting additional services. This is a success, not a failure. Making this decision proves your strength, responsibility and most of all your love. Making certain that the elder is well cared for should come before your guilt and your desire to prove anything. Love is letting go.

Beyond caregiver burnout, there are other reasons to consider alternative arrangements for your elder's care. The elder may desire it. Perhaps the situation is not to the elder's liking. He or she may prefer more peace and quiet than your busy household can provide or may want more interaction with people of his or her own age group.

The elder's physical care may have become more than anyone anticipated. The elder may want the security of having a nurse on call twenty-four hours a day.

You may live in an area where at-home services are unreliable or nonexistent. In this case the care the elder needs could be some distance away.

The caregiving situation may be endangering the rest of your relationships. An unhappy spouse or children can strain family relationships to the breaking point. Sometimes a caregiver may be handling the caregiving portion of life at the expense of other responsibilities.

You also have a natural concern for your future and that of your family. The caregiving situation may have escalated to the point where it puts you in financial trouble or your career in jeopardy. The repercussions of this threat can cause strife and damage long after the need for caregiving has passed.

If these situations are occurring, it is time to consider other options. Assess your elder's needs and look at the alternative care possibilities listed in chapter 3. Remember that no decision is permanent or irrevocable.

Follow the same procedure as outlined before:

1. Decide what you will and will not do.
2. Discuss the situation with your spouse.
3. Call a family meeting with your siblings and work out a plan.
4. Offer choices to your elder.

You may face some opposition from your family or your elder over your decision to give up personal caregiving. Notice the word *personal* in the previous sentence. Simply because you are no longer handling every detail of your elder's life personally doesn't mean that you are no longer a caregiver. It only means that you recognize that twenty-four-hour-a-day care is something you can not give at this time.

As a caregiver you will still be in touch with the elder, still supervising his or her care, still protecting the person and watching out for his or her welfare and, most of all, still loving the elder. Only your constant physical presence is missing. Telephone calls and frequent visits will show that the elder has not been abandoned.

To those who might criticize your decisions, take a firm stance. You were there. You gave the care. You did the best you could, and that is all any reasonable human being can expect, of himself or herself and others. These statements are true even if you have to say them to the elder. If they need to be said to your spouse or to a sibling, you might even suggest that that person take a turn at handling the caregiver situation. There is never any reason for you to automatically accept criticism or to assume guilt.

FOURTEEN

How to Say Goodbye

Some might hesitate to read this chapter because saying goodbye is very, very sad. It's bad enough when the loved one is returning home after a visit and will be back next June. *This* goodbye is permanent. The loved one isn't going home but dying. You may not believe it right now, but this goodbye can also be filled with love, hope and a feeling of peace.

You know that time with the elder is growing short. Even if the elder is in relatively good health and care needs are mostly Level I, now is the time to work on your relationship with the elder. This is not only a matter clearing up old business but a time to put some finishing touches on your personal growth in the relationship.

As a caregiver, you will have ample opportunity to facilitate growth with open, honest communication. It will be a time of stretching and discovering your capacities. You will learn a great deal about yourself and your family, both primary and extended.

As the elder approaches the end of life, he or she will go through a period of reviewing the past. Most will think about mistakes and regrets as well as successes. How each elder handles this is an individual matter. Some will dwell on the bad, others will ignore it (or will seem to ignore it). Be receptive to the elder's changes by being available to talk. Listen, don't criticize.

Balancing this, however, must be a heavy dose of common sense and kindness. This is a time to come to a closeness, not a time to dump out years of frustration, anger and pent-up memories. Handle those on your own, later if need be. Even if there is a particularly bitter memory from your childhood, now is the time to let go of it, not to use it as a weapon.

The Myth of the Perfect Parent

There is a pervasive myth of a perfect childhood. It comes complete with wondrous days filled with joy and unconditional love presided over by benevolent parents who are perfect and who fulfill every need while showing us how to attain every dream.

Then there's reality.

The "perfect parent" is a myth. No one ever had perfect parents. No one ever reached adulthood without hurt feelings and the remembrance of a time when Mom and Dad were totally unfair. Usually we get over these feelings for the most part. What seemed so horrible and wrong at the age of fourteen can be humorous at forty. There are no appreciable scars. Hopefully this will be your situation, and you'll be providing care for an elder with whom you get along just fine. In this case, you won't need all of the information and suggestions in this section. It's still advised that you read through it.

For others a small sting of hurt remains when these feelings haven't been totally resolved. And sometimes the wounds go much deeper. If they're too deep, and if the conflict between you and the elder is bitter, perhaps you should reconsider the idea of providing care. At very least, it's advisable that you get professional help so that the hurts and conflicts can be resolved.

There are many books on the subject of resolving childhood traumas. Therapists run groups and oversee peer self-help encounters. You can also take advantage of these opportunities or talk with your clergy or social worker.

Some claim that the best way to heal these feelings is to air them with the person responsible, to dump the load of pain on that person in a "See how you've ruined my life" attitude. Does this really help? It may make the "injured" person feel better *momentarily* to get it off his or her chest, but it doesn't solve the problem. Even if the elder says "I'm sorry" or "You're right, I was wrong," it doesn't change what happened. You may feel gratified by hearing the words, by finally "winning," but this is a shallow victory.

What usually happens in a confrontation of this nature is that the elder gets angry and maintains his or her version of the incident(s). Whatever relationship the two people had deteriorates even further. Instead of healing a rift, the encounter opens a chasm, one that may never be breached this close to the end of the elder's life. Whatever opportunity existed to form a new, healthy relationship is gone. The elder and the adult child both end up with an additional and unnecessary load of guilt and regrets, and at exactly the *wrong* time.

There are many ways to resolve old hurts and issues other than a direct confrontation. The first step is to recognize that your parents are humans, just like you—and that they made mistakes, just like you do. Couple with this the present popular trend of blaming everyone else, including the past. In more and more cases people "remember" wrongs done to them that never even happened.

Sometimes false memories are planted. Most often this is done by someone who means well but who has some hidden prejudice or agenda. More often it's brought about by misinterpretation of the event itself, and then by years of mulling over it.

In one experiment, a story is told in secret to one person. This person tells it, also in secret, to another. This continues through a number of people until the last in the group tells the story as he or she heard it. The story will invariably change as each person interprets it. Often at the end it bears very little resemblance to the story that started.

Irrelevant? Not really. An incident from your childhood has gone through your mind over and over again, like going from one person to the next. Even with the best of us, the most accurate memories aren't quite accurate. The harsher the memory, the more likely that it will have been distorted over time.

Accept the *possibility* that you've had it wrong all these years.

Next, assume that the incident really did happen just as you think you remember. You're now faced with a very simple fact. The past cannot be changed. But the future can be better, and you have only the present to make it that way.

Estranged Relatives

As a caregiver, you may be called on to be the mediator between an elder and an estranged sibling or other family member. You may be asked to arrange a meeting or a phone call. As you can see from the previous discussion, the situation can be loaded with dynamite, much of which you can defuse. Explain the elder's medical situation and possible ramifications of excess tension (if any) to the person the elder wants to talk to. Encourage the person to listen and to try to be nonconfrontational.

All the varying degrees of hurt can happen in the same family with the same parents but to different children. If you put three adult siblings together and ask them to describe their childhoods, you may wonder if they came from the same family. They will have different incidents that stand out in their minds and different views of their parents and of their relationship to them. They may describe each other's childhood in ways the others don't even recognize.

"You were always the favorite."

"That's not true. They let you do anything you wanted, but when I asked it wasn't allowed."

"You two had it good. I had to work after school to pay for my car; you got one for your seventeenth birthday."

The same dynamics can carry over into adulthood.

"Mom and Dad gave you a bigger wedding."

"It wasn't that big. Besides, look at all the money you've borrowed from them and never paid back."

"Every year they drive to see you. If we want to see them, we have to go there."

And on it goes.

As the caregiver, and mediator, you could find yourself suddenly faced with injuries and bitterness of all kinds, and from all directions. You could find, for example, that your beloved sister gets along great with the elder but has held a grudge against *you* for the past thirty years, or perhaps doesn't get along with your brother.

Ellen's father, Ralph, had always been a man of strong opinions and never hesitated to voice them. Ralph lived with Ellen, her husband and their two children. Two of Ellen's brothers had a reasonable if somewhat prickly relationship with their father. That was not the case with Jeremy, Ellen's youngest brother. Though she and Jeremy were close, the one subject they could never discuss was Ralph.

Ralph and Jeremy had never gotten along. Ralph was an outdoorsman who loved to hunt and fish. He was proud of his work on the docks. "Real man's work," he called it. Jeremy was a quiet boy who loved school and had a talent for photography. His two older brothers were high school sports stars. Jeremy won the school's chess championship and was president of the science club.

The oldest brother became a career military officer, the other a college football coach. Despite his father's taunts and cruel comparisons to his brothers, Jeremy became a professional photographer and managed to make a living in a very competitive field.

They saw little of each other over the years. When they did meet, it usually ended with Ralph demanding that Jeremy get a real job and Jeremy yelling at the narrow-minded old man to get off his back. The final fight came when Jeremy married. Ralph said he'd never be able to support a family like a real man.

Almost twenty years passed before Ralph, then approaching eighty, so much as asked about Jeremy. Once he asked Ellen if she knew how Jeremy felt about him. Ellen replied that Jeremy wouldn't talk about it to her. Then she asked if Ralph would like to talk with Jeremy. He said no, that it was Jeremy's place to be a man and to come to him.

Ellen was in quandary. She was certain he wanted to reconcile with Jeremy and was equally certain that he would never make the first move. On the other hand, Jeremy had refused to talk about their father and seemed to harbor a lot of anger and pain. Yet if *she* tried to get them together, the results could be disastrous in terms of both the relationship and her father's heart condition.

In the end, Ellen decided to call Jeremy. She stressed their father's medical condition and that he seemed to want to talk. Eventually Jeremy flew east for the visit, which took place behind closed doors. Afterwards, neither would speak of the meeting. Jeremy left the next day.

A month later Ralph died of a massive coronary. Jeremy attended the funeral, where he told Ellen, "I sat there and listened to him. I didn't say a word all through it. I felt so much rage I almost choked. I kept thinking you were wrong about him wanting to make peace. He wound down after about an hour and finally asked me if I had anything to say for myself. About a million thoughts chased themselves around in my head. Then I looked at him. Really looked at this tired old man slumped in the chair. He had tears in his eyes and he was afraid. I told him that I lived my life the way I believed. Then I told him I loved him. He didn't say a word for a minute. I hadn't told him that since I was seven and he said, 'Real men don't tell other men they love them.' Anyway, he straightened up in the chair, looked at me and said, 'At least you have the courage of your convictions. Now get out.'

"That meeting wasn't what I'd envisioned. I thought we'd finally say all those father-son things you're supposed to say. All the way back to Nebraska I kept cursing myself for being an idiot and trying one more time. I felt I'd never get his approval. I'm forty-two years old, and I still wanted him to say he loved me or was proud of me or something. I was miserable. All I could remember him saying was to get out. It wasn't until you called to tell me he was dead and I decided to come to the funeral that I finally understood. All my life he talked about how a real man stood up for himself and for his beliefs. I think he really did want to say all those father-son things but didn't know how."

Undertaking the role of mediator is risky and must be weighed in the context of the others' belief structure. Ellen was fairly sure that Ralph wanted to at least talk to Jeremy. How would she have felt if Ralph had died and she had not tried to put together a meeting? What if the meeting had ended with Ralph having a heart attack? When elders indicate they want help in finishing unfinished business, a caregiver can be caught in the middle. You must look at all the what-ifs and decide which you can live with and which you can't.

Jeremy's situation wasn't unique. For years, he had a problem expressing what his father meant to him despite their differences. Paying a final compliment, expressing appreciation, saying thank you and showing your love are all parts of unfinished business. The emotional finality of expressing these feelings is often so difficult that many people, including the caregiver, never get around to it. This is one time when actions don't speak louder than words. If these things aren't expressed, guilt makes the grieving process that much harder.

Communication

There are two major stumbling blocks to expressing feelings at this time. First is that the feelings are so deep that you fear expressing them in a way the person can understand. You fear stumbling over your words and making a mess of the whole thing. Second is the fear that your expression might be rejected.

Whatever the cause, communication blocks make it difficult to deal with unfinished business. Yet emotional issues need to have closures if we are to find the resolution we need to grow and say goodbye. You might try one of these solutions.

Tell the elder that your feelings are so deep that they are difficult to talk about. Write down what you need to say and read it to the elder. Or write and leave it for the individual to read when alone.

Writing is sometimes easier than talking. You can take your time and correct things without fear of embarrassment. When the writing is accomplished, its recipient can read and reread the letter. This gives a better chance of understanding. If the elder has a difficult time reading, consider reading your words into a tape recorder. Whether feelings are expressed in written or recorded form, you know you have conveyed them and have made a giant stride toward finishing the emotional side of unfinished business with no regrets over having remained silent.

Express what your relationship has meant to you. Reminisce about shared experiences. Your elder needs to know that his or her life was of value to you. Discuss plans for your future. The elder may not be there physically to see those plans and dreams come to fruition, but the elder feels a sense of continuation into the future for knowing about them. Knowing that you shared the future if only in the planning, dreaming stage brings the elder into your future when their physical presence is absent. This lessens "survivor's guilt."

Survivor's guilt is the term used for what we feel when we find our lives continuing when our loved one has died. For a caregiver this type of guilt can be particularly devastating because the survivor may have been involved with the day-to-day care of the elder. It intensifies the "what if" and "maybe if I had done more" aspects of guilt.

When you are informed that your elder is terminal you eventually find yourself involved in anticipatory grief. This means that the grief over losing a loved one has started while the loved one still lives. Survivor's guilt and what-if varieties also play a part in the anticipatory grief process.

Anticipatory Grief

Some people fear that anticipatory grief will cause a premature emotional separation with the dying elder or that the family will abandon the elder. This is a valid concern in some cases where the elder has been institutionalized or has a deteriorating mental condition and is unable to interact, and in some caregiving situations where the need for care has encompassed years or has involved extreme self-sacrifice on the part of the caregiver and the family. Usually they are able to deal with anticipatory grief and still maintain an emotional involvement with the elder.

The key to balanced anticipatory grief is to gradually emotionally detach yourself from a future in which the elder has a physical presence. Continue to be involved with the elder in the here and now. The stages of separation you will go through will be those similar to what is outlined for the elder as he or she faces the end of life.

All those connected to the elder, including children, will undergo the grief process in anticipation of death and/or at the time they learn of it. The depth of their grief will depend on a number of factors. How emotionally close they felt to the elder, their awareness of the elder's condition and their concept of what happens to a person after death are three of the most important.

Preparing people for the elder's death can help minimize grief and can facilitate closure both for the elder and the survivors.

Preparing the Children

Preparing a child for an elder's death is a great benefit for both the elder and the child. Children are frightened by the unknown and upset by shocks to their world, as we all are. Trying to shield them from death and dying only makes it harder for them to accept.

Children are much more observant than most adults think they are. Even the youngest child will respond to your fear, worry and sadness on an emotional level. If they do not understand the circumstances, the children may well think they are at fault or somehow to blame for your unhappiness. Even if you were the greatest actor in the world, you could not keep a child from suspecting that something is terribly wrong. The whispered conversations, the furtive looks between adults, being sent out of the room so grownups can talk, hurried excuses about "not being able to talk now," increased unexplained absences, sudden silences when they walk in a room, not being able to see Grandma or Grandpa anymore, overhearing parts of conversations, the change in your mood: All are clues to children that something terrible is about to happen. They feel alone, left out of the protective warmth of the family circle. Remember, they are already learning about grief and problems from you and the way you handle the situation.

Telling older children (ten and above) is easier because they have already formed a concept of death (which we will discuss in the next chapter). These children usually want to know more of the medical reason why. The bigger fears for them may be contagion and heredity. They may ask questions about when the elder will die or what happens afterward, depending on their religious background. Straightforward answers work best.

Talk about what the elder means to you and how your future will be handled when the elder is no longer physically present. All children are concerned for their future and want to feel secure. This is especially important if caregiving has been taking place in the children's home or if the elder expects to die there. Always let the children know they can ask questions about the situation at any time.

Remember to give them permission to be upset. One way to do this is by allowing them to see that you are distressed and sad. If you don't grant this permission, the children might think they have to be strong for you, in which case they may well withhold expressing their own pain so that they don't upset you. When people don't allow themselves to feel or to express what they are feeling, it can set a pattern into adulthood that causes them to be emotionally withdrawn, even from the people they love. Let the children know they can talk about their feelings with you at any time.

Children under ten need a less factual account of the reasons leading to death in most cases. They want to know why it is happening and gain reassurance that they and their parents aren't threatened. When you are explaining to young children that the elder will die soon, you need to make some distinctions. To simply say "Grandma is very old and sick. Very soon she will die and not come back (or go to heaven)" may cover all the basics, but the statement is very confusing.

To youngsters, forty is positively ancient. Will *you* die now? How about the next time you get the flu? They may now fear that all sickness leads to death. If the grandmother is in the hospital, children may connect the hospital and/or doctors with dying.

Take time to explain a little more fully. Be prepared to tell the truth on a level the children can understand. This is dependent on their emotional development, not their age. Answer their questions. If you don't know the answer, say so. Children can accept "I don't know, but I'll try to find out for you" a lot easier than the discovery of a lie or half-truth.

It's not necessary (unless the children ask) to name the particular illness, only to differentiate between the kinds of sickness you recover from and the kinds you don't. Don't be surprised if, the next time you or your child is sick, you are asked if it's a dying sickness. Because you laid the groundwork for understanding sickness, the child will accept your answer: "No. It's just a headache." Still, you may need to do some further exploration of death with your children. This subject is covered in the next chapter.

If the elder will be living in your home during this time and you have younger children, or if they will be visiting, be sure to prepare them for any medical equipment that might be used. Children can be frightened by things they don't understand. Simple explanations usually solve the problem. If they will be seeing the elder at another location, be sure to tell them what they can expect.

After everyone has begun getting used to the fact that the elder's condition is incurable, there will still be even rougher ups and downs. A new treatment is offered; the elder seems to respond well to a new medication; the elder seems to be "holding her own" or even showing signs of improvement, perhaps even recovery. You are unprepared. Everyone's emotions are mixed, including the elder's. You are caught between letting go and hanging on. So what do you do now?

Predictions of death are notoriously wrong when they attempt to set a date. Everyone has heard of cases where someone was given a year to live and died in a week. There are cases where the prognosis was a year or less and the person lived another ten.

That's why death, even when you are expecting it, comes as such a shock. The best way to minimize the highs and lows in this terrible waiting game is to stop waiting and live. Live each day, with the majority of your thoughts on today. Cherish the good and the peace you find in the moment. Tomorrow will come whether or not we are ready. The elder knows this, too.

Be Honest With the Elder About the Prognosis

The elder knows more than many people give him or her credit for. The elder has aged, the thinking processes may have slowed, but the elder is not stupid. The elder lives inside the body everyone has been so concerned about. It doesn't take too long or too many clues for the elder to figure out he or she is dying. If the doctor has told you that the elder has an incurable illness, have the doctor tell the elder. The elder also has a need to know that he or she will not be abandoned to pain and simply sent home to die. The elder still needs information, reassurance and hope for the future, which is why the doctor is the best choice for breaking the news to the elder.

If for some reason the doctor refuses, ask a minister or professional counselor to tell them or tell them yourself. In any case, it's often a good idea to be there. Someone must tell the elder, because the elder will find out anyway, and the longer that takes the more difficult time he or she will have.

"He (She) can't be told, he'll (she'll) never handle it" is an argument that is frequently used by adult children in an effort to keep the truth from the elder. They want to protect the elder from the pain of knowing that a medical opinion gives him or her only a short time to live. This is only part of the reason. The adult child *also* wants to avoid facing the elder's demise. It's painful to contemplate. So if the elder isn't told, no one has to face the situation or talk about it.

The reality is this: Elders can feel changes happening in their bodies, especially if the changes are accelerating due to illness. They receive new medical treatments and visit the doctor more often; nurses give them anxious looks; they overhear doctors in the hallways consulting with still more doctors; sometimes they peek at the comments written in their own medical charts—and all this becomes evidence for what they suspect. They know that radical surgery isn't performed for minor ailments and harmless lumps aren't cured by radiation and chemotherapy.

Then there are the friends and family who visit: the expressions on their faces, the avoidance of certain topics, the carefully worded questions and replies, the catch in the voice, the tears that threaten to spill over. Elders put these clues together pretty quickly. So why doesn't your elder say anything? Because of you. By your silence, you have shown your elder you can't handle the situation. The dying elder has become the protector of the living.

In the conspiracy of silence, everyone loses. The elder is stripped of free expression, shared feelings, the opportunity to say goodbye and the opportunity to put personal affairs in order. No one can share the elder's tears, fears or anxieties. No one can comfort the elder, and the elder cannot comfort anyone else.

The elder has been reduced to the status of "child," unable to have determination or control over his or her life. The elder has been denied the reassurance of being allowed to face the end of life without physical pain. Most people fear pain and believe it automatically comes with terminal disease. Pain can be controlled with medications, though in very severe cases a person may have to choose among lucidity, sedation to the point of unconsciousness, or something in between. This is a very personal choice that belongs solely to the person going through it. The elder must be given a say whenever possible as to how and where he or she will live out the final days and moments. Awareness and choice allow rational thinking and lessen the fear of death.

How the elder accepts the news of a terminal illness depends on the type of person the elder is and on his or her personality. If the person has always played ostrich when faced with decisions, he or she may verbally deny the condition or pretend it doesn't exist. A person who has always met a crisis head on will likely handle terminal illness in the same manner. The elder may bluntly ask, "How long?"

Regardless of how the elder appears to handle the news in the beginning, he or she will eventually deal with its implications. If the elder was told by the doctor it will be easier for the elder to rely on the doctor's promise of support and prevention of pain. The elder needs to know that everything possible will be done, that he or she will not be abandoned or ignored even in the most advanced stages, that he or she will be given options to decide the course of treatment. Psychologically, the fact of being told makes it easier for the elder to communicate while passing through the stages of dying.

Stages of Dying

Dr. Elisabeth Kübler-Ross is a medical doctor, psychiatrist and thanatologist. Her work with terminal people of all ages has given us insight into the needs of the dying and the stages they go through as they face their mortality.

After learning of a terminal illness, the elder will go through five stages: denial and isolation, anger, bargaining, depression and acceptance. These stages will not necessarily be sequential, and the elder may go through them more than once. Be aware that you, too, may go through these stages when dealing with anticipatory grief.

DENIAL AND ISOLATION (NO! NOT ME!)   Denial functions as a buffer against shocking news and allows the elder to assimilate the news until other defenses and coping mechanisms can be marshaled to deal with the situation. Denial is usually a temporary defense. Later on, the elder may be quite grateful and relieved simply to sit and talk with someone about his or her feelings concerning impending death.

ANGER (WHY ME?)   Anger is difficult to cope with because the elder lashes out at everyone and everything, often seemingly at random. The only way to get through these incidents with your relationship intact is to understand what is happening from the elder's point of view. The elder has just lost control of his or her life. Depending on the stage of the illness, the elder may be physically limited, which makes dealing with a mobile world difficult. The elder only has to look out a window, watch TV or see someone enter the room to be reminded that everyone else has a life that they can reasonably expect to continue, which is something now denied to the elder. Irrational anger can only be handled with understanding, love and patience. Anger caused by inappropriate care is justified and needs to be addressed immediately to those responsible.

BARGAINING (I PROMISE...)   If we can make a bargain, we sometimes feel more in control. This might be come out as something like, "God, if you'll let me live just one more month I promise I'll donate $5000 to the church." There might also be bargains between the elder and others. "If I agree to take these treatments do you promise to come help me plant the flower garden?"

The bargaining might be bold or subtle, spoken or held inside. Understand that however it comes, it's natural. Your main concern, as the primary caregiver, is to keep it in perspective. Realize that the elder may make impossible promises (and try to keep them) that are damaging. There is also the risk of making promises on your own that can't be kept, at least not without great sacrifice.

DEPRESSION (WHAT'S THE USE?)   Depression for the terminally ill is a preparatory phase for acceptance. Depression is intimately connected to the loss the elder feels in all areas of life. At this stage the illness has progressed so far that the elder can no longer deny its existence. There are many causes for depression. These differ from person to person and from situation to situation. One common cause is the reaction to the loss of a job, self-esteem, etc. Someone aging may have already faced this, which opens them even more. An elder who is facing death, for example, may already feel depressed from retirement and a growing sense of uselessness, and now faces the coming loss of everything. Still another cause of depression can result from being forced to accept treatments (sometimes degrading and embarrassing ones) or being asked to struggle for life when the individual has already accepted death.

Reassurance will often help. "You are still a valuable human being" can go a long way (if convincing) to someone bedridden after a lifetime of hard work. Bringing up memories and reminders of contributions may also help. This is also a good time to be a good listener without the platitudes "Don't be sad." It's an even better time to open your mind and heart. The dying person may have truly come to terms with death and may be "hanging on" for you.

Is it depression? Often this is not easy to determine, even for those who have had years of education, training and experience. Even if it is depression, is it "normal" or a matter of concern? Can you help, or are you contributing to it?

This can be one of the most difficult times. There can easily be a discrepancy between the elder's wishes and your own (and those of the doctors). True depression ignored can lead to more serious problems, even suicide. At the same time, it's easy to impose your own depression upon the elder who has come to accept reality.

It's a fine line that is easily misread and that requires great awareness.

ACCEPTANCE (IT'S OKAY.) When the elder has come to terms with the shock, anger and depression of facing the eventual loss, the elder will contemplate the end of life with a quiet expectation. It is not the hopelessness of "I give up" or a sense of "What's the use?" It is instead a sense of peace. The elder may or may not wish to talk at this point but will appreciate the touch of another caring human being. Often all you need to do is sit in companionable silence and hold the elder's hand.

The acceptance stage can be hardest on the caregiver and the family, because an elder who accepts that he or she is going to die begins to say goodbye and to detach emotionally. It feels like rejection or even a death wish.

How could the elder not want to live? Not want to be with us? The elder is not rejecting the living and the life he or she has known but is as accepting the end of life with peace and dignity. The elder has mentally prepared for the final journey into whatever the person believes lies beyond—a journey each must take alone.

The elder is dying. The elder knows it. The elder accepts it. *You* must know and accept it, too. Now is the time to say, "I love you. I'll miss you." Reassure your elder you will be fine. Now is the time to hold your elder's hand and kiss goodbye.

Closure

Once you have accepted the fact that the elder you are caring for is facing death, you can move forward and help him or her with closure. Exactly what is needed will vary from person to person.

As caregiver, your primary task is to help your elder. Sometimes this means helping with necessary bodily functions, without making the elder feel ashamed. Another large part is simply being there. Listen as your elder reviews his or her life. Try to give the support and acceptance the elder needs to cope with mourning for the loss of relationships, people, things and life itself.

Give consideration to the elder's wants and emotional needs. Separate the person from the illness. You might consider getting some extra physical help at this time so that you can spend more time on the emotional closure of the relationship and less time on the needed physical care.

Make allowances for the elder's condition. Many months of pain and emotional turmoil can make for emotionally stormy situations between the elder and family members. It is a good idea to keep all visitors informed of the elder's condition and mental outlook. This prevents many cases of hurt feelings and misunderstandings.

Remain as involved as possible. You might find yourself wanting to withdraw. A psychologically healthy person wishes to avoid pain. Knowing that someone you love is dying is emotionally painful. But if you emotionally disconnect, it dehumanizes the elder and leaves you with more regrets to work through than is otherwise necessary.

Communication is a gift you give not just to others but to yourself. With it there are fewer regrets. It helps everyone come to closure in their own lives. Closure is needed if they are to experience peace and acceptance of their own death.

Attending to the elder's last wishes is important but can also be strenuous. You need to prepare yourself ahead of time by deciding what you will and will not do. Some of these wishes will involve the more mundane things, like seeing to it that a will is executed and bills are paid. Others may mean trying to open communication with a "lost" relative or friend. As we have discussed, this isn't always easy, especially if there are old injuries and grudges.

Discuss (tactfully) how and where your elder wants to spend his or her remaining time. Some will choose a nursing home or other facility, such as a hospice center. Most will want to die in their own home. Being surrounded by a lifetime of memories and the more casual atmosphere that home care provides brings a feeling of emotional and psychological safety and security. With hospice services, which are available in cases of a terminal illness, living the remainder of life at home becomes possible for most elders.

A painful part is talking about death itself, and the funeral arrangements afterward. The sad fact is that if you don't discuss it now, it will be too late. Honor your elder's wishes about things like taking no "heroic measures," such as life support machines. One person might want a traditional funeral with burial; another might prefer cremation.

If you find that your personal beliefs are at odds with the elder's wishes, turn the tasks over to someone who can handle them.

Sometimes there is a hesitancy in letting the elder die at home because you simply don't know what to expect. The following chapter on death and the aftermath will give you some insight into this particular situation.

FIFTEEN

Death, Grief
and the Aftermath

As little as a hundred years ago you wouldn't have needed to read this chapter. Death was closer because fewer people went to hospitals or other facilities to die. More people died at home, often surrounded by the family. This meant that more people witnessed death firsthand. The advantage was that the family as well as the community tended to be closer. The loved ones not only helped the dying elder but each other as well.

The trend is shifting back. The medical profession recognizes that many elders prefer to die at home. The use of home health services and hospice makes this possible, yet often there is reluctance on the part of the family to let this happen. The reason is fear. Most baby boomers have seen few people die, if any, other than in movies. They simply don't know what to expect.

Is dying gruesome, full of pain or screaming? Rarely, especially if hospice is involved and/or your primary-care physician has kept a promise to medicate for pain. Each illness is different, of course. The home health nurse or your primary-care physician can explain what is to be expected in your elder's case.

For the elder, there will be little, if any, fear or anxiety at the time of death, especially if there has been an opportunity for closure. The elder will be at peace, separating from the world as we know it. In the final hours or moments before death, some elders will talk of seeing a bright white light and feeling drawn to it, much as people have recounted in near-death experiences. Others will talk to loved ones who died years ago. They may talk to these visions directly, or may describe them to you, saying they are being greeted by them or that these loved ones are waiting for them. Some will even smile as death comes. Others will simply become still and quietly slip their bonds to this life.

In other words, although some of the signs of death can be disturbing, the process isn't necessarily at all what you've imagined it to be.

Observable Signs of Impending Death

Sometimes there are no physical signs. The elder seems stable, goes to bed and dies in his or her sleep. Even if you're there, you may not notice anything at all until you become aware that the elder is no longer breathing.

An elder may complain of being tired or feeling worn out and spend time in bed. He or she may grow physically weaker and eat and drink very little. This is probably something you have seen before so it is not really alarming. The elder may then slip into semiconsciousness or unconsciousness and die. This kind of death is also rather undramatic.

When an elder has suffered a long illness and actually begins the process of dying, it is sometimes difficult to tell. Again you may notice a lack of interest in food or drink. On the second or third day you will notice that fluid intake has really dropped and that the elder does not have his or her usual bathroom habits. The person may tell you he or she is not going to get up, and may continue to refuse food, liquids and most or all medications (except pain medications). The person may even say, "I'm dying."

If you call the home health nurse or physician, and if no heroic measures are to be taken, you will probably be advised to let nature take its course. The nurse or hospice worker, if you have such services, will check to make sure the elder is physically comfortable. If the professional's assessment of the situation is that the elder is indeed dying, insertion of a catheter may be recommended. Agree to it unless the elder strenuously objects. A dying person usually becomes incontinent. A catheter and bag will keep the elder from becoming uncomfortable from being wet and having to be moved and to be cleaned.

As body functions fail, the elder will become less responsive. The elder will sleep more and could lapse into a comatose or nonresponsive state approximately one or two days before death. Through this, keep in mind that the last sense a person loses is hearing. Talk to the elder. Comfort the elder and say, "I love you." The elder may not respond but can probably hear you.

Body temperature begins to drop. You may notice some blueness around the heels of the feet, on the buttocks or on the hands. This is known as lividity. As the heart ceases to be an effective pump, the blood will pool at the lowest points as the body temperature drops. Death is near.

Depending on the disease, the lungs may become involved. In the case of lung disease, lung cancer or severe heart problems, the lungs will fill with fluid. This can cause a gurgling noise. It sounds alarming, but the elder is usually in little or no discomfort. If the elder has this type of history or is on oxygen, check with the nurse or physician, who may recommend that the elder be propped up in a sitting or semi-sitting position. This can be done with pillows if you don't have a hospital bed.

Almost everyone has heard of the "death rattle" type of breathing. Clinically it is called Cheyne-Stokes, pronounced "chain stokes." Most dying people have this type of breathing, but some do not. The elder usually breathes very quickly and in a noisy manner; then the breathing stops for up to a minute. This is followed by a long breath and more fast breathing (stoking), then no breathing again. It sounds rather like the chugging of an old-fashioned train. This type of breathing may continue on and off interspersed with periods of normal breathing. Inevitably the elder will draw the last breath, which is frequently released as a long sigh.

The pulse stops. The elder's spirit finishes separation from the body. The elder has died. The urinary and anal sphincters usually relax and open. Anything that passes now is usually minimal, though there may be an odor. Don't feel guilty about using an air freshener.

Sometimes, but not always, the person who has been comatose or semi-comatose, even after Cheyne-Stokes breathing has started, will experience a short period of extreme lucidity shortly before dying. The elder will recognize you, know what is going on and make appropriate responses to questions. At this point, the elder may or may not speak of what he or she has been experiencing. This period can be quite brief or may last thirty minutes or more. The elder then lapses back into a coma. Death usually follows quickly.

The actual process of dying usually lasts about four days. It can be much shorter (one or two days) or a bit longer, though it very rarely takes more than a week.

Facing Death

Many caregivers wonder if they can emotionally handle being with someone as that person dies. It's an individual decision, and no one should pressure you to stay or leave. There is no doubt that lending your presence and giving comfort to a beloved elder who is dying is an intensely emotional and personal experience.

Earlier in the book it was suggested that you keep a journal of your thoughts and even mundane day-to-day details. The following is an excerpt from just such a journal.

Aunt Marie put Grandma's favorite music on again. She had been taking good care of Grandma for almost two years. The music was barely audible over the only other sound in the room, the incessant hiss of the oxygen machine. Grandma was lying still in the hospital bed, making barely a sound at all, though she seemed to struggle for breath.

"Grandma. It's me, Debbie," I said. Gently, I cradled her small fragile hand in mine. I cleared my throat, hoping to ease the ache of trapped tears. Her eyes were half open. Can she see me? I wondered. Does she know I'm here?

Smoothing her hair, I leaned over and kissed her forehead. "I love you," I whispered. I could barely feel the
fluttering movement of her hand as she tried to return a
gesture of love and comfort.

Grief ripped at me. She looked so tired, yet selfishly I
wanted her to speak just one more time. To tell me
something, anything I could hold onto, to take with me. All
I heard was the music and the whooshing of the machine.

After a while my father came in, and I knew he needed to
be alone with his mother. Part of me wanted to escape from
the room, the dying. Part of me wanted to stay.

When I returned, Aunt Marie was removing the oxygen
tubing, though that monstrous machine was still hissing
away. She reached up and gently closed the half-open eyes. I
watched as a tear followed the course of a deep wrinkle down
Grandma's cheek. Softly, I wiped it away. The tear was still
warm. Inside, where the truth of me lives, I knew Grandma
just acknowledged our presence, the only way she could. She
waited a day and a half for us to arrive so she could say
goodbye. She never spoke a word. But she knew we were
there. I gazed at her face, remembering how it crinkled in
laughter, and I told myself, "She's only sleeping."

"It's over, Deb." Aunt Marie's voice was a rough whisper.
"Turn off the machine."

I was standing right beside it, but I just couldn't make
myself touch the switch. No! was still echoing in my mind,
half defiance and half prayer. She still needs... she's
only... and the thoughts faded.... Reality is not always
nice. Tears flowed freely as I flipped the switch that made
the machine silent. The whole room was silent. It was over.

I felt a little numb as I looked out over the garden from
Grandma's room. Death has never been so personal before.
At thirty-four I know I should have decades of life before me.
But I can't help but wonder when my turn to face God will
come. Grandma lived seventy-eight years, will I? Suddenly
that seemed like such a short time.

I turned to the door. Once more I looked back. In that instant, Grandma gave me one more gift. I had walked into that room with a world full of problems, and needing acknowledgment of my worth. I closed the door knowing nothing would ever be as important as the spirit and the purpose with which I choose to live.

Debbie's experience was traumatic but fairly positive. She stayed until the last few minutes and would have stayed longer. Doing so may have made things better for her, or worse.

What criteria do you use to judge your capability? Should you stay or leave? Can you take it?

It's one thing to hold your elder's hand during a sickness, quite another to hold it as life slips away. The gasps of troubled breathing that can be cured with the tube from an oxygen tank are quite different from the Cheyne-Stokes death rattle. It's different for everyone. There are no guidelines to offer. It comes down to what you feel.

Telling the Children

In a crisis, the last thing we want to do is deal with another problem, make another decision. With so much going on it's easy to temporarily discount the emotional needs of children. Actually the children often need more help and reassurance than any of the adults, including a surviving spouse. At the very least, an adult has had more years of living experience in which to learn how to cope. The child still looks to you. Turning away at a time like this can be devastating.

More often than we want to admit, the world is a complicated and confusing place. We think of childhood as idyllic when compared to the pressures we face today. "Let kids be kids" is a refrain from a loving parent. Parents think that by protecting a child from sadness and pain they are doing the child a favor. They aren't.

Some parents will rush children to a neighbor's house. The

children know something terrible is going on and need trusted adults to provide reassurance, yet here they are being shuffled away to tremble alone in their fear.

Children naturally talk openly and honestly about their feelings and thoughts. Their very directness strips away the protections we use for ourselves and forces us to deal with the loss and the reality of the situation. Another reason we let children mourn alone is we simply don't know what to say.

Put yourself in the child's place. Mom and Dad simply tell you Grandmother "has gone away." You wait, perhaps for years, for her to come back, all the time wondering why Grams didn't say goodbye, what you did to make Grams so angry that she never calls or writes anymore. Doesn't Grams love you? Then one day you find Grams's obituary in the family bible or photo album, or you overhear someone refer to an incident that happened at the time of Grams's death. Suddenly you know. It's a shock. You might very well be angry. Why didn't anyone tell you? You loved Grams, too.

Children are more aware of death than we might imagine, but often their interpretation of it has been skewed. They are educated about it daily but are getting confusing information. Children may have seen dead animals along the road. Beloved pets may have died. They have seen people killed in television shows and cartoons. Some children "know" very well that the dead don't stay dead—they come back with metal fingers, as vengeful monsters or as ghosts. Children still point their fingers and yell, "Bang! You're dead!" and their friends obligingly fall down, play dead, then get up to play again.

Even religion can engender confusion about death. For instance, in Christian Sunday schools children are taught about the miracle of Easter. Jesus died on the cross and went to be with His father, God. After three days He came back. If Grams went to be with God, wouldn't she come back, too? To many children, usually from about age two to sometimes as late as seven or eight, death is not a permanent event.

In our culture the words *death* and *die* belong to newspapers and television as something that happens to other people. When death touches our personal lives, it is somehow transformed into a series of euphemisms. The person has "passed away," "passed on," "gone to a greater reward," "expired," "departed," "gone on," the person is "lost" to us, or "no longer with us." These terms applied to death may appear to be a gentler way to speak to an adult, but they are certainly confusing for a child.

If you say to a child, "We lost Grams," don't be surprised if the child responds, "Where did you lose her?" or "Don't worry. We can find her." Similarly, telling children that someone has passed on, passed away, departed or even gone to a greater reward sounds more like the person has gone on a trip and is expected back. Doesn't "Grams went to be with God" sound like "Grams went to be with Aunt Susie"? And before didn't Grams always return from Aunt Susie's?

Also be careful what you tell children about God. "God was lonely for good people to be in His garden, so He took Grams to live with Him" may seem like a wonderful image for the child to have. Look at that statement through a child's eyes. The child loved Grams; God took Grams away. Wouldn't you be angry with God? God is now perceived as the enemy who "took away" the loved one.

"Grams was so good that God took her to live with Him." Now think about the times you've told the children they were "good." Can you see how they may now fear they, too, are going to die? They can become afraid of being too good because then they will be ripped away from their parents, siblings and friends and made to stay in some strange place. Then of course the child has figured out bad people die, too. They do in the movies and on TV. Children know where God sends bad people. Good or bad, the ultimate end is death.

"Grams has gone to sleep for a long time. She won't wake up anymore." While the concept of sleep is peaceful, telling children that the dead are only sleeping can be scary. The children sleep every night. Does this mean they won't wake up when they go to bed tonight?

So what *can* you tell children about death? First, tell them the truth. Children are born with an intuition that resembles radar. They instinctively pick up on falsehoods and half-truths. If *you* don't believe what you're telling them, they won't either. Be prepared to answer their questions and soothe their fears.

Young children, between the ages of two and six, usually believe death is reversible. Grams will get up and walk again. It's magical thinking based on the images they are trying to comprehend from all the things they've seen, heard and guessed at when trying to fill in the blanks.

Six- to nine-year-olds have begun to understand the finality of death but may develop the fear that death is contagious. Death is looked on as a taker. Many will fear worms or dirt getting on Grams. Some may blame themselves: "If I had been good, Grams wouldn't have gone away." With some variations, the guilt phase can carry over into the next general age bracket.

Usually by the age of nine the concept of mortality is developed. Many view death as punishment and still have some thoughts of "It was my fault." The child who didn't see Grandma when she was sick and thought, "I'm missing my ball game. If only she wasn't around!" may be plagued by guilt when she dies. It's important for children to know that wishes don't kill.

As children grow older, there can be a greater personal attachment to the elder, which in turn can make the loss more painful. Older children begin to see death as universal and as a natural enemy. Teenagers spend a lot of time philosophizing, criticizing, daydreaming and even fantasizing. Although they may pretend to know, they need to know more concerning their role (what to do, what to say) and purposely look to adults for cues in handling their emotions.

All children mature at different rates, and few will fit precisely into a category. Always tailor your explanation to each child's understanding, and answer questions honestly.

To tell children of their elder's death, take them somewhere quiet where you will not be disturbed.

"Something very sad has happened. Remember how we talked

about Grams having a dying sickness and that one day she would die? Well, it happened today. Grams died. Do you know what that means?"

The last sentence questions the children's concept of death. Do not simply launch into a discussion of death. Before you can explain, you need to know what the children think and feel so you can clear up any misconceptions. This will also give you a clue as to how far to go—and when to stop.

Some experts suggest the easiest way to explain death is to liken it to the cycles of nature the children have grown up with. Look at a tree and remind them of the leaf that buds in the spring, is full grown in the summer, ages and changes color in the fall, then dies in the winter. While this analogy can help children accept death, make certain they don't think that the elder will come back in the spring like the leaves on a tree.

"Why did she have do die?"

"Sometimes the body of a very old person just wears out, and then they die."

You can say the body stopped working, can't eat, can't breathe and so forth. Most children understand when a toy stops working or wears out. Children draw on their own experiences in order to understand new concepts.

"Where did Grams go?"

Discussing the afterlife according to your religious beliefs is fine. Tell the children what you honestly believe. If you don't have any answers you feel comfortable giving the children, tell them you don't know. Reassure them that if they're interested you will help them try to find the answers.

"Some people say when you die your spirit goes to heaven. Others say you become part of all living things. I don't know what really happens. I do know that you'll always remember all the nice things you did together and how much she loved you."

The last caution is to make certain the children tell you what other well-meaning friends and relatives have hold them. Children overhear things, fantasize, mix it all together and draw their own conclusions, some of which can be terrifying. Knowing what they've done with all the information will help you help them during the grieving process.

Children at the Funeral?

One question that always comes up when there is a death is whether or not children should attend the viewing, wake, funeral or memorial rites.

These ceremonies are part of your family tradition, and they help provide the family members with a way to say goodbye, a means of closure. Children who felt close to the elder need a means of saying goodbye the same as everyone else.

The unknown is scary for most children. Take their fear away by explaining the rites the family will participate in. Do this in detail. Even things that seem self-explanatory to you can frighten or anger some children. For instance, seven-year-old became upset when he saw his beloved grandfather in a casket. The casket was only half open, so the child only saw the upper portion of his grandfather's body. He mistakenly assumed the lower half was lost, because the child had seen the "saw the person in half" trick at a magic show. Similarly, a young girl was convinced her Nana wasn't really dead and that they were burying someone else, because a new hairstyle and cosmetics had made the woman in the coffin look vastly different from the Nana the child had known.

Some families have very personal customs that involve touching the dead person, such as kissing goodbye to promise remembrance. Children can find this scary, especially if they have not been told of the coldness or different feel of a dead person's skin. Do not force children to participate if they are upset by this.

The solution to all these problems is a clear, detailed explanation of what will happen and what they will see. This includes the other people who will be there. Tell them Aunt Mimi will have hysterics, that Uncle Jed will say not to cry, that Uncle Brian will sit in a corner and not talk to anyone. Explain that someone may tell them that Grams is asleep just to make them feel better, but that it's really not true.

When you've explained all the rites, what they are for and how everyone acts, ask the children if they want to go. If you have decided to allow them to participate in some portions, give them a choice. Perhaps going to the grave site or mausoleum afterwards with just the family is preferred. If the children do not attend the services, take them to the cemetery afterwards for their own closure.

One way you can help facilitate closure is to ask the child if they want to place something, such as a prayer, a note or a flower, in the coffin to be buried or cremated with the elder. One high school sophomore got special permission to have the first trophy he'd ever won buried with his grandfather, who had been his coach.

Some well-meaning relatives and friends may virulently disagree with your approach to telling the children about death and letting them participate in the funeral or other ceremonies. They may not believe in the type of openness we've discussed. That's their problem. Your priority is the children and what you want them to believe and know.

Children also make their own ceremonies and grieve in their own personal ways. Seventy-three-year-old Martha was scandalized that eight-year-old Kevin was permitted to wear a T-shirt to his grandfather's funeral. Wearing the T-shirt was important to Kevin. It was the "lucky" shirt he always wore when his grandfather took him fishing.

When There Is No Ceremony

The rites and the ceremonies we have been discussing offer comfort to the living. Throughout this book we have advocated the elder's rights to have things his or her way. There is one slight modification that needs to be expressed in deference to those left behind. When an elder has adamantly expressed the desire not to have any form of closure rites whatsoever (no viewing, cremation, ashes scattered without ceremony, etc.), it is all right to agree to those plans. However, the effect of this lack of ceremony on the living can be devastating.

Under these circumstances, people are left with no formal way to say goodbye. If this is the case in your family, consider picking a day to gather those who need to participate and hold your own private memorial. This is not disrespectful to the dead. It is helpful, even necessary, to the living. Obviously, the elder who requested the absence of rites had reasons, but those left behind are usually more comfortable with their grieving process if it has some formality to it.

The Grieving Process

Grief begins before death. This anticipatory grief was covered in the last chapter. Basically it stems from knowing the life of your loved one is winding down. The grief immediately following the death is obvious and intense. For many, the closure of a formal ceremony helps because it brings a sense of finality. But grief doesn't stop here. It can continue for some time.

The funeral is past. Relatives and friends have gone home. Everything is settling into a new routine. It has been maybe two or three weeks, and friends and family expect things to be back to normal—normal being "precaregivng" life. Regardless of what people expect, it doesn't feel normal to you. You might feel sorrow, isolation, anger, relief, guilt or a pervasive numbness. Certainly nothing feels "normal." But this *is* normal. It is grief, and everyone experiences it differently.

Someone says to you: "It's all for the best." "At least the suffering is over." "It's God's will." "He had a good life." "At least she's at peace." "He lived to a ripe old age." There is little consolation in clichés.

Then someone tells you, "I know exactly how you feel." This makes you want to scream, "No, you don't!" And you're right. The other person is not you and didn't have your relationship with the elder. It doesn't help to know everyone has lost someone to death. *You* are in shock.

No two people grieve in the same way, not even two children for the loss of the same parent. You have a right to grieve in your own way. Grief does not follow a formula.

This is especially true if the elder's death was anticipated and you were giving care on a frequent or daily basis. You began your grieving while the elder was still alive (anticipatory grieving). Do not be concerned if you feel less emotion now than you expected to.

Grief involves mourning not only for the person but also for the loss of hopes and dreams that are connected with that person— Mom's approval, Dad's respect. In the case of a surviving spouse, mourning the loss of a lifestyle, security and social place is also normal.

Three Stages of Grieving

Everyone goes through several stages of grief. The duration of each varies. Some may have been started and mostly completed in the anticipatory phase of grieving. We flit back and forth between these stages. The trauma can recur sporadically. A song, a flower, a holiday—anything can send us tumbling back to square one.

DENIAL   Not being able to grasp the fact that the elder is dead is denial. Even people who have been involved in the caregiving process can have trouble accepting the death of a loved one. Intellectually they know that the person has died, but emotions don't follow the dictates of logic. They may talk of the person in the present tense: "Dad always likes his coffee in that mug." Encourage remembrance in the past tense: "I remember how Dad always liked his morning coffee in that mug."

DISORGANIZATION   You realize the person is gone forever, but feelings of helplessness, rage and guilt may have set in. You may feel at loose ends, not knowing how to conduct your day. You feel disorganized.

One thing that helps in this stage is to find ways to grab normalcy. It's often the ordinary, day-to-day tasks that help the most. Shaving, reading a book, making a salad, attending a play at school, washing the car—it doesn't matter, but do try to avoid those things that would remind you of the loss.

It also helps to bring others back into your life. Take the kids to the park or zoo. Attend a pot luck supper at your church. (Better yet, offer to help in the kitchen.) Sometimes the activity can be something as simple as having a conversation. Don't be afraid to talk about your feelings and your relationship with the person, both the good and the bad.

All these things will help to make your life seem more normal again, and with that comes the sense that you are once more in control of your life. That in turn helps to get rid of the sense of disorganization.

SURVIVING   Eventually you will realize emotionally what you've known intellectually all along, namely, that life will go on. Once you've reached this stage you again begin to see options for the future.

Keep in mind, however, that grief is an ongoing process. Just when you think that you've survived the worst of it, you might find yourself dropping back into one of the earlier stages. Eventually, though, it passes, and we are left with memories without pain.

Coping With Grief

The trauma of losing a loved one can be lessened by understanding. At the beginning of this chapter, the actual process of dying was detailed to help you know what to expect. Obviously not every death is "textbook." There will be differences. Even so, that basic understanding and preparation can help you through it.

Coping with grief is much the same. It's different for every individual in both intensity and the length of time it lasts. Understanding what is going on helps, but grief is emotional, not logical. In coping with grief, you can't reason or think your way out of it. What's needed is to deal with the emotion. This is true of grief within yourself and of the grief felt by others.

It's important to understand what to expect, but also realize that when the death of a loved one comes, your world does tend to go temporarily numb. You may have been keeping a vigil for hours or days. It might be that you've been told to make an emergency flight cross-country before it's too late. Perhaps news of the death reached you by phone.

There is no easy way. Regardless, the death has happened, and there's no way it can be undone. Suddenly, there are dozens of people to call and a hundred small details to remember, even if most of the arrangements have been made. It feels like another crisis.

But remember, you're not the only one for whom this is a crisis.

Be honest about your emotions. This should be your number one rule. Suppressing your feelings does not make them go away. Trying to hide your grief only drives it inward for a time, where it will later erupt as an overreaction to something else.

CRYING   Crying is a natural release valve for emotions. It is biologically available to both sexes, but this precious gift of release has generally been deemed by society to be acceptable only for females. For men who have been taught that crying isn't allowed, the denial of such a natural release makes sadness even harder to deal with. Be aware also that this repression isn't restricted to men. Some women have also been taught to "control" their emotions, at least as far as outward signs go. Please, if anyone, male or female, adult or child, needs to cry, help that person to do so. Show your acceptance. Simply put your arms around the person and hold on gently. A loving human touch is so important.

ANGER   Death is the ultimate abandonment. Every child feels angry to some degree when abandoned by a parent, even if the "child" is an adult with children of his or her own. If the elder has left a spouse behind, the spouse will feel abandonment even more strongly, because the absence of his or her life's companion has torn an enormous hole in the fabric of life.

This anger can show itself in an almost infinite variety of ways. It may be obvious but is more likely to be subtle. Within yourself especially, but also with those around you, be aware that feeling anger that someone died is perfectly normal and natural.

FEAR   There is fear for the future. "How will I manage without this person in my life?" A surviving spouse may fear the future for any number of reasons, including financial and social. There is also the fear that nothing will ever be the same and that the past is lost forever. Coupled with this is often the fear that since the past is lost, so is the future.

As a caregiver, you may feel the additional loss of purpose if caregiving has been your main activity for any length of time. Loss of purpose can lead to a sense of uselessness and futility. This can bring on a whole new set of fears.

GUILT   "Could I have done more?" We go over a litany of our own perceived misdeeds, often blowing them way out of proportion. Sometimes we may wonder if it's our fault the person is dead. Children are likely to feel guilt because they often see themselves as direct causes of everything, good or bad, that happens in their world. They need reassurance that they are not the cause and that there is a vast difference between a thought and a deed. The same is true of yourself.

"If only I had spent more time with my elder." "If only I had been a better son or daughter." You keep remembering all the things you wanted to say and didn't, and wish you could take back some of the things you *did* say.

Watching a beloved elder suffer is horrid. It's not unusual to wish the suffering would end, then after the death feel guilty for wishing the person's life had ended. Guilt seeps in, adding to the grief.

Sometimes people feel guilty for even being alive. This is particularly common for a surviving spouse. It's not uncommon for the survivor to have thoughts like "I wish it had been me."

RELIEF   Part of us is glad that the caregiving situation has ended. We didn't want our beloved elder to suffer. Yet the relief we feel can make us feel guilty, because part of the relief is for ourselves and for no longer having to give care in demanding circumstances.

It's like the proverbial double-edged sword. If you feel happy that the suffering is over, guilt kicks in. Then you might feel guilty about feeling guilty. How dare you wish that the elder was still alive and suffering! How selfish of you! Then, being convinced that you must be selfish, more guilt comes.

The key is the same as always. Be honest with yourself. Feeling relief is natural. There's nothing wrong with it, and nothing wrong with you for feeling it. Let relief be the healing potion you need, not the source of guilt.

The Children's Grief

Telling children about a death, as we have discussed, can be difficult. Dealing with grief can be even more difficult. Children have the same feelings of anger, sadness, isolation, loneliness and guilt that you do, and sometimes these are amplified. The less the child understands what is going on, the more likely it is that fear of the unknown will add to the problem.

Remember that children learn by watching. If they see you feeling free to express these emotions, they will, too. It is much easier for children to talk about painful feelings and to deal with them than to suffer the consequences of repressing "bad" feelings.

How close was the child to the deceased? The closer the relationship, the deeper the grief. How do children deal with grief? They learn from you and incorporate it into their own personalities. Quiet, reserved children are likely to become more quiet. This does not mean they are not thinking about the death and what it means personally. It means they are having trouble verbalizing it.

Children who are more outgoing and used to communicating their feelings will need to communicate on the subject of death, too. Their communication skills will make it easier to help them, because they will tell you what they think, feel, fear and know.

Especially when children have withdrawn (or are that way by nature), it's important to watch for outward signs that they need help in dealing with their grief. Be aware that what children say may not necessarily reflect what they feel deep inside.

You can't take their pain away. Like it or not, they have to deal with it themselves, same as you. However, and especially when children are uncommunicative, you can watch for signs of distress and try to help them through it. Keep in mind that the symptoms discussed below are normal. (Also don't be surprised if you see the same signs exhibited by adults.)

In the case of a death in the family, it is always a good idea to alert your children's teachers. During the conference, advise them of the circumstances and what the children have been told. The teachers can keep you up to date on the children's school performance and help head off any problems in that regard, and can also be a valuable source of information on how your children are behaving when away from home.

Depending on the age of the child, you can expect to see some of the following manifestations in varying degrees.

SLEEPLESSNESS OR NIGHTMARES   It's not at all unusual for a grieving child to find it difficult to sleep or to have sleep interrupted by nightmares. Some of these dreams will have to do with the person who has died. Other dreams seem to have nothing to do with death at all. The usual and best treatment is to simply be there for reassurance. If the child is too old to cuddle back to sleep, sometimes merely your presence in the same room gives the needed feeling of being safe.

With rare exceptions, this symptom will pass on its own. If it doesn't, the problem is deep-seated and may require professional help.

EXHAUSTION OR HYPERACTIVITY   Many grieving children will appear listless or will sleep too much. Others may skip from activity to activity in an effort to stop thinking about what they're always thinking about—the dead person.

One way to help is to monitor what the child is doing, and if need be replace one activity with another. It can also be of great help to become a part of the activities.

NONVERBAL COMMUNICATION   Are the facial muscles tight? Is the body language stiff? Does the child seem unresponsive, tense, hostile or hard to talk to? These are symptoms that the child is having trouble communicating feelings and needs. Without forcing it, let the child know that you are there and willing to listen.

DEPENDENCY   Needing extreme support, the child may revert to dependency, always needing to be near another person, usually a parent or a sibling. In the need for reassurance the child may become clingy, want directions for everything or be afraid to be alone.

Like nightmares, this phase will usually pass on its own. The best thing you can do for a child who is afraid to be alone is to be there. But remember that your goal is to get rid of dependency. Wean the child from it.

FEELINGS OF UNREALITY   The child may feel that the entire episode is happening to someone else (denial). The child may still be functioning in school and talking with friends but feel inside that none of the things he or she is doing is "real."

It's not easy to tell when this is happening. Often the only way to know is by doing all you can to open, and keep open, communication. If it continues, be aware that retreating into a fantasy world can signal a number of very serious conditions. Don't hesitate to consult a professional or even to seek counseling for the child.

PANIC OR FEAR   The child fears that something devastating is going to happen (as it just did) or may have nameless fears. This child needs lots of reassurance and a solid feeling of safety. Be patient. Encourage the child to talk about the fears, but keep in mind that your goal is to dispel them. Don't dwell on them. Doing so can reinforce the problem, making it worse and more difficult to handle.

PREOCCUPATION WITH THE DEAD PERSON   Sometimes everything reminds the child of the dead person. The child may even imitate the dead person's mannerisms or repeat the person's favorite expression. This is a way of keeping the dead person alive.

Somewhat related, and of more concern, is a preoccupation with death. For some children, this will be their first experience with death. All of a sudden they come face-to-face with the reality that they will die some day, and that you will, too. Losing Grandma was tough. Losing you will be tougher. Losing their own life is too frightening to think about.

Depending on how far this has gone, professional help might be needed.

DESTRUCTIVE BEHAVIOR   Feeling helpless, angry, hopeless and/or ignored, a child may lash out verbally or physically. Increased negative behavior with siblings and/or friends is possible, as are falling grades. Your job is to attempt to bring the child back to a more normal world. Let the child know anger is okay but the behavior is not. Help the child to find other ways to vent that anger.

AVOIDANCE   Sometimes a child shows no immediate symptoms of grief. If the child was not particularly close to the elder, he or she may be adjusting well, accepting your explanations and having no problem. If the child had been seeing the elder frequently, or had a close emotional bond with the elder, the child may be denying the elder's death. Initiating a quiet talk about the elder and the death will reveal which is the case. Be aware, however, that if there is no problem, pressing the matter could cause one.

Helping a Surviving Spouse

When the death of an elder leaves a widow(er) behind, the trauma of losing the elder is compounded by worry for the survivor. Can he or she cope alone? Should you protect him or her completely? What should you do?

Stop!

Unless there is an overwhelming need for intervention, let the person find his or her own balance. If you establish a protective pattern, you interrupt the grieving process and run the risk of having the surviving spouse become overly dependent on you. Provide emotional support by talking with the survivor and simply being there.

It seems that doing things for the newly widowed would be an act of kindness and love. *Offering* your help is a form of support. *Forcing* someone to accept your ideas or services is control and an interruption in the grieving process.

When Mrs. Morrison was suddenly widowed, she was stunned into numbness. Her two daughters rushed to her side, and she was grateful for their understanding. After the funeral, they urged her to relax and return to one of their homes until she felt better able to cope. She chose to visit with her elder daughter for a week. By the end of the third day she wanted to go back to her own home where she had lived with her husband for over forty years. Her daughter convinced her to wait the week. She did and then went home.

Mrs. Morrison knew something was wrong the moment she opened her front door. She was shocked into speechlessness as she wandered from room to room.

"We knew it would be painful for you to deal with so many reminders of Dad, so we did it for you. We even rearranged the furniture so it wouldn't remind you of him so much."

The daughters had carefully erased every trace of their father from the house. His clothes were gone, as were his personal effects. Even his favorite coffee mug was missing. Family photos that contained his picture had been removed. The spot by the fireplace where he had his favorite chair was empty.

Even in her grief, Mrs. Morrison knew her daughters meant well, but it took a good deal of time for her to forgive the intrusion. What they had done was strip forty years of tangible reminders of warm, treasured memories, leaving her with nothing to touch as she separated naturally from her grief. Instead of being a familiar oasis, her own home felt strange. Instead of being comforting, it was bleak. Even worse, the plans for her husband's things that they had discussed in the past would never come to fruition.

The first six months to a year following the death of a spouse is a time of grief and reordering one's life. Any decisions made during this time should be small or considered temporary. The only overwhelming reason to make a major decision is necessity, such as needing to sell the home so the remaining spouse has funds for financial support.

Becoming "Normal" Again

Throughout caregiving and afterwards, your own life goes on. There will be times when this isn't such an exciting proposition, but it remains a fact. Tomorrow will come. The pain of grief will lessen. Your life will begin to return to something more normal. So will the lives of those around you.

Although the recovery process can't be forced, it can be aided.

- Accept reality. The elder has died. Life as you knew it has changed.
- Feel the feelings. Allowing yourself to feel, and accepting what you feel without internal criticism, is the first step toward recovery. Be patient with yourself.
- Take care of yourself. Monitor your health. Don't fall into the trap of abusing alcohol or drugs. Many caregivers let their own medical needs go while taking care of an elder. Schedule a full physical exam.

- If you are torturing yourself with what-ifs and if-onlies, stop feeling guilty. Remember that your caregiving made life much more pleasant for the elder than it would have been otherwise.
- Give yourself the gift of time. If you don't have to resume work immediately, don't. You need to replenish yourself. You need time to heal. Allow time off from responsibility. Time to yourself is important. This is a good time to think and take stock of your life. Accept that not every day will be good.
- Try not to make permanent major changes at this time. Do what needs to be done. Little decisions help restore confidence. For example, don't insist that the elder's house or possessions be sold. Put a six-month moratorium on major decisions if possible while you plan for the future.
- Rearrange the furniture. Clean out the closet and restore the elder's room to its former function or a new one. This can be extremely difficult and will bring a flood of memories. If so, ask a close friend or your spouse to help. Once it's done, you will have succeeded in another step of closure.
- Set a new routine or schedule for yourself.
- Art, music and physical activity all help to break routine. Join organizations or clubs, that use your talents. Volunteer at a hospital or for a charity. Try something new.
- As you begin to feel better and put things in a more balanced perspective, consider the new priorities in your life without the duties of caregiving.
- Do not set a schedule for grieving to be over. It is a process, not a goal.
- Determine to live again.

Sometimes the feelings of sadness or rage don't go away or seem to be overly intense. You may simply feel that you can't cope. Friends and family may criticize the way you are handling your grief and just want you to "knock it off." If you or your family are having trouble handling these feelings, call your minister, doctor, social worker or funeral director and ask for a referral to a grief support group.

The caregiving situation you've been involved in may have been very short or may have gone on for years. As time passes, you will gain more perspective on the impact caregiving had on your life and the lives of family members.

In an earlier chapter it was suggested that you keep a journal in which you were to write your feelings and the situations you were dealing with. This may not be the time to read that journal, or it may be the perfect time. Only you know that. Don't push it. In either case, get the journal out and write about your current feelings and the overall impact caregiving had on your family. Then put the journal away until it's time for its next use.

That time might be when you feel the need to review what you've been through. The journal then serves both as a reminder and as another means of closure and gaining perspective.

Another use of the journal will come the next time you are asked to take up the role of caregiver. Yes, the need will probably arise more than once. If you are married, you probably have four elders (two sets of parents), or more if there have been remarriages in your family. There are other relatives, including siblings. You and your spouse are aging. With all of this, it's very likely that you will eventually find yourself back in a caregiving situation.

Before you again undertake caregiving, read your journal. The immediacy of the words you'd written then will have more reliability than your memory of the experience. Time tends to blur the daily reality of the job.

For most there will thankfully be a space of time between caregiving roles. Family dynamics and your personal needs will have changed. The journal will help you see the strains and triumphs and give you a reference point to begin assessing your capability again.

Resources

In your caregiving experience you will be networking with various agencies, companies, groups and individuals. When you find a business or service that makes your life easier or solves a problem, please let us know. When this book is updated, we want to be able to include the new information you provide. If you have questions or comments regarding this book, we would like to hear them as well. (Enclose a self-addressed, stamped envelope if you wish to receive a response.)

To contact us with source listings, questions or comments, write Gene Williams or Patie Kay in care of the publisher. Remember to include your name, address and phone number.

The fastest, most efficient and often most reliable sources are at the local level. Your primary-care physician, home health nurse, social worker, state and local government agencies, local churches and the Yellow Pages of your phone book are all excellent places to start. As we have mentioned throughout the book, assistance and information of many kinds can be obtained from the local Office on Aging, Red Cross, Salvation Army or senior citizens centers.

The resources in the following list are separated alphabetically by the need they fill or the service they perform.

Caremanagers

National Association of Professional Geriatric Caremanagers
1604 N. Country Club Road
Tucson, AZ 85716
(602) 881-8008; FAX (602) 325-7925
Information and referrals to local caremanagers. For information send a self-addressed, stamped (first-class) envelope.

Clothing and Shoes

Golden Threads Mobile Healthcare Fashions
8341 East Evans Road, #109
Scottsdale, AZ 85260
(602) 951-0889
Offers a variety of clothing with a number of features to aid those with assorted physical challenges.

National Odd Shoe Exchange
7102 North 35th Avenue, #2
P.O. Box 56845
Phoenix, AZ 85079
(602) 841-6691
Provides shoes and referrals for those people who require only one shoe or two shoes of different sizes.

Hearing

AT&T National Special Needs Center
(800) 233-1222; TDD (800) 233-3232
Free catalog of adaptive equipment, emergency call systems, telephone amplifiers, etc.

Helping Aids Companies

Appliances for the Physically Challenged
(800) 235-7054
Free catalog.

Comfortably Yours
(800) 521-0097
Free catalog of a wide array of products to aid the physically challenged.

Hospice

National Hospice Organization
1901 North Fort Meyer Drive

Suite 307
Arlington, VA 22209
(703) 243-5900
Provides names of Hospice organizations in your area.

Medical ID Jewelry

Medic Alert
Medic Alert Foundation
2323 Colorado Avenue
Turlock, CA 95832
(800) 432-5378, twenty-four-hour phone enrollment
Nationwide registry. Provides bracelet or necklace with contact phone number for client's medical information in case of emergency. Fee.

Needs of the Dying

The Elisabeth Kübler-Ross Center
South Route 616
Head Waters, VA 24442
(703) 396-3441
Noted expert on death and dying has established a retreat to promote her ideas. The center provides educational services and audiovisual material.

Sheepskin Products

Walden Sheepskin Products
RFD 2 Box 421
Hardwick, VT 05843
(802) 563-2380
Provides a variety of sheepskin products including slippers. Will do some custom orders.

Visual Aids

American Foundation for the Blind, Inc.
(800) 232-5463
Catalog of products for those with impaired eyesight.

Index